To:

_____

From:

_____

Date:

_____

I Will
Sing
with
JOY

CHRISTIAN ART
PUBLISHERS

Published by Christian Art Publishers
PO Box 1599, Vereeniging, 1930, RSA

© 2014
First edition 2014

Cover designed by Christian Art Publishers

Images used under license from Shutterstock.com

Scripture quotations are taken from the *Holy Bible*,
New International Version® NIV®.
Copyright © 1973, 1978, 1984, 2011 by Biblica, Inc.®
Used by permission.
All rights reserved worldwide.

Scripture quotations are taken from the *Holy Bible*,
New Living Translation® NLT®.
Copyright © 1996, 2004, 2007 by Tyndale House Foundation.
Used by permission of Tyndale House Publishers Inc.,
Carol Stream, Illinois 60188.
All rights reserved.

Set in 14 on 16 pt Palatino LT Std
by Christian Art Publishers

Printed in China

ISBN 978-1-4321-1122-9

15 16 17 18 19 20 21 22 23 24 – 12 11 10 9 8 7 6 5 4 3

I have put my *hope* in Your laws.

I will walk about in *freedom*,

for I have sought out Your *precepts*.

I *delight* in Your commands

because I *love* them.

~ Psalm 119:43, 45, 47

Contents

Preface

January   Living Close to God

February   Relationships

March   Spreading the Good News

April   Jesus Suffers for You

May   On the Road with Peter

June   Honor and Glorify God!

July   Suffering

August   A Letter of Hope

September   People Who Care

October   Characteristics of God's Children

November   What Makes a Christian Different

December   Through God's Eyes

Reading List

Preface

When the Day Breaks

Your unfailing love, O Lord, is as vast as the heavens; Your faithfulness reaches beyond the clouds. Ps. 36:5

Love is God's defining characteristic. John sums it up perfectly when he states: God is love. God's love takes our breath away – it is unfathomable, incomprehensible, unconditional, eternal, inextinguishable and infinite. It has existed since before Creation and nothing can ever separate us from it.

According to Peter Kreeft, "All the things in this world are gifts and signs of God's love for us. The whole world is a love letter from God." You and I need to decide how we are going to respond to this love letter from heaven.

When you respond in love and choose God, He comes into your life and with Him comes a life-changing love that makes you more and more like Jesus. When you belong to God, you live in the vast expanse of His love.

Slowly but surely, wrapped in the cocoon of God's love, your previous selfish nature is transformed into a beautiful butterfly fluttering around and exhibiting the glory of God's redemption in acts of sacrifice. You become what God intended you to be.

January

Living Close to God

The secret to happiness is to live close to God. You need to diligently seek His presence. The following prayer by St. Patrick reveals a desire for God's presence:

I arise today
through God's strength to pilot me,
God's might to uphold me,
God's eye to look before me,
God's ear to hear me,
God's word to speak for me,
God's hand to guard me,
God's way to lie before me,
God's shield to protect me,
God's host to secure me,
from everyone who desires me ill,
Christ with me, Christ before me, Christ behind me,
Christ in me, Christ beneath me, Christ above me,
Christ on my right, Christ on my left,
Christ where I lie down, Christ where I sit,
Christ where I arise,
Christ in the heart of every man who thinks of me,
Christ in the mouth of every man who speaks of me,
Christ in every eye that sees me,
Christ in every ear that hears me.

Heavenly Father,
This year I truly want to draw closer
to You every day – I want to set aside
more time to spend with You,
and seek Your advice before I do anything.
Thank You for the assurance that You
will be with me every day of the new year.
I praise You because You have planned
a prosperous future for me and You
have a special vision for my life.
Teach me to understand how important today is.
Help me to use the time given to me to
the best of my ability and to take hold
of every opportunity that comes my way.
I want to anchor my hope in You and work only
for You – I choose now to have faith in You.
How good You are to promise to carry me day by day!
Make it possible for me to live as You ask me to,
to be holy, to be ready to continue believing,
even when there is no visible evidence for my faith.
I want to hold fast to this faith
and run the race of faith in such a way
that I will one day win the heavenly prize.
Even if my expectations are not fulfilled
I know for certain that You will help me when I need You.
I confess my absolute dependence on You, Lord,
which is why I want to wait on You, avoid sin
and unburden all my fears on You.
My heart longs for You.
Amen.

First Seek the Lord's Advice

Jehoshaphat also said to the king of Israel, "First seek the counsel of the LORD." 1 Kings 22:5

When the King of Israel asked King Jehoshaphat of Judah to go to war with him against Aram, he was immediately willing to do so, but he had one condition: that the Lord be consulted first before they do anything.

If you follow this advice in the new year things will fall into place for you. This year, before you follow your own lead, bring your plans to God first. He already knows exactly what is in store for you.

When you regularly seek the Lord's advice and surrender your year and your life into His hands, you can be certain that even if trials and tribulations lie ahead of you, the wisdom of God will be available to you each and every day – that He will carry you even when things are extremely tough. Even then will He be with you to help and support you.

The very best New Year's resolution is to set aside more time for God this year and to work on your relationship with Him. This year, live close to God, listen for His voice and be ready to obey Him. Talk to Him and study His Word. Then you will experience the blessedness of His presence in your life every day.

Heavenly Father, I commit to seeking Your advice every day of the year that lies ahead rather than following my own bent. Please lead me daily and show me Your will for my life. Amen.

God Is with You

"Do not fear, for I am with you; do not be dismayed, for I am your God. I will strengthen you and help you; I will uphold you with My righteous right hand." Isa. 41:10

God did not promise us a life of eternal happiness on earth or a problem-free existence, but He did promise that in the stillness and in the darkness He will be with us, beside us, in us and He will help us to exist. This is what Philip Yancey claims in his book *Reaching for the Invisible God.*

The people of God were often confronted with big problems in biblical times, but He was always there to help and protect them and to show them His strength. For that reason they were almost always able to get the better of their enemies.

It is highly unlikely that you will have a problem-free year this year; in fact, you can probably count on it that problems and crises will cross your path, but in the midst of those crises you need never be afraid or worried. After all, you have the promise that God will never let you down, that He will be with you every day of the new year to lead you and help you, that He Himself will strengthen you whenever you need extra strength, that He will hold you tight with His own hand and will help and protect you. This is why you can enter the unknown year that lies ahead with great faith.

Heavenly Father, it is wonderful that You have promised to be with me, to strengthen me and to help me, to hold me tight and to save me. I come now to lay claim to that promise! Amen.

Are You Close to the Lord?

"Is the LORD among us or not?" Exod. 17:7

If, after all the miracles that God worked for Israel during the exodus and the journey through the wilderness, they still doubted whether the presence of God was with them, they must really have been very short-sighted. They began to question God every time things went slightly wrong for them. Before we get too critical of the Israelites, we should first acknowledge that we very often do exactly the same thing!

There is a story of a group of Christians during the American Civil War who went to visit President Abraham Lincoln. "We hope that God is with us, President Lincoln," they said to him. "I reckon that's not the most important thing," Lincoln answered. The visitors stared at him in shock, until he added, "I am more concerned about whether we are with the Lord."

Perhaps this is the question that you should answer for yourself today. Are you still absolutely certain of the fact that you are with the Lord? That the Lord is with you is a promise that is emphasized in various places in the Bible. But what about you? Are you with the Lord? Do your actions, attitudes and words all bear witness to the fact that you love God and are truly with Him?

Heavenly Father, I praise You for the promise that You will never leave me. You are with me each day of the new year. Please forgive me for the times when I act like I am not with You. Amen.

A New Future

*"I know the plans I have for you," declares the LORD, "plans
to prosper you and not to harm you, plans to give you hope
and a future. Then you will call upon Me and come and pray
to Me, and I will listen to you." Jer. 29:11-12*

The advice that Jeremiah gave to the Israelites in exile
was that they continue with their lives in the foreign
land and should not long for the past. God promised that
He would one day return them to their own land. He
had a future for them. He guaranteed them something
to look forward to if they were prepared to call to Him
and seek His will.

Usually at the beginning of a new year, people have
all kinds of expectations about what the year ahead
will hold for them. God wants His children to have
positive expectations. It is His will that we should leave
the disappointments of the past behind us, and that
we should reach forward to a new future with Him.
With the help of God you too can manage to make
your dreams come true this year, to embrace a new and
brighter future.

There is, however, one condition that you must not
lose sight of: If you want to be able to take God's promises as your own, you must be prepared to call on Him,
to seek His will and obey Him. Only then will the Lord
undertake to answer you and to fulfill your expectations
for the new year.

*Heavenly Father, thank You so much for the promise that
You have planned to prosper me in the year that lies ahead,
that You want to give me a future and a hope. I want to call
upon You now and I want to obey Your will. Amen.*

A Vision for the New Year

"I am the LORD, *and there is no other; apart from Me there is no God. I will strengthen you, though you have not acknowledged Me." Isa. 45:5*

God gives each of His children a special vision – a task He gives specifically to them.

Katie Brazelton in *Pathway to Purpose* says that to have a vision is to know how God wants to use you in a powerful way to accomplish His will. It is to sense your God-given destiny and to see what remarkable, humanly impossible task God has in mind for you. It is to receive a taste of His multi-dimensional strategy for you – to be aware of the kind of person that He would like you to become and the work that He would like you to do for Him.

Try to find out what the personal task or vision is that God has planned for you. Pray that He will reveal it to you and that He will equip you to bring it to pass.

If the Lord gives you a vision, He also promises to be with you and to help you fulfill it. All that He asks of you is your willingness. The only way you will be truly happy this year is if you discover your vision and, with the strength of God, bring it to pass.

Heavenly Father, please show me what task and what special vision You have set aside for me this year. Equip me to be able to do it to the best of my ability for Your glory. Amen.

The Only Important Time

Whatever your hand finds to do, do it with all your might.
Eccles. 9:10

There is a time for everything, and a season for every activity under heaven, says the writer of Ecclesiastes. There is a time to be born and a time to die, a time to plant, a time to uproot, a time to break down and a time to build. God made everything to fit into a determined time (see Eccles. 3). And it is God's will that you use the time that He has entrusted to you with caution.

Therefore, do not waste your time in the year that lies ahead. Do everything that comes your way with enthusiasm and diligence. There is just one moment that is really important, and that is right now. "Make the most of every opportunity," Paul advised the community in Ephesus (Eph. 5:15). You cannot change anything that has happened in the past and neither can you predict the future. You do not even know what awaits you tomorrow. That is why you need to make the best use of today.

Philip Yancey, in *Reaching for the Invisible God*, rightly says that today is the only time over which we have any power. Therefore, remember, there is only one time that is really important – now! Use today as if there will be no other time.

Heavenly Father, please help me to use my time in the year that lies ahead with insight, to do everything I do in the very best way possible and with absolute commitment. Amen.

There Is Always Hope

We have this hope as an anchor for the soul, firm and secure.
It enters the inner sanctuary behind the curtain. Heb. 6:19

In his autobiography, *A Long Walk to Freedom,* Nelson Mandela talks about how he was imprisoned on Robben Island for fourteen years before he was permitted to see his daughter. It was a magnificent experience for him to hold her close again after such a long time. He had last seen her when she was a young child, and now she was a woman with a baby in her arms.

She placed Mandela's first grandchild in his arms. He said that to hold a newborn baby, so vulnerable and soft in his rough hands, hands that for so long had worked with nothing but picks and shovels, was a great joy. He could not believe that any man could ever have been happier than he was that day.

According to the tradition of Mandela's tribal culture, the grandfather can choose the name of a new baby, and Mandela decided to call him Zaziwe, which means hope.

The children of God also have a hope to which they can hold fast: the hope of heaven that waits for us. You can enter the new year with hope, no matter what your circumstances, because even if your hope is not fulfilled in this lifetime, you can still hold on to God's promise that heaven awaits you in the future.

Heavenly Father, thank You so much that I can put my hope in heaven. This hope is a secure anchor in my life because I know that this hope will come to pass. Amen.

Do Your Work for God

Serve wholeheartedly, as if you were serving the Lord, not people. Eph. 6:7

Philip Yancey tells how he visited Calcutta where the nuns who had been trained by Mother Teresa serve the poorest and most wretched people on the planet with great love. These nuns get up at four in the morning, and sing and pray together before they begin with their daily work. The calmness of these women's spirits astounded Yancey.

Mother Teresa instituted a rule that her nuns should set aside Thursdays for prayer and rest. "The work will always be here, but if we do not rest and pray, we will not have the strength to do our work," she told them.

Yancey reports that these sisters work with a wonderful calmness. They do not work to complete a specific workload for a specified charitable organization. They work for God. They begin their day with Him, they bring their day to a close with Him – and everything in between is an offering to God. Only God determines their worth and measures their success.

Let this be your motto – to do your work for God. Look to God for guidance, because He is the only One who can determine your worth and measure your success. Make sure to set aside specific and sufficient time to be alone with Him and that you get sufficient rest.

Heavenly Father, please help me this year to do everything I do for You, and to look only to You when I want to achieve success. Amen.

Carried by God

"You whom I have upheld since your birth, and have carried since you were born. Even to your old age and gray hairs I am He, I am He who will sustain you. I have made you and I will carry you." Isa. 46:3-4

There is a beautiful contrast presented to us in Isaiah 46:1-4: While His covenanted people forsook Him and carried worthless idols in their hands, God did not stop carrying them. There are various promises in the Bible that God will carry His children – that He will care for them from their birth through to their old age, that even through times of difficulty He will carry them when their strength is weak.

Perhaps it would be good to take a personal inventory: Are you still burdening yourself, like the Israelites of old, with worthless idols that are weighing you down because you refuse to let them go, or are you allowing God to carry you? Someone who is being carried has to make no effort of his or her own – they simply have to be still and allow the other person to carry the load.

For people who are willing to become still and allow God to carry them, the beautiful promise found in Isaiah is still valid today: The God who created you has undertaken to carry you every day, to save you and to hold you close, and to give you sufficient strength for each day right through to your old age.

Heavenly Father, forgive me for sometimes being weary because I carry so many unnecessary burdens with me. Lord, today I want to allow You to pick me up and carry me. Please hold me tight and save me from all danger. Amen.

With Jesus in Your Boat

Jesus got up and rebuked the wind and the raging waters; the storm subsided, and all was calm. "Where is your faith?" He asked His disciples. Luke 8:24-25

Some time ago I had a moving experience. A church congregation invited me to spend a morning with a class of disabled children.

There were five teachers who cared for about sixteen children. Each teacher was given the chance to tell the same Bible story in their own words and show the pictures in a children's Bible to their little group of children. The story was the one where Jesus was awoken by His disciples when a storm broke out on the sea. I listened in awe to the group of five teachers who repeated the same story five times and wondered how much the children, whose ages ranged from four years to twelve, had actually understood of it. Not one of them was in a position to be able to communicate verbally in any way. When it was the turn of a young teacher to show his group the pictures, he ended his story with words that I will never forget: "If you have Jesus in your boat with you, you can laugh in the storm."

Make sure that Jesus is in your boat of life. Then the storms of life can come against you, but you will not need to fear. Not only can He calm any storm, but He also keeps you safe, even after you die.

Lord Jesus, thank You for the privilege of being able to laugh in the storm because You are in my boat of life. I can be certain that You are on my side and that I am completely safe at all times. Amen.

Live as God Asks You To

He has showed you, O mortal, what is good. And what does the LORD require of you? To act justly and to love mercy and to walk humbly with your God. Mic. 6:8

Some psychologists suggest a treatment in which patients should act as if a certain situation is true, even though the circumstances might reflect the complete opposite. For example, if you are unhappy in your marriage you need to treat your husband like you did when you were first married; if you are struggling to forgive someone, act as if you have already done so. These actions can influence your whole life positively.

Through the mouth of the prophet Micah, God showed His people how He wanted them to live. Their relationship with Him needed to be right and their love for Him should be reflected in the way they live: they should do what is right, be faithful to Him, love Him and live humbly.

Try to apply God's command to the prophet Micah in your own life. Behave in the way that the Lord asks you to; do the things that are good and right in His eyes. If you ask Him, God will make it possible for you to treat all people fairly, and to let your love and faithfulness for Him and others be evident in the way that you live before your God.

Heavenly Father, this year I truly desire to live as You long for me to do. It is my prayer that You will teach me to do what is right, to approach You as well as all other people with love, faithfulness and humility. Amen.

Be Holy

To be made new in the attitude of your minds; and to put on the new self, created to be like God in true righteousness and holiness. Eph. 4:23-24

If you want to be like Jesus, it is necessary for you to start living a holy life, just as He is holy, to begin thinking in a new way and to fulfill God's will.

In *Reaching for the Invisible God*, Philip Yancey refers to Thomas Merton's reflection and meditation in which he ponders how we can even begin to know God if we do not at least begin to be somewhat like He is. We do not see and then act, but act and then begin to see.

An active relationship with God is only possible if you make up your mind to obey His commands, to set aside sufficient time to spend with God, if you get to know Him better through studying His Word and doing His will.

We can begin to understand God's holiness if we try to behave as Jesus did. John writes, "Whoever claims to live in Him must walk as Jesus did" (1 John 2:6). If you do not really understand what this means, then go and read the four Gospels through from beginning to end so that you can see how Jesus lived and behaved. And then, as Jesus recommended to His disciples after He had told them the parable of the Good Samaritan, "Go, then, and do exactly the same!"

Lord Jesus, it is my deepest desire to become more like You each day. Renew my thoughts and my soul; help me to live a holy life and to obey Your will in all things. Amen.

First Do and Then You Will See

Then Jesus told him, "Because you have seen Me, you have believed; blessed are those who have not seen and yet have believed." John 20:29

Thomas refused to believe that Jesus had really risen from the dead; he insisted that he could not believe it unless he saw Him with his own eyes. Then Jesus appeared to Thomas and invited him to look at His nail-pierced hands and to put his hand into the wound in Jesus' side. Thomas was awestruck. All that he could manage to utter was, "My Lord and my God!"

If you truly want to become like Jesus, it is necessary to start behaving as if you believe it and then you will see how the things that you believe will become true.

Thomas Merton goes on to say that the person who first wants to see clearly before they believe never actually sets out on the journey. The writer of Hebrews is very clear on this matter. He writes, "Now faith is being sure of what we hope for and certain of what we do not see" (Heb. 11:1). Trust God even if you cannot see what lies ahead in the future. Trust Him to help you in all your undertakings that lie ahead of you. If you take Him at His Word – even though His promises have not yet come true for you – you will reap the fruit of your faith.

Lord Jesus, sometimes I really struggle to believe when I don't see. Please forgive me, and make it possible for me to take You at Your word this year. Amen.

Faith Is a Choice

"'If you can'?" said Jesus. "Everything is possible for one who believes." Mark 9:23

The children of God need to commit themselves to imitating Jesus; to believe in Him without insisting that what they believe in must be made visible. And yet it is not that easy to keep believing when the promises of God just do not seem to come to pass in your own life. There is then only one thing left for you to do: choose to believe in God.

Sheldon Vanauken declares that to choose is to believe. All that we can do is to choose. It is not that we do not ever doubt, but we do ask for help to overcome our doubt after we have made the decision. We are, in effect, saying, "Lord, I believe; help my unbelief!" (v. 24).

You can choose to believe in God once again. Perhaps there will be days when you may still doubt. On those days simply hold fast to the promises of God that He has mapped out for you in His Word and be obedient to the things that He highlights for you in His Word.

The prophet Isaiah reminds us that He is the one you can trust every day of your life (see Isa. 33:6), and of all the people who have trusted in God through the ages, not one has been disappointed.

Lord Jesus, I want to put my trust in You today and choose to continually believe in You in spite of my negative circumstances. Please help me in the areas where I still doubt. Amen.

Two Extremes

What is mankind that You are mindful of them, human beings that You care for them? You have made them a little lower than the angels and crowned them with glory and honor. Ps. 8:4-5

The Bible is full of paradoxes: the last shall be first; a person needs to lose their life in order to gain it; children are the most important people in the kingdom of God; if you truly want to be great, you need to be prepared to serve others.

An old Jewish rabbi once remarked that every person should carry two stones in their pocket. On one should be written: "I am but dust and ashes;" while the message written on the other should be: "The world was created for my benefit." The rabbi went on to explain that we should use each stone as needed.

Be aware of how worthless and incomplete you are every day, but know also that God has placed you on this earth as His image-bearer and that He sacrificed His Son so that the price of your sins could be covered.

On the days that you feel really good about yourself, remind yourself that you are made of dust, but when you sit on the ash heap with Job, think about the fact that you are the crown of God's creation, His image-bearer. Between these two extremes you should live a balanced life.

Heavenly Father, help me never to become proud and arrogant, but to always remember my shortcomings. Yet I worship You because You have made me so wonderful that I can be Your image-bearer. Amen.

Life Is Difficult

"I have told you these things, so that in Me you may have peace. In this world you will have trouble. But take heart! I have overcome the world." John 16:33

It is interesting to note that the book that has spent the longest time at the top of *The New York Times* bestsellers list is *The Road Less Traveled* by M. Scott Peck – a book that begins with the words: Life is difficult.

Job says that man is born to trouble (see Job 5:7). Before Jesus was crucified He also warned His disciples that life is hard. Because we are people who live on a planet that is interspersed with sin, it is inevitable that hardship will at some or other time come your way. It might be that you fall ill or that you might experience financial setbacks. But in the midst of all these difficulties you can depend on the fact that Jesus has already overcome the world and that He is on your side.

Hardships always have a positive side as well – it is in fact your hardships that cause you to draw closer to God, that help to reveal your own inabilities. Trials are good because they nurture perseverance, as Paul writes to the church in Rome; and in its turn, perseverance develops sincerity of faith, sincerity of faith develops hope (see Rom. 5:5). Use your allotment of hardship to help you to grow in faith.

Lord Jesus, over and over again I have found that life is difficult. Thank You that hardship can be an advantage because it keeps me very close to You, and because it develops perseverance and sincerity and faith. Amen.

Hold Fast to Your Faith!

Let us run with perseverance the race marked out for us, fixing our eyes on Jesus, the pioneer and perfecter of faith. Consider Him … so that you will not grow weary and lose heart. Heb. 12:1-3

Philip Yancey says that faith will always mean that you believe something that cannot be proved, and that because of it you commit yourself to something of which you can never be absolutely sure. Someone who lives by faith is compelled to proceed on incomplete evidence and to believe in something up front that will only make sense in retrospect.

It is rather difficult to keep believing when there are few visible signs around you to which you can attach your faith. Perhaps it would be good if every Christian were to realize that it is not all that easy to believe. And that it is impossible to believe on our own if God does not put faith into our lives. God makes it possible for you to believe. The fact that you believe in Him is not the result of your own cleverness, but is pure grace.

The road of your earthly journey will at the very best of times be full of potholes and it is doubtful if you will succeed on your own in living the way God expects you to. You can be sure that if you hold fast to your faith and keep your eyes focused on Jesus, you will not become spiritually weary, but will eventually one day arrive at your heavenly destination.

Lord Jesus, I praise You that You have made it possible for me to hold fast to my faith, to keep my eyes focused on You so that I will one day arrive at the right destination. Amen.

Unfulfilled Expectations

Hope deferred makes the heart sick, but a longing fulfilled is a tree of life. Prov. 13:12

Perhaps you should make peace with the fact that not everything you hope for will happen. The reason that we sometimes become disillusioned and disheartened is simply because we want things to be different from what they actually are.

If you apply for a job and are reasonably certain that you will get it, you are floored if your application fails; if you have planned a trip overseas in great detail and your plane is delayed, you will be upset about the time that has been wasted. It is also understandable if you are disappointed because your child has not done as well in his course at university as you expected him to.

There is, however, a way in which you can limit disappointments. Learn to not nurture so many expectations that will probably not work out, and trust God with your dreams. Focus on Him, be prepared to exchange your will for His and ask Him to intervene on your behalf; He will give you the strength to handle your crises in the right way.

Hold fast to the promise in Romans 8:28, that ultimately the Lord will cause all things – even the disasters – to work out for your good if you love Him.

Heavenly Father, please help me this year to handle my expectations that do not work out in the right way. Thank You for Your assurance that ultimately You will work all things for my good. Amen.

When You Need Help

Lord, there is no one like You to help the powerless against the mighty. Help us, Lord our God, for we rely on You.
2 Chron. 14:11

Take some time to read through the exciting story of war in 2 Chronicles 14. King Asa of Judah was confronted by a huge army. Asa had 500,000 soldiers who were armed only with shields, spears, bows and arrows while the Cushite Zerah's army consisted of a million men and 300 chariots. It was crystal clear to King Asa that only God could help them now, and he prayed that things would work out as they had so many times before in the history of Israel.

As always, God listens when His children come to Him asking for help. He answered King Asa's prayer for help and in verse 12 we read that the Lord caused the Cushites to be defeated by Judah. So many Cushites were slaughtered that King Zerah was never able to restore his army.

The Lord is fighting on your side. When you have to face moments of crisis that you are not able to deal with on your own, you can confidently seek His help. He can still help the weak against an army. With Him on your side you can be sure that you will be on the winning team every day.

Heavenly Father, it is wonderful to know that I can simply come and ask for Your help this year when crises unravel in my life. I know that I am always a winner because You are on my side. Amen.

Seek the Lord Purposefully

The LORD is near to all who call on Him, to all who call on Him in truth. Ps. 145:18

Walter Cizek wrote a remarkable book called *He Leadeth Me*. All through his life, Cizek struggled to reconcile the negative situations he faced every day while he was in a labor camp in Siberia with God's will. His hard life taught him bit by bit to trust in God with a childlike faith, but he continued to seek a clearer experience of the presence of God in his life. Eventually he found it in a somewhat unlikely place: in the camp where he was being held prisoner.

Cizek came to the realization that through faith we can know that God is present everywhere and is always there if we simply turn to Him. It is therefore we who need to place ourselves in the presence of God; we who need to turn to Him in faith. Cizek had to learn that life is really not fair and that God does not simply smooth the road for us with the wave of a magic wand.

Even though all things will not fall in exactly the right places for you, you can know that you will find God if you seek Him, that He is close to all those who call on Him in righteousness, and that He will lead you if you ask Him to do so.

Heavenly Father, thank You very much for the assurance that You are always there when I call on You in righteousness – even in those times when things go wrong for me – in the year that lies ahead. Amen.

Dependence on God

You do not even know what will happen tomorrow. Instead, you ought to say, "If it is the Lord's will, we will live and do this or that." James 4:14-15

Sometimes we wrongly imagine that we are in control of ourselves, our time and our future. People who think this are mistaken. Not one of us knows what will happen tomorrow. At the beginning of a new year you do not know if by the end of the year your whole life will have turned upside down.

The future remains a closed book to people. And yet the children of God can dream dreams and make plans for the future – just as long as they realize that their plans must fit in with God's purposes for His kingdom, and as long as they are willing to submit their plans to the will of God. Ultimately He is the only One who holds the future in His hands. And because you know for certain that He loves you, you also know that nothing happens by chance in the life of a Christian.

Acknowledge your absolute dependence on God right now. In the Sermon on the Mount, Jesus told the people that those who know that they are dependent on God will receive the kingdom of God (see Matt. 5:3). To live within the will of God and to be completely dependent on Him is the only guarantee that you will be successful and happy.

Heavenly Father, forgive me for so reluctantly surrendering control of my life to You. This year I want to live within Your will, in complete dependence on You. Please help me to do so. Amen.

Leave the Baggage of the Past!

One thing I do: Forgetting what is behind and straining toward what is ahead, I press on toward the goal to win the prize for which God has called me heavenward in Christ Jesus. Phil. 3:13-14

P aul tackled the challenges that lay ahead of him with the right attitude. He was not concerned with the things that had gone wrong in the past, but reached forward to the new things that lay ahead of him. He made every effort to be the first to cross the finishing line so that the heavenly prize to which God had called him, could be his.

Many people start the new year while they are still staggering under the heavy baggage of the year that has passed. Harvey Cushing says that even the strongest man will give way when the burden of yesterday is carried together with that of tomorrow.

Perhaps you too have made mistakes in the last year. Begin this year without the burden of the things that are behind you and gird yourself up to reach the finishing line. Usually there is only one winner, but the children of God can all be winners. There is a heavenly prize that waits for each one of us.

Right now, stop stressing about all the things that went wrong in the year that has passed. Forget about your mistakes. Or better yet, learn from them and do not make the same mistakes again.

Heavenly Father, help me to leave the unnecessary baggage of the past behind me, to live this year with commitment and enthusiasm. Amen.

Hold Fast to God's Promises

Being fully persuaded that God had power to do what He had promised. Rom. 4:21

Abraham succeeded in continuing to hope in God and to believe in His promises long after it seemed completely impossible for the promises to ever come true. And God rewarded Abraham's persistent faith. Even though he and his wife were much too old to be able to have children, God fulfilled the promise that He would give them a son. Isaac was born because Abraham held fast to the promises of God, because he was one hundred percent convinced that God's power was sufficient to do what He had promised.

When someone ends up in the depths of despair, it is good to be reminded of the promises of God. The Bible even tells us that we should remind God of His promises (see Isa. 62:6).

Every promise of God is built on four pillars, so writes L. B. Cowman in her well-known devotional *Streams in the Desert*. The first two are the righteousness and holiness that will never allow God to deceive us. The third is His mercy that will not allow Him to forget. The fourth is His truth that will ensure that He will not change, but guarantees that He will carry out all that He has promised.

Heavenly Father, just like Abraham, I hope in You and believe that You have the power to do what You have promised. Thank You that I can hold fast to Your promises in the year that lies ahead. Amen.

Your Time Is Precious!

Do this, understanding the present time: The hour has already come for you to wake up from your slumber, because our salvation is nearer now than when we first believed. The night is nearly over; the day is almost here. Rom. 13:11-12

Paul delivered this sermon almost 2,000 years ago – in this letter he wanted to teach the Christians in Rome that time is precious; that the return of Jesus is imminent. There is no better time to reflect on this Scripture verse than at the beginning of a new year. Not one of us knows how much more time we have to live. We simply do not have the time to live a life that is not established according to God's expectations.

There is a story about the renowned evangelist Dwight L. Moody who, one night, addressed a large crowd about sin and the judgment of God. He then invited everyone to return the next evening so that he could talk to them about the mercy of God and His salvation. That night the hall in which the meeting had been held burnt down and Moody never again had the chance to speak to that specific group of people. He reproached himself his whole life because he had not used the time he had to present the salvation message.

Use every opportunity that comes your way; live as God asks you to do, so that you will not later regret making better use of your time. Time that is wasted can never be reclaimed.

Lord Jesus, I realize that the time of Your return comes closer day by day. Teach me to use my time properly and to live as You ask me to. Amen.

Quiet Time

"Let My teaching fall like rain and My words descend like dew, like showers on new grass, like abundant rain on tender plants." Deut. 32:2

How I get up in the morning determines my whole day. If I jump out of bed in a hurry in the mornings and have only five minutes to read my Bible and pray, my whole day goes wrong from the beginning. Everything I plan seems to fail, I run on a short fuse and am rushed; nothing seems to work out well.

But if I wake up early enough so that I can spend an hour alone with God and His Word and can discuss my day with Him, everything runs smoothly. I am relaxed and can solve every problem that arises with God's wisdom and His strength. As the day progresses I am more and more aware of the presence of God.

You too can enter each day with self-confidence and confidence in God with the certain assurance that this day will be a day of victory for you. But you need to make time for God's instructions – you need to let His words refresh you every morning.

Always remember: the busier your day will be, the more you have need of your quiet time with God. The most foolish thing you can do is to neglect your quiet time because you have too many other things that demand your time.

Heavenly Father, I praise You for the privilege of being able to spend times of refreshment and restoration with You. Thank You that the words of Your Word can refresh me like the morning dew. Amen.

Continue to Wait on the Lord

On one occasion, while He was eating with them, He gave them this command: "Do not leave Jerusalem, but wait for the gift My Father promised, which you have heard Me speak about." Acts 1:4

Jesus asked His disciples to remain in Jerusalem and to wait for the gift that His Father had promised them. If they had not listened to Him they would not have been there when the Holy Spirit was poured out.

When someone once asked Abba Anthony, one of the desert fathers, what a person should do to bring pleasure to God, he was immediately ready with his answer. There are three things. The first two are obvious: we should always be aware of the presence of God and we should obey His Word. The last one is, however, somewhat surprising: we should not be too hasty to leave the place where we find ourselves at present.

Perhaps you are trapped in a town, job or marriage at the moment that does not seem to work out for you. Perhaps, you have the desire to pack up your stuff and move somewhere far away. Take heed of Abba Anthony's advice: stay where you are. This is the place where the Lord wants to use you, even though you are not quite happy there at the moment.

Stop being dissatisfied with your present circumstances. Make peace with your situation and ask God to use you in a special way right where you are.

Lord, I am sorry that I am so dissatisfied with my surroundings and situation. Make me willing to be used by You right here where I am. Amen.

Principles for a Better Life

I saw that wisdom is better than folly, just as light is better than darkness. Eccles. 2:13

During a series of interviews with juvenile prisoners, the writer Katie Brazelton asked each one what three things they would do should they be released that day. She then summarized the answers:

- Live one day at a time. If you realize you are beginning to go off track, make a plan to get back on.
- Think positively. Avoid negative people and influences. Find good role models and mentors.
- Relax. Live light. Do not take yourself so seriously. Laugh more readily at yourself and with others.
- Give to others much, much more than you expect from them.
- Talk to God about every decision so that you can learn to focus on the bigger picture of your purpose in life. Don't focus on your own desires all the time.
- When you discover that certain something that inspires you, respond to it immediately. It will help you to stay out of trouble.

These are the perfect New Year's resolutions. If you could manage to keep these six principles, you will also find that it is much easier to stay out of trouble!

Heavenly Father, will You please help me to follow these principles for a better life so that this year will be a good year for me. Amen.

Don't Be Afraid!

There is no fear in love. But perfect love drives out fear, because fear has to do with punishment. The one who fears is not made perfect in love. 1 John 4:18

The command to not be afraid appears 365 times in the Bible, more than any other command, precisely because each day we encounter things that can make us afraid. It is hard not to be afraid of the unknown. We don't know all that lies ahead for us this year. We are afraid that we might not get through it.

The good news is that you do not need to be afraid if you love God. God's love for you should be able to drive every fear from your life. In *Reaching for the Invisible God*, Philip Yancey writes that the antidote to fear is not a change in your circumstances, but a deep understanding of the love of God. When you want to give in to fear, think of God's immeasurable, incomprehensible love for you. If you grasp the extent of that love, your fear will simply dissolve of its own accord.

John describes this love for us in 1 John 4:19: "We love God because He first loved us." God loved you long before the world existed, declares the Bible. Right back before time began He had already chosen you to be His. This year you can with absolute confidence take all your fears and worries to Him – He wants to give you His peace in exchange for them.

Lord Jesus, thank You that Your love will cause every fear in my life to dissolve. I praise You that I can live the year that lies ahead under the banner of that love. Amen.

Beware of Sin

If I had cherished sin in my heart, the Lord would not have listened. Ps. 66:18

One of the things that disturbs our relationship with God the most is sin. Unconfessed or deliberate sin has a way of building a wall between God and us so that He no longer hears our prayers.

Unfortunately we live in a society where sin has become cheap. Nothing is actually seen as wrong anymore in the eyes of the world. Living together, adulteress relationships, swearing, using drugs, watching explicit movies, lying and cheating have all become such a part of everyday life that even Christians have become used to it. But God's rule against sin remains the same – the Bible's understanding of sin has never changed.

If the wrong things around you cause you to live the wrong way, it is time that you see the red danger lights flickering ahead. What you do still matters to God. He still asks you to obey His Word and His commands if you want to live close to Him. He sees sin in such a serious light that He let His Son die so that you could be forgiven for the wrong things you do.

Make an effort to study the Bible again so that you will know how God wants you to live. Only then will He listen to your prayers and you will live close to Him every day.

Father, please forgive me for becoming so accustomed to sin that it no longer disturbs me. Show me once again through Your Word and Your Spirit what Your will for my life is. Amen.

Live Close to God

This is what the LORD Almighty says: "In those days ten people from all languages and nations will take firm hold of one Jew by the hem of his robe and say, 'Let us go with you, because we have heard that God is with you.'" Zech. 8:23

The prophet Zechariah prophesied that a great number of people would go to Jerusalem to seek the will of God and to ask His advice. These people would say to the Israelites that they wanted to go with them because they could see that God was with them.

If you live close to God you have the assurance that God will also be close to you and that He will even change the way in which you think and live. Day by day you will become more like Jesus.

"Come near to God and He will come near to you," writes James. He also goes on to tell us how to do it: "Wash your hands, you sinners, and purify your hearts, you double-minded" (James 4:8). If you are serious about drawing closer to God, you will need to be prepared to bid your sins farewell, because sin will always bring about distance between you and God. You ought to live in such a way that others will become jealous and will want to follow your God because they too long for the joy and peace that they see radiating from your life.

May it be true for you that people who look at you will want to go with you because they can see that God is with you.

Heavenly Father, I want to live in such a way that all who look at me will be able to see that You are with me. Please help me to inspire other people to also learn to know You. Amen.

Desire God

As the deer pants for streams of water, so my soul pants for You, my God. My soul thirsts for God, for the living God. When can I go and meet with God? Ps. 42:1-2

A person can only survive for three days without water, although they can go for forty days without food. It is therefore much more serious to be without water than it is to be without food.

The psalmist compares his longing for God in a time of hardship with the physical thirst of a deer. It is God Himself who places this desire to want to live closer to Him in our hearts and lives. The church father St. Augustine once wrote, "I invite You into my soul which has been prepared to receive You through the desire which You have placed in it."

When you truly live close to God, you cannot get by without Him and you constantly long for His presence in your life. Then you will be like Peter and John who, in spite of the fact that the Jewish Council forbade them to speak about Jesus, answered that they would rather obey God than people (see Acts 4:19).

When you find yourself in a crisis situation, you want God to be with you. You walk around all day with a longing to live even closer to Him, to have an even more intimate relationship with Him. Satisfy your spiritual longings for God through living close to Him every day and making His Word part of your life.

Heavenly Father, I long for Your presence in my life as a deer thirsts for water. Thank You that I can experience Your closeness every day. Amen.

February

Relationships

In *Everybody's Normal Till You Get to Know Them*, John Ortberg comes to the conclusion that there isn't a single normal person on earth!

We all have a weak spot, no matter how hard we try to hide it from others. All of us are sinners from the moment we are born, but fortunately there is hope for us!

Jesus is the only Person who was ever perfectly normal; no, perfect. He was prepared to become like us so that our sins could be forgiven by God.

Although we are abnormal (sinful) at the moment, God is planning to make us normal again one day.

In heaven we will be able to get rid of all the abnormalities in us, forever.

In the month ahead we are going to focus on relationships, discover our own weak points – and hold on to our hope in heaven.

Lord, I realize now how imperfect
and sinful I am and how much I need
to change before my relationship with You
and others can be whole again.
Thank You for the people that
I love and for those who love me;
thank You that You love me
unconditionally and hold me close.
Make me willing to prove my love for You
and others in practical ways –
by keeping in touch and caring about them.
I praise You for the Christian friends
that You have sent me.
Grant that I will truly care for my friends,
share my faith with them
and make time for fellowship with other believers.
I pray for my relationship with my spouse and children –
the people I don't need to wear masks in front of;
people who accept me and who
I can accept just the way they are.
Keep me from talking too much,
so that I won't hurt others with my words;
to be friendly towards everybody,
and to solve conflict situations with Your wisdom.
Make it possible for me to forgive others
like You forgive me; to always tell the truth,
say no to temptations
and not discriminate against people.
Grant that I will treat each and
every person as if they are You.
It is wonderful to know that heaven is my final destination,
where You will put an end to all negative things
and I will meet You face to face.
Amen.

You Are a Sheep!

All of us, like sheep, have strayed away. We have left God's paths to follow our own. Yet the LORD laid on Him the sins of us all. Isa. 53:6

One Sunday my husband preached on Psalm 23 and at one stage he said that we are all God's sheep. A little boy sitting in front disagreed. Above the laughter of the congregation, he said loudly, "No way. *I'm* no sheep!" And yet, Isaiah is quite right; we are actually all sheep, only too keen on going our own way. The brush of sin has touched each one of us. None of us can escape it. Like Israel of old we just cannot manage to stay on God's road. We try very hard to hide our negative characteristics from others, but in the end, we do not succeed in doing so.

In fact it is the people who live closest to us – our parents, husband, children and friends – who bear the brunt of this imperfection and are often disillusioned by it. Fortunately Jesus made a plan. He died on the cross so that the price for our sins could be paid once and for all; so that God could forgive our sins and call us His children.

Yet, our sinfulness can teach us a precious lesson. Because we are imperfect sinners we dare not expect other people to be perfect. Treat their imperfections with the same tolerance and love that God shows you.

Lord Jesus, thank You very much that You bore my sins on the cross. Change me so that I may become more like You. Amen.

Imperfect Bible Characters

There is no one righteous, not even one. All have turned away; there is no one who does good, not even one.
Rom. 3:10, 12

If you would like to know what imperfection looks like, just start reading your Bible. Perhaps you are under the impression that the people described in God's Book should at least be "normal." Think again. Eve lands the whole of humanity in sin because she wants to be like God. Cain murders his brother because he is jealous. Noah gets drunk and puts a curse on his son. Abraham sleeps with his wife's slave, Hagar, and then allows Sarah to chase her and her son away. Lot goes and lives in evil Sodom and offers his daughters as prostitutes to his visitors; and after he leaves Sodom, his daughters sleep with him and conceive two children, and so it goes on and on …

However, before you judge these imperfect Bible characters too harshly, first go and read what Paul says in Romans 3:12: "All have turned away, they have together become worthless; there is no one who does good, not even one." We are *all* imperfect and sinful so we all deserve to be punished. But, fortunately for us, God had already made a plan after the Fall: He sent His only Son as a sacrifice to deliver us from sin. Through the justification that faith in Jesus gives us, God is now prepared to forgive our sins.

Heavenly Father, how wonderful You are to have sent Your Son as a sacrifice for my sins so that I can be saved! Amen.

We Need Each Other

The LORD God said, "It is not good for the man to be alone. I will make a helper who is just right for him." Gen. 2:18

After God had created all things, He came to the conclusion that it was not good for a person to be alone. So He created a partner for Adam; someone like him. It was only when Eve was created that Adam came into his own and was able to achieve the purpose that God had created him for.

No one is perfectly happy being alone. We need someone to communicate with, someone to love and touch, someone to do things with. People need each other. If we cannot give and receive love, we become neurologically handicapped. Yet, often we are hesitant to open up to others because we are afraid of getting hurt.

We need other people and they need us. A Harvard researcher, Robert Putnam, discovered that when lonely people join a group, their chances of dying within six months drop by 50%!

Relationships are like paintings, and trust is the frame around the painting that keeps everything together. Trusting people is always risky, but you must believe that the risk is worthwhile, because without taking it, there is no chance of a healthy and steady relationship. Therefore, reach out to others. Cherish your spouse, family and friends. Dare to be a people's person, because others need you.

Lord, thank You for relationships, for people that I can love and cherish. Make me willing to trust the people around me wholeheartedly. Amen.

God Holds You

"Don't be afraid, for I am with you. Don't be discouraged, for I am your God. I will strengthen you and help you. I will hold you up with My victorious right hand." Isa. 41:10

When things were going very badly for Israel, God had a reassuring message for them, brought by the prophet Isaiah. He said that in spite of their negative circumstances, in spite of the fact that they were in exile at the time, they did not need to be afraid or worried any longer because God was still with them. Their God of the Covenant had promised to strengthen them, to help and uphold them.

Babies want to be held. And it is an instinctive reaction to pick up a baby or toddler and hold them when they cry. Usually the baby stops crying when they feel the arms of someone they know around them. And this is not only true for babies and toddlers, but for us too!

Being held provides comfort against the world's hurt. When you are sad, it is comforting to feel a friend's arms around you. Sadly, there are times when we don't have people to comfort us. But God is always with His children, and He is the very best Comforter. Because He is with you, you need never feel lonely, afraid or worried. The Bible assures you that God will hold you in His arms in times of suffering, close to His heart and that He will surround you with love every day.

Heavenly Father, it is wonderful to know that being close to You will always comfort me, that You will hold me and help me. Amen.

Hugs Are Necessary

Then He took the children in His arms and placed His hands on their heads and blessed them. Mark. 10:16

Jesus was displeased with the disciples when they tried to stop the children from coming to Him. "Let the children come to Me. Don't stop them! For the Kingdom of God belongs to those who are like these children," Jesus said to them (Mark 10:14). Mark says that Jesus then put His arms around the children and blessed them.

I have often wished I could have been one of those lucky children who felt Jesus' hand on their head, or arm or shoulder. Today it is not possible any more, but we can still be Jesus' hands by giving people in need of comfort and encouragement a hug.

Kathleen Keating wrote a charming little book on the therapy of hugs. She says that all people, irrespective of their age or status, like to feel safe. If we do not feel safe, we cannot function effectively and we find less pleasure in our interaction with others. If, however, someone gives us a hug, we become aware of the support of a fellow human being and take heart from it for our daily task.

Maybe there is someone close to you who is longing for a hug. Stop being so stingy with your hugs and bestow them liberally to everyone who crosses your path.

Lord Jesus, help me to show my personal care for others by comforting them with a hug or a touch. Amen.

The Value of Friendship

Seeing their faith, Jesus said to the paralyzed man, "My child, your sins are forgiven." Mark 2:5

One of my favorite Bible stories about relationships is the one where the paralyzed man's four friends brought him to Jesus. It was impossible for him to get to Jesus by himself. There were no wheelchairs in Jesus' time so the handicapped people had to rely on others to do everything for them.

This paralyzed man was completely helpless; but that didn't put his friends off. They cared so much for him that they carried him on a mat to the house where Jesus was. But when they got there they discovered that the place was crowded; there wasn't even space outside to put their friend down. They couldn't even get him close to Jesus! But they refused to give up. They made a hole in the roof of the house and lowered the paralyzed man on the mat, right at Jesus' feet. (I wonder what the owner had to say about this!) Mark says that Jesus saw the faith of the four friends and He healed the man because of this.

Nothing could stop these men from getting their friend to Jesus. And because of their care, Jesus healed the paralyzed man. What about you? What are you doing to bring your friends to Jesus?

Lord, thank You for Christian friends who introduced me to You so that You could touch me and forgive my sins. Help me to do the same for my friends. Amen.

Friends Care about Each Other

There are "friends" who destroy each other, but a real friend sticks closer than a brother. Prov. 18:24

Yesterday we read the story of the paralyzed man's four friends who wanted to get him to Jesus so badly that they left no stone unturned in the process. They firmly believed that Jesus could help their friend, and Jesus saw their faith and rewarded them for it. But Jesus did not heal the paralyzed man immediately. He simply said to him that his sins were forgiven – something that is impossible to see. When we communicate with Jesus, the very first thing we become aware of is our sin. It is only when we have confessed our sins that we can really get to Jesus so that He can forgive our sins and touch us.

The spiritual well-being of your friends should also be important to you. It is easier to love others when you are alone than when you have to live among them and are confronted by their imperfections every day. This is why the writer of Proverbs says that friends can break you. Yet friends are precious, they care about you and you care about them – some are even closer to you than your own family.

If you really care for your friends, it is your duty to pray for them and to bring them to Jesus, so that He can forgive their sins and heal them spiritually.

Lord Jesus, I am sorry that I don't try hard enough to bring my friends to You. Help me to make every effort to share my faith with them and to pray for them. Amen.

The Fellowship of Believers

They worshiped together at the Temple each day and shared their meals with great joy and generosity – all the while praising God and enjoying the goodwill of all the people.
Acts 2:46-47

Having relationships with other people is time-consuming. Mark says that the first church made a lot of time for the fellowship of believers. They met every day and ate together. It seems that everybody set aside ample time to be together and share meals together as believers. This was also one of the reasons why this church was so richly blessed and grew so quickly.

The Bible strongly emphasizes the fellowship of believers. It is God's will that His children spend time together. Most people today don't even have time for their own families, let alone for other believers.

In Romans 12, Paul gives guidelines for Christians: We must be glad with those who are glad and sad with those who are sad; we must share the interests of others.

Make time to fellowship with other believers. There is a saying, "Wise people do not try to microwave friendship, parenting, or marriage." Therefore, stop rushing, slow down and spend time with other children of God. It won't be long before you see the fruits of your fellowship with believers in your life.

Lord, please forgive me for going through life so fast that I do not make nearly enough time for other believers. Teach me to give them more of my time. Amen.

How Much Do You Love Others?

If someone has enough money to live well and sees a brother or sister in need but shows no compassion – how can God's love be in that person? 1 John 3:17

This Scripture verse makes me feel very guilty. It is a serious accusation: If the fate of people who are cold and hungry does not touch you, it is impossible for you to truly love God. We have become so used to seeing underprivileged people that we have become desensitized, and we feel less and less sympathy for them. Just feeling sorry for them is not enough, John writes. Our sympathy ought to result in action, otherwise it serves no purpose. Only then will other people be able to see that we love God (see 1 John 3:18).

Dallas Willard writes: We cannot have one posture toward God and a different one toward other people. If love is truly the fulfillment of the law, then a lack of love is the very worst sin one can be guilty of. And each and every one of us is guilty of this.

God measures our love for Him by our love for other people. What do you think? Do you pass the test? If not, it is not too late to change your attitude towards others and to ask God to help you love them sincerely and prove your love through your actions.

Heavenly Father, once again I am so guilty before You. There are so many people who need my help and yet I still turn a blind eye. Show me where You want to use me today so that my love for other people can be proved through my deeds. Amen.

The Very First Relationship

*The man said, "This is now bone of my bones and flesh of
my flesh; she shall be called 'woman,' for she was taken out
of man." That is why a man leaves his father and mother and
is united to his wife, and they will become one flesh.
Gen. 2:23-24*

Adam, the first human being, was used to the animals in the garden. He knew all of them and named
each of them. These animals came in pairs, each of them
had a mate – only Adam was alone. And God saw that
this was not good. God made him a mate who suited him
perfectly. Even more than that, she could communicate
with him – something none of the animals could do.
"Eventually there's someone like me," was Adam's
joyful reaction to this.

The first human couple was perfect and without sin.
They knew each other completely and accepted each
other wholly. There has never again been such a perfect
relationship. They walked with God in the garden –
their relationship with each other and with God was
good, without flaws. It was part of their normal day to
communicate with each other and with God.

Unfortunately there are very few marriage
relationships that can compare with the very first
relationship. Yet a happy marriage is still possible:
provided the marriage partners love each other and
God sincerely and are willing to serve Him together.

*Lord, thank You for the spouse that You have given me.
Please bless our relationship so that it will be happy and fulfilling. Amen.*

Relationship Breakdown

"You won't die!" the serpent replied to the woman. "God knows that your eyes will be opened as soon as you eat it, and you will be like God, knowing both good and evil."
Gen. 3:4-5

A dam and Eve's happiness lasted only until the snake entered Paradise. The snake knew exactly how to cause trouble in the perfect relationship between the first human couple.

The devil still knows how to disrupt the relationship between humankind and God, as well as among people. He is, after all, the Father of Lies. What the Serpent told Eve was not the truth, but he succeeded in misleading her and caused her to be dissatisfied with her circumstances.

When he promised that she would be like God, she yielded to temptation, and then involved Adam in her disobedience. To this day, the devil works in exactly the same way. He makes us dissatisfied with our circumstances and persuades us to put ourselves and our own interests before those of God and others.

He also knows exactly where our weaknesses lie, and that is precisely where he will attack us. Fortunately God is much stronger than the devil. If you are willing to resist him in God's strength – something that Eve couldn't do – he will flee from you (see James 4:7).

Lord, with Your power please help me to resist and defeat the devil so that he will not be successful in destroying my relationships. Amen.

Sin Enters the World

At that moment their eyes were opened, and they suddenly felt shame at their nakedness. So they sewed fig leaves together to cover themselves. Gen. 3:7

Satan made the eating of the forbidden fruit so irresistible to Eve that she gave in to temptation. But she didn't stop there; she also gave Adam some to eat. By eating the fruit, they both disobeyed God, and their eyes were opened – just as the devil promised. But what they saw was not what they expected. The nightmare of sin became a reality to them for the first time. They became aware of the fact that they were naked and tried to cover their nakedness with fig leaves. But the very first consequence of their disobedience was that their relationship with God was in troubled waters.

This story is well known to us – and we only have to look at the newspapers or watch the news to see the consequences of sin around us. Because of Adam and Eve's transgression, all people are sinful from the moment of birth. Not only has their communication with God gone awry and their relationships been disrupted, but they are also out of sync with nature.

Only God can deliver you from sin. Although you are programmed to sin, you can still choose to obey God. In Jesus you can choose again, you can make the right choice; you can choose God and from now on say no to sin and temptation.

Lord Jesus, I praise You that, in spite of the fact that I am born a sinner, You make it possible for me to choose again; to choose to serve You. Help me to do this. Amen.

Hide-and-Seek

The LORD called to Adam, "Where are you?" Gen. 3:9

God knew very well that the first human couple had been disobedient to Him. Instead of communicating freely with God as they were used to doing, they hid from Him when they heard Him walking in the garden. When God asked where they were, they immediately started blaming each other for their disobedience. Thus the breach in their relationship with God led directly to a breach of trust in their relationship with each other.

Hide-and-seek is normally a fun game, but when Adam and Eve hid from God it was not fun at all. They were ashamed of their poor behavior and disobedience. They were also hiding from each other, because they were no longer comfortable with their nakedness. They covered themselves with fig leaves to be acceptable to one another.

When you have a close relationship with God, and sin in your life disrupts that relationship, you tend to hide from others and from God. And this deals a deathblow to any relationship, because if we want to have a healthy relationship we have to be open with each other. We should rather confess our sin before God and each other and put an end to it so that the relationship can be restored.

Lord, please forgive me for often wanting to hide from You when I have sinned. Point out my sin to me so that I can confess and stop it and then my relationships will be restored. Amen.

Mutual Accusations and Punishment

[Adam] replied, "It was the woman You gave me who gave me the fruit, and I ate it." Gen. 3:12

When God confronted Adam, Adam immediately blamed God: "The wife that *You* gave me brought me some of the fruit."

Eve did exactly the same: "No, it wasn't me, Lord; the Serpent deceived me."

You and I have that same inborn tendency – to blame other people and not take responsibility for our mistakes. And this is exactly the key to our failure: blaming others for things that go wrong. When we blame others for our mistakes instead of taking responsibility for them ourselves, it causes a breach in our relationship with God and others that is very difficult to fix. Stop blaming others for things you did and be brave enough to admit your mistakes. In the end, this is the only way to correct them.

Before Jesus took the punishment for your sins on the cross, you would have had to take them yourself. God imposed heavy punishments on Adam, Eve and the serpent. But He also gave them the awesome promise that one day Someone would come and crush the serpent's head.

This promise is meant for us too. Jesus made it possible for you and me to be redeemed from the sin in which we were born.

Lord Jesus, I praise You that I don't have to plod along in sin anymore, because You have already paid for my sins in full on the cross. Amen.

Off with the Masks!

O Lord, You have examined my heart and know everything about me. You know when I sit down or stand up. You know my thoughts even when I'm far away. Ps. 139:1-2

People sometimes wear masks so that other people cannot see who they really are. We all want others to think we are prettier, cleverer and better than we really are. Most women won't venture out of doors without their make-up; they color their hair and pay a fortune for cosmetic products that promise to keep them forever young. And it's not just women – men do it too! They also use miracle creams and work out at the gym and watch their figures.

Most adults do their utmost to please others, while children are not hesitant to go without masks.

There's a reason why Jesus says we must become like children again. What children think can be read so clearly on their faces. They have no hidden agendas. To me the most precious thing in the world is seeing our two-year-old granddaughter's face beam with happiness when we visit.

Perhaps we should learn to share our vulnerable areas with our friends, to open up to each other, to live without masks and be honest with each other. Masks don't work with God because He sees straight through us, He knows about the things we try to hide. Get rid of your masks and give your friends the gift of openness.

Lord, I hide my true self behind so many masks. Thank You that You know me through and through. Help me to live without my masks in future, in all sincerity. Amen.

Accept Each Other

Accept each other just as Christ has accepted you so that God will be given glory. Rom. 15:7

I recently read a quote by Dorothy Day that gave me quite a jolt because it made me feel very guilty: "You only love God as much as you love the person you love the least."

To accept someone else means that I stop criticizing that person and stop saying and thinking negative things about them. It means that I look at them through the cross of Jesus and be prepared to love them in spite of their faults and shortcomings. This is something I fail at time and again!

Paul Tournier, the brilliant Swiss psychologist to whom people from all over the world flocked to study his "techniques," liked saying that he had no techniques – all he did was accept people.

The next time you struggle to accept someone, remind yourself of your own sinfulness and lack of love and ask God to set you free from these sins. Always try to see the best in everyone who crosses your path. If you can manage this, it becomes so much easier to accept others and no longer magnify their faults, but rather become aware of your own. Then you will no longer look down on other people, but be willing to accept them just like God accepts you.

Lord, grant that the things I say about others will always reflect love and acceptance and not judgment. Amen.

Acceptance and Approval

Then Jesus stood up again and said to the woman, "Where are your accusers? Didn't even one of them condemn you?" "No, Lord," she said. And Jesus said, "Neither do I. Go and sin no more." John 8:10-11

In today's Scripture reading the Scribes and Pharisees brought a woman who was caught in adultery to Jesus so that He could say what should be done with her. Jesus replied quite simply that the one with a clear conscience should cast the first stone. When they heard what Jesus said they walked away one by one, until Jesus was left alone with the woman.

Acceptance and approval are not the same. Even though Jesus didn't approve of her sin, He accepted the adulteress and did not condemn her. He told her to stop sinning in this way: "Go and sin no more." Accepting others does not mean that you must accept their sins. You have the right to confront someone – always in love, of course – who is on the wrong track.

"It is not possible to accept someone and withhold your forgiveness from him," writes John Ortberg. God accepts your sins and is prepared to forgive you again and again. Ask Him to make it possible for you to not only accept other people, but to also forgive them whole-heartedly.

Lord Jesus, I realize now that acceptance is not the same as approval of something. Teach me the right way to admonish others in love, and to forgive their transgressions towards me. Amen.

Don't Talk Too Much!

Too much talk leads to sin. Be sensible and keep your mouth shut. Prov. 10:19

One of my weaknesses is that I talk too much and I talk before I think. When we are busy with Bible study I just have to tell my friends about a lovely story or quote. I also tend to interrupt people while they are still busy talking. I did it with my husband for a long time without noticing until, one day, he told me about the old man who said to his wife, "Hold that thought, *I'm* talking now!" Although I still catch myself allowing my words to run away with me, I have improved.

The message from Proverbs today is unsettling: There is a correlation between the number of words you speak and the sins you commit.

William Backus discovered through research that the average person tells themselves and others approximately 200 lies a day. His research was most probably only done on women – I can't imagine men talking that much! Then there are also many other word sins like gossip, boasting, insults, not keeping your promises and criticism. And it is precisely these word sins that are the most important stumbling blocks in relationships. In future, make David's prayer in Psalm 19:14 your own: "May the words of my mouth and the meditation of my heart be pleasing to You, O LORD, my Rock and my Redeemer."

Lord, You know how often my words make me sin. Please teach me not to talk too much. Amen.

Smile!

Always be humble and gentle. Be patient with each other, making allowance for each other's faults because of your love. Eph. 4:2

P aul advises the church in Ephesus to be humble, gentle and patient at all times. Kindness should be an essential characteristic of each Christian. It is not surprising that it is listed in Galatians 5:22-23 as one of the fruits of the Spirit.

There is a poster in our garage that says, "Of all the things you wear, your expression is the most important." We all know people whose smiles are not reflected in their eyes. And sometimes you simply cannot look kind and friendly and be sincere about it (no matter how much you want to!), like when someone wants to take a photo of you on stage in front of a crowd of people … the best I can manage then is a grimace! A spontaneous smile is by far the best enhancement. It draws other people to you and works wonders for any relationship. Everybody likes friendly and kind people.

William Auden writes, "Among those whom I like or admire, I can find no common denominator, but among those whom I love, I can: all of them make me laugh!" Research shows that happy people smile up to 400 times a day. Decide today to make a point of trying to be friendlier!

Lord, please make it possible for me to be kinder to everybody around me. Amen.

Conflict Solution

"Don't sin by letting anger control you." Don't let the sun go down while you are still angry, for anger gives a foothold to the devil. Eph. 4:26-27

John Ortberg writes, "Nobody is normal, but conflict is. To be alive, means to be in conflict." To handle conflict correctly is one of the biggest challenges in building relationships because practically no relationship is without conflict.

In Matthew 18:15, Jesus says that you must reprimand your brother if his conduct was wrong. Thus it is necessary to go and talk to the person you are angry with or who is angry with you, and that takes some nerve. Paul cautions the people of Ephesus that they must never end a day in anger because it gives the devil a foothold.

Therefore, always be sensitive to the feelings of others. Bottled-up anger can be very dangerous. Always be very careful that you handle conflict situations in your own home, family or circle of friends with sensitivity. If possible, defuse the conflict or approach the matter in love and with forgiveness. The main aim of solving conflict situations should be to reconcile the two parties. Ask God to help you achieve this.

Heavenly Father, forgive me that I am still in conflict with others so often and cannot find the right way to solve things peacefully. Please help me to defuse the conflict situations in my life in the right way. Amen.

Forgive Each Other

Be kind to each other, tenderhearted, forgiving one another, just as God through Christ has forgiven you. Eph. 4:32

Forgiveness is essential to good relationships. If you refuse to forgive other people, your relationships are never going to work. In his book *Vengeance or Mercy*, Lewis Smedes explains what forgiveness is *not*: It is not apologizing, forgetting, or reconciliation. Forgiveness means forgiving someone even though they don't deserve it or ask for it.

C. S. Lewis once wrote to his friend Malcolm that he had at long last succeeded in forgiving someone who had been dead for thirty years! Lewis detested the fact that this person was never punished for his crime, and had therefore gotten off scot-free.

The closer the relationship between two people, the more it hurts if one breaks his promise to the other. Then we sometimes get the "eye-for-an-eye" and a "tooth-for-a-tooth" reaction. Forgiveness means putting such thoughts out of your mind. Jesus told Peter that we should be willing to forgive someone seventy-seven times. Even though Jesus knew that one would betray Him, another would deny Him and all of them would desert Him when He needed their support most, He still forgave them wholeheartedly.

If you refuse to forgive someone else, you are going to be the one who suffers most because of your unforgiving attitude.

Lord, help me to forgive people who wrong me as freely as You forgive my sins. Amen.

Stick to the Truth

Jesus said to the people who believed in Him, "You are truly My disciples if you remain faithful to My teachings. And you will know the truth, and the truth will set you free." John 8:31-32

It is sometimes difficult to own up to the truth about ourselves. And it is even worse when someone else has to tell us! The truth seems to be missing in our society today. Not many people live honest and open lives anymore – most have an agenda. People glibly tell lies in order to look better in other people's eyes. It is difficult to tell others the truth about ourselves because we don't want them to reject us or take offense. It is much easier to avoid conflict in our relationships by sidestepping the truth.

But God expects His children to tell the truth at all times. Jesus was truthful at all times. He promised His disciples that when He sent them the Spirit of truth, He would lead them in the whole truth, and then He prayed for them that they would consecrate themselves to God through the truth (see John 17:17).

The truth here refers to that which is right and genuine. If you undertake to speak the truth at all times, and do the things that are right in God's eyes, you can rest assured that His truth will set you free.

Lord Jesus, teach me to know the truth, to be devoted to You in truth, so that the truth will set me free. Amen.

Temptations

"Keep watch and pray, so that you will not give in to temptation. For the spirit is willing, but the body is weak!"
Matt. 26:41

When Jesus' disciples failed to stay awake with Him in Gethsemane, He cautioned them to watch and pray so that they would not give in to temptation.

The problem with most sin is that it is easy to start doing the wrong thing, but very difficult to stop. This is true about anything that threatens the human character, like bitterness, pornography, greed and fraud. And it is absolutely fatal to think you can handle temptations in your own strength. After all, this is what Eve wanted to do. The devil is way too strong for you to handle on your own. One of the surest signs that you are in trouble with a certain temptation is when you don't want to tell anyone about it.

Jesus teaches us in the Lord's Prayer to pray that we are not led into temptation. Is there perhaps a secret sin (temptation) in your life? Pray about the thing that you can't overcome even though you know it's wrong, like smoking, alcohol and drugs. Share your personal temptation with a friend you trust and ask her to pray with you. God promises that He will never allow temptation to become too strong for you – He will show you a way out every time so that you will not give in to it (see 1 Cor. 10:13).

Lord Jesus, give me the strength to resist temptations.
Amen.

Part of the Inner Circle

They [James and John] replied, "When You sit on Your glorious throne, we want to sit in places of honor next to You, one on Your right and the other on Your left." Mark 10:37

God's people, Israel, were part of a privileged group. God chose them from all the nations to receive His covenant promises. Yet, not everybody was welcome: tax collectors, heathens, women (!), Samaritans and lepers were definitely not part of this inner circle in Old Testament times. Those who were part of the inner circle, like the Scribes and Pharisees, who were held in high regard by the community, looked down on these people.

John and James were already part of Jesus' inner circle, but that was not good enough for them. They wanted to fill a place of honor one day at Jesus' left and right hand. The other disciples were indignant when they learned about this, and understandably so.

We all want to be important so that we can be part of the inner circle. We want to get front-row seats and we enjoy it when people make a fuss of us. We want to be accepted by others. However, the kingdom of God doesn't work like this. This is a place where we must adhere to Jesus' rules, where the last will be first and the first, last. It's a place where we must accept each other and not judge people because they are not like us. Are you part of that inner circle yet?

Lord Jesus, thank You for making me part of Your inner circle. Help me to accept others with all my heart, like You do with me. Amen.

No Favorites!

Then Peter replied, "I see very clearly that God shows no favoritism. In every nation He accepts those who fear Him and do what is right." Acts 10:34-35

Peter was under the impression that the Jews had a privileged position. But Jesus gave him a vision of unclean animals and ordered him to eat them. When Peter refused, he heard a voice speaking: "Do not call something unclean if God has made it clean" (Acts 10:15).

Shortly afterwards three men arrived who had been sent by the Roman officer Cornelius. Peter then realized what God wanted to tell him with the vision and was then willing to visit the house of the Roman officer straight away. Peter told Cornelius about his dream and shared the gospel with the Gentiles in Cornelius's house. While they were there together, the Holy Spirit came down on all of them, and they were baptized in the name of Jesus. Only then did Peter understand that God makes no distinction between people; He accepts all who believe in Jesus – regardless of their nation.

God has no favorites: "Remember, you both have the same Master in heaven, and He has no favorites" (Eph. 6:9). You may never make decisions about other people on the grounds of your personal bias. Always remember that everybody is the same in Jesus' eyes, so learn to look at others through His eyes.

Heavenly Father, forgive me for being biased towards certain people because of their background or appearance. Help me so that, like You, I will have no favorites. Amen.

Love and Forgiveness

Simon answered, "I suppose the one for whom he canceled the larger debt." Luke 7:43

T he well-known story of Jesus' meal at Simon's house focuses on the sinful woman who washed Jesus' feet with her tears, dried them with her hair and then anointed them with expensive perfume.

What this woman did was unheard of in the society she lived in, and all the others guests must have been bewildered by what she was doing. Then Jesus explained why it happened: Simon, who was the host, did not accept Jesus with the customary hospitality and honor. There was no water for Jesus to wash His feet in, no towel to dry them on, and no oil to anoint them with. Jesus then asked Simon who would show more love: someone who has been forgiven for a few sins or for many. The latter, Simon answered correctly.

Simon failed to treat Jesus with the politeness that the customs of that time dictated. The woman, on the other hand, professed her love for Jesus for forgiving her sins by washing His feet with her hair and anointing them with expensive aromatic oil. The woman was aware of her sin; she offered Jesus her love and received His forgiveness.

It's easy to look down on criminals for their crimes, but we also need to acknowledge that we sin too, and in God's eyes all sin is equal.

Lord, forgive me for sometimes behaving in an unloving manner – make me thankful towards You and others, and make me willing to show love. Amen.

As if for Jesus

"Now I am giving you a new commandment: Love each other. Your love for one another will prove to the world that you are My disciples." John 13:34-35

I f there is one overriding message that Jesus came to deliver on earth, it is that we must love each other. This is one of the last things He asked His disciples before His death on the cross. The love that Jesus talks about here is not merely a feeling of love, but love that shows itself in deeds – like Jesus' love on the cross.

Mother Teresa often said that if one should see someone on the street, critically ill and disfigured by sores, one must treat that person with the same love and care that a priest handles the tokens of Holy Communion, because that poor person is none other than Jesus in disguise. This is the meaning of true love for your fellow humans: to treat every person you come across as if that person is Jesus Himself.

Just imagine what an unbelievable place our world would be if we could succeed in loving all people; even those who robbed our house or hijacked our car or injured our loved ones. Ask God to give you more love and that He will make it possible for you to prove the love He asks from you by the way you live, so that people will see that you belong to Him.

Lord Jesus, please make it possible for me to love other people as if they are You. Amen.

Final Destination

"He will wipe every tear from their eyes, and there will be no more death or sorrow or crying or pain. All these things are gone forever." Rev. 21:4

Every Christian believes and knows that when our life on earth is over, heaven awaits us. Exactly what heaven is going to look like, we don't know. A book has been written about the first five minutes after death that has become a runaway best-seller. I haven't read it myself, but I can't help wondering how the author (who is still very much alive) could write a book on something he doesn't have first-hand experience of.

In Revelation 21, John describes his vision of the new heaven and the new earth. Going by this, we know that heaven will be an awesome experience for God's children; a place where He will wipe every tear from our eyes, where the things that were difficult for us on earth, like death, heartache and pain, will not exist at all. A place of everlasting joy and light, where God Himself will be our lamp. Perhaps it is possible to write a book on heaven after all!

Jesus is busy preparing a place for you in heaven right now. Thomas Brooks writes that Christ's blood is the key to heaven. The only way to know for certain that heaven will be yours one day is to have faith in Him. Make sure you have the key to that heavenly final destination.

Lord Jesus, I praise You that You have made heaven possible for me by dying for my sins on the cross. Amen.

Face to Face

The throne of God and of the Lamb will be there, and His servants will worship Him. And they will see His face, and His name will be written on their foreheads. Rev. 22:3-4

In the Old Testament, God was so holy that people could not see Him and still live. But in the New Testament Jesus comes to show us what the Father really looks like. In Revelation 1:17-18, Jesus says to John, "Don't be afraid! I am the First and the Last. I am the living One. I died, but look – I am alive forever and ever! And I hold the keys of death and the grave."

Because Jesus was raised from the dead we don't need to fear death anymore. He has first-hand experience of how the first five minutes after death will be. Because He was resurrected we know that we will live with Him in heaven forever one day.

So you need not be afraid of the unknown, of death or of the end of your earthly life. It is nothing more than passing on to real life, the start of your everlasting life, where you will at long last meet Jesus face-to-face and be happy, living with Him forever. Therefore it's alright to long for and look forward to the day that Jesus comes again – just make sure that you are ready when it happens!

Lord Jesus, it is wonderful to know that one day I will meet You face-to-face and be in heaven with You forever. Amen.

March

Spreading the Good News

I f you have God in your heart, you cannot help but spread the good news of Jesus.

Jesus promised His disciples that the Holy Spirit would make them witnesses so that His message could be spread in Jerusalem, Judea, Samaria and to the ends of the world.

The whole book of Acts is a testimony of what exceptional witnesses the early Christians were.

Paul writes to the church in Corinth that we can speak to others about our faith because we have the Spirit of faith to empower us (see 2 Cor. 4:13).

During this month we are going to focus on how to be spontaneous witnesses so that the good news of the love of God will be spread through our words and our deeds.

Lord Jesus,
In the past month I have learned
so much about spreading Your Good News
throughout the world.
I know that it is You who sends me,
that You will be with me
and will equip me, that You will teach me
what to say so that I can be a light for the nations.
Forgive me for sometimes being
embarrassed to speak about You,
and please bring about the right opportunities for me
so that other people will be able to hear about Your love.
Forgive me for sometimes feeling discouraged
when there is no fruit of my witnessing –
make me prepared to persevere as Your witness
until the hearts and lives of people open up to You.
It is impossible for me to remain silent
about Your love for me!
I truly want to use every opportunity
to present Your message of salvation to others.
I also want to live in such a way that
my faith will be clearly visible through my actions,
so that all those who look at me
will know that I belong to You.
Thank You for the privilege of being able to share my faith
with my children and for the joy of knowing
that they too can love and serve You.
I praise You for Your Holy Spirit
who makes it possible for me to be
an enthusiastic witness and for the power
that He makes available to me so that it
becomes easy for me to proclaim Your Good News.
Amen.

Help for the Task of Witnessing

The LORD said to him, "Who gave human beings their mouths? Who makes them deaf or mute? Who gives them sight or makes them blind? Is it not I, the LORD? Now go; I will help you speak and will teach you what to say." Exod. 4:11-12

In the Old Testament already we hear that God wants His children to spread His message. He tells Moses that he does not have to be afraid to testify because God, who gave people their mouths, would help him to speak and tell him exactly what to say. Moses, however, just like us, continued making one excuse after the other. In his defense, we must admit that Moses had a physical problem – he stammered!

Perhaps you too have a physical reason that makes it hard for you to witness. If so, take God's promise to Moses for yourself. He will help you to be a powerful witness. He will help you speak and teach you what to say if you are willing to be used by Him.

Like the disciples long after Moses discovered, God never gives us the task to be His witnesses without being with us. "I am with you always, to the very end of the age," Jesus promised them when He sent them out as witnesses (Matt. 28:20). You too can trust God to do that for you!

Lord Jesus, thank You for the assurance that You will teach me what to say when I speak to people about You and for the promise that You will be with me. Amen.

God's Witnesses

On the evening of that first day of the week, when the disciples were together, with the doors locked for fear of the Jewish leaders, Jesus came and stood among them and said, "Peace be with you!" Again Jesus said, "Peace be with you! As the Father has sent Me, I am sending you." John 20:19, 21

The first time that Jesus appeared to His disciples after His resurrection, He had a very important message for them, "As the Father has sent Me, so I am sending you." The work that Jesus came to accomplish on earth was to proclaim the message of salvation – an obligation that He carried out with great diligence up to His crucifixion and death.

The time came for Jesus to return to His Father, but He left His followers behind to continue His work on earth. As Jesus was sent by God, He also sent His disciples to proclaim His joyful message. During the three years that they had worked with Him, they were prepared by Jesus for this important work. Jesus breathed on them and said, "Receive the Holy Spirit" (v. 22).

If you belong to God you are automatically one of His witnesses – you actually have no choice in this matter. A disciple is at the same time also a disciple-maker, otherwise they completely miss their purpose.

Fortunately for you, you have also received the Holy Spirit to help you with this task.

Holy Spirit, I praise You because You are with me to equip me to witness for God in the world. Please help me with my work on earth. Amen.

Today Is the Day!

"In the time of My favor I heard you, and in the day of salvation I helped you." I tell you, now is the time of God's favor, now is the day of salvation. 2 Cor. 6:2

P aul urges the church in Corinth not to receive the grace of God in vain. God answered their prayers at the right time; today is the day of their salvation. They had to treat their salvation seriously; the salvation that God brought about for them and which Paul explained to them. In verse 11, Paul writes that his heart is wide open to the people of Corinth and he asks that they open their hearts to him.

The worst thing that any witness can do is to put off their work of witnessing. There is no better time to testify of your faith than today. You can confidently put God to the test in this matter – He wants you to be His witness today, and to tell other people of His love (even if you are shy, or young, or find speaking difficult).

You cannot afford to remain silent – if you do so, someone might forfeit their last chance to accept God into their lives.

Heavenly Father, I am sorry that I often put off witnessing for You. Help me to realize the urgency of Your message of redemption so that I will no longer keep it to myself, but will share it with other people today. Amen.

Out of the Overflow of His Heart ...

"A good man brings good things out of the good stored up in his heart, and an evil man brings evil things out of the evil stored up in his heart. For the mouth speaks what the heart is full of." Luke 6:45

To be a witness for Christ is the natural outcome of faith. The mouth speaks of what the heart overflows. Jesus said this to His disciples after He told them that a tree is known by its fruit.

The truth of this saying can be seen very clearly if you listen to grandmothers swapping stories about their grandchildren! The things that you talk about show other people what is truly important to you. From your words people will very quickly hear that you are a Christian, just as they can see from your deeds that you belong to God.

"I believed; therefore I have spoken," Paul wrote to the church in Corinth (2 Cor. 4:13). From the day of his conversion on the road to Damascus, Paul never stopped witnessing. His whole life was dedicated to telling people why they should believe in Jesus.

If you are a Christian, other people should know about it. Are you able to speak about your faith in such a way that people can see that your heart is filled with the love of God?

Lord Jesus, my heart is indeed full of You – give me the right words to tell other people about You, so that my mouth will overflow with the things that live in my heart. Amen.

Who Will Go?

Then I heard the voice of the Lord saying, "Whom shall I send? And who will go for us?" And I said, "Here am I. Send me!" Isa. 6:8

God gave the prophet Isaiah a vision of His majesty: Isaiah saw God sitting on a high throne and the train of His robe filled the temple. Surrounding Him were angels who praised Him with the words, "Holy, holy, holy is the LORD Almighty; the whole earth is full of His glory" (v. 3). When Isaiah saw this vision and realized how mighty and holy God is, he was immediately aware of his own sinfulness and confessed his impurity before the Lord. At this, one of the angels touched his lips and God forgave his sins.

Directly after this the Lord asked whom He could send as a messenger for Him, and Isaiah was ready for the challenge. "Here am I. Send me!" he answered. Unlike Moses before him and Jeremiah after him, Isaiah did not have a list of excuses for why he could not carry out God's command, but he was immediately willing to do it.

God still uses people in His service to carry His message to others. Like Isaiah, you are a sinner, but God can purify you and forgive your sins so that He can use you as His messenger. God wants to call you and send you today. Are you willing to be His messenger?

Lord God, You know me very well and You know that I am a sinner. Touch me as You did Isaiah so that my sins can be forgiven and that I will be prepared to be sent as Your messenger. Amen.

A Light for the Nations

The LORD says, "I will also make you a light for the Gentiles, that My salvation may reach to the ends of the earth." Isa. 49:6

God had a specific task in mind for the exiles from Israel who were now returning to Jerusalem – it was His will that they would not just keep the covenant promise to themselves but that they would carry it to the rest of the world. He had called them for this task even before they were born, wrote Isaiah, and He promised to make their mouths like sharp swords (see vv. 1-2). The prophet Isaiah told the people of this commission, "I am making you a light to the nations so that you will bring My salvation to the ends of the earth."

God has also called you before you were born to be His witness on the earth and to carry the message of His joyous salvation to others. He wants to make you a light for the nations so that His salvation will reach all people and everyone will have the opportunity to believe in Jesus.

Are you prepared to do this? Then the promise in verse 5 is also for you: "I am honored in the eyes of the LORD and my God has been my strength."

Heavenly Father, it is wonderful that You have called me, as You called the Israelites of old to be a light to the nations and to spread the Good News of Your gospel so that it will reach the farthest corners of the earth. Thank You for the promise that You will give me the strength to do this. Amen.

The Testimony of a King

"He rescues and He saves; He performs signs and wonders in the heavens and on the earth. He has rescued Daniel from the power of the lions." So Daniel prospered during the reign of Darius and the reign of Cyrus the Persian. Dan. 6:27-28

By listening to his jealous officials, King Darius issued a decree that anyone in his kingdom who, in a period of thirty days, worshiped anyone except him would be thrown into the lions' den.

When Daniel defied this decree and continued to worship God, King Darius had no other choice but to throw him into the lions' den. After a sleepless night, early the next morning the king went to the lions' den to see what had happened to Daniel. When he saw him fit as a fiddle among the lions, the king knew that the God of Daniel was the only true God.

He did not hesitate to issue another decree; this time the instructions read that the God of Daniel was to be honored and feared throughout his kingdom. On top of this the king gave a wonderful testimony of God: "He rescues and He saves; He performs signs and wonders in the heavens and on the earth," he said.

Daniel's unshakable faith in his God leads his king to come to repentance and to also worship God. Furthermore, on the command of the king the whole country was instructed to follow his example.

Heavenly Father, I pray for a faith like that of Daniel that will encourage other people to believe in You and to testify of You. Amen.

Jesus' Command to Testify

"As you go, proclaim this message: 'The kingdom of heaven has come near.' But when they arrest you, do not worry about what to say or how to say it. At that time you will be given what to say." Matt. 10:7, 19

It was of the utmost importance to Jesus that the message for which He had come to earth was spread further. He therefore sent His disciples to go and do this. They were to proclaim through the whole of Israel that the kingdom of God was at hand. He also warned them that this work of witnessing would not always be easy; they could expect to be persecuted.

Yet He promised that they need not worry about what they would say because God Himself would give them the right words to speak. He also added, "It will not be you speaking, but the Spirit of Your Father speaking through you" (Matt. 10:20).

Jesus still sends His followers into the world to carry His message that the kingdom of God is at hand. If you are willing to be one of them, you also need not worry about what you will say. Through the working of His Spirit who lives in you, God will give you the right words to say each time. But the warning of Jesus also still applies to you: to be a witness is never an easy task – you can expect opposition. Prepare yourself for this!

Lord Jesus, I am prepared to be one who proclaims the coming of Your kingdom. Thank You for Your promise that Your Spirit will give me the right words and that You Yourself will support me. Amen.

John's Life Mission

There was a man sent from God whose name was John. He came as a witness to testify concerning that Light, so that through him all men might believe. He himself was not the light; he came only as a witness to the Light. John 1:6-8

E ven before the birth of John the Baptist, his father, Zechariah, prophesied that his son would one day be the predecessor of the long awaited Messiah. "You will go on before the Lord to prepare the way for Him," he prophesied in Luke 1:76-77. And John fulfilled his father's prophesy. He fulfilled his mission that he had received from God. He himself said that he came to bear witness to the Light so that all those who listened to him would come to believe in Jesus. John also made it abundantly clear that he was not the Light, but that he had only come to tell people of the Light. "The life appeared; we have seen it and testify to it, and we proclaim to you the eternal life, which was with the Father and has appeared to us," writes the apostle John (1 John 1:2).

Through his testimony, John did his part to ensure that the light of Jesus shone brightly in the darkness, and that the darkness could not extinguish it. Every person who testifies for Jesus helps to spread His light through the world, and ensures that the reign of the devil over the world receives a deathblow. Because no matter how cruel the world looks to us, Jesus has overcome the world.

Lord Jesus, use my testimony so that Your light can be spread throughout the world. Amen.

The Testimony of an Elderly Woman

There was also a prophet, Anna. She was very old. Coming up to them at that very moment, she gave thanks to God and spoke about the child to all who were looking forward to the redemption of Jerusalem. Luke 2:36, 38

Anna, who spent so much time in the temple, was an example for every believing Israelite. Even though women did not play an important role in biblical times, she, in spite of her advanced age, did not stay away from the temple where she served God night and day through fasting and praying.

When she saw the Baby Jesus in Simeon's arms, she immediately believed the words of Simeon: "Sovereign Lord, You now dismiss Your servant in peace. For my eyes have seen Your salvation, which You have prepared in the sight of all nations" (vv. 29-31). She did not keep the good news to herself, but began to speak to all those who had been waiting for the Messiah.

Anna is still a worthy example for us to follow today. Perhaps you neglect your church attendance because you are no longer all that young; perhaps you no longer pray as much as you did before; perhaps you shy away from witnessing to others.

There are still many people these days who have not heard the message of Jesus. If Jesus is a part of your life, it is your responsibility to speak to them about salvation.

Heavenly Father, make me a witness like Anna was, and help me to not hold back from speaking to others about salvation. Amen.

Do Not Be Ashamed to Witness ...

Do not be ashamed to testify about our Lord or of me His prisoner. Rather, join with me in suffering for the gospel, by the power of God. 2 Tim. 1:8

P aul was never ashamed to speak to others about the message of Jesus, and he was also not ashamed to go through hardships for the cause of Jesus. For this reason he could speak to Timothy with authority about witnessing. Paul told Timothy he should not be embarrassed to proclaim the message of the Lord.

Some people find it much easier to witness than others do. Some of my friends can spontaneously initiate a conversation with perfect strangers and ask them about their faith. If I try to do this, I blush and every word I think of saying flies out of my head. At least, this was until I learned the secret of witnessing without being embarrassed. If you happen to be one of the shy ones, I possibly have some advice for you. Stop stressing about when you should witness and about what exactly you must say. Do not concern yourself with what people will say or think of you. Make yourself available to God and wait until He gives you the right opportunity and the right words. Then you will discover that your embarrassment will dissolve like mist before the sun and that you will easily be able to share your faith with others.

Lord Jesus, please forgive me for finding it so hard to share my faith with others. Help me to be able to witness freely about You. Amen.

The Testimony of Philip

Andrew, Simon Peter's brother, was one of the two who heard what John had said and who had followed Jesus. The first thing Andrew did was to find his brother Simon and tell him, "We have found the Messiah." John 1:40-41

Philip, one of the followers of John, was there when John the Baptist declared that Jesus is the Lamb of God. As a result of John's testimony, he decided to follow Jesus. He went after Jesus and asked where He was making His home. When Jesus invited him to come and see, he went with Him and spent the whole day with Him. After this, he went with great excitement to find his brother Peter, and told him that he had found the long-awaited Savior of Israel.

Philip did more than just witness; he physically took Peter to where Jesus was. After this, both Philip and Peter became Jesus' disciples. Later, when Peter, in answer to Jesus' question, said that He was the Christ, the Son of the Living God, Jesus said, "Blessed are you, Simon son of Jonah, for this was not revealed to you by flesh and blood, but by My Father in heaven. And I tell you that you are Peter, and on this rock I will build My church" (Matt. 16:17-18).

Eventually this person to whom Philip had witnessed played a far greater role in God's kingdom than Philip himself. Who knows, perhaps the same can happen to someone you witness to?

Lord, make me willing to witness to others about my relationship with You – and then use these people who have heard my testimony for the good of Your kingdom. Amen.

A Witness from Samaria

Many of the Samaritans from that town believed in Him because of the woman's testimony, "He told me everything I ever did." John 4:39

To me, one of the most beautiful stories of witnessing in the Bible is the one of the Samaritan woman whom Jesus met at the well. To her amazement, Jesus asked her for water. He also told her that everyone who drank of the water that He gives will never again be thirsty. When the woman said to Him that she too wanted some of that water, Jesus asked her to go and call her husband. At this, she told Him her life story and He told her that He was the long-awaited Messiah.

She was so enthusiastic to tell the people in her village about the Messiah that she left her water jar at the well. And her testimony had an amazing effect: Many Samaritans believed in Jesus based on the words of the woman who had witnessed. They all went to the well to meet Jesus personally. After this they asked Jesus to stay with them for a little while, and after two days many more Samaritans believed in Him. The people in the village also had a testimony: "We no longer believe just because of what you said; now we have heard for ourselves, and we know that this man really is the Savior of the world" (v. 42).

Lord Jesus, make me as enthusiastic about telling people about You as the Samaritan woman. Thank You that I also know for certain that You are my Savior. Amen.

Peter Denies Jesus

A servant girl saw [Peter] seated there in the firelight. She looked closely at him and said, "This man was with Him." But he denied it. A little later someone else saw him and said, "You also are one of them." "Man, I am not!" Peter replied. About an hour later another asserted, "Certainly this fellow was with Him, for he is a Galilean." Peter replied, "Man, I don't know what you're talking about!" Luke 22:56-60

The most eager of Jesus' twelve disciples, Peter failed his witnessing test – he denied Jesus. He allowed no less than three opportunities to pass him by in which he could have witnessed about Jesus.

While he was denying Jesus, the cock crowed and Peter remembered the words of Jesus: that he would deny Him three times before the cock had crowed. Luke tells us that he went outside and wept bitterly (see Luke 22:62).

After His resurrection, Jesus appeared to Peter and three times asked him if he loved Him (see John 21:15-19). This time Peter was ready to testify each time that he loved Jesus. He was also willing to look after Jesus' sheep. Jesus prepared him for the things that his witnessing would require of him: "When you are old you will stretch out your hands, and someone else will lead you where you do not want to go" (John 21:18).

Are you, like Peter, prepared to care for your fellow believers and to pay whatever price your witnessing might ask of you?

Lord Jesus, like Peter, I want to testify of my love for You. Make me willing to do so. Amen.

The Testimony of Mary Magdalene

Mary Magdalene went to the disciples with the news: "I have seen the Lord!" And she told them that He had said these things to her. John 20:18

Mary Magdalene had an intimate relationship with Jesus. He had in fact cast seven demons out of her (see Mark 16:9). We, however, never read that she had the boldness to personally speak to others about Jesus.

This fact changed after the resurrection of Jesus. When Jesus appeared to Mary, He asked her not to touch Him, but to go to His disciples and to tell them that He had risen from the dead and was ascending to His Father. Her task was now not to cling to Jesus, but to go and be a witness for Him. Jesus Himself empowered her testimony.

For the first time in the Bible we hear that a woman received an equal command to witness: "Go and tell them!" Jesus said to Mary. And Mary obeyed immediately. Straight away she went to the disciples with the good news that Jesus was not dead, but alive, that she had seen Him with her own eyes. She also told them what Jesus had said to her.

The resurrected Jesus really wants you to be His messenger and to tell other people that He has risen from the dead. Are you willing to respond to His request?

Lord Jesus, help me to be prepared to obey Your command to witness, to tell others what You mean to me and to share with them the message of Your love for us. Amen.

Thomas Does Not Believe His Friends

So the other disciples told him, "We have seen the Lord!" But he said to them, "Unless I see the nail marks in His hands and put my finger where the nails were, and put my hand into His side, I will not believe." John 20:25

Sometimes, even though you carry out your calling to be a witness, there are people who do not believe your testimony. This is exactly what happened when the ten disciples to whom Jesus appeared after His resurrection went and told Thomas what had happened.

When they told Thomas that they had seen Jesus, his immediate response was that he wouldn't believe it was true unless he put his own fingers into the nail marks in His hands and his own hand into the spear wound in Jesus' side. Eight days later, when Jesus appeared to the disciples again and invited Thomas to do exactly that, Thomas was ashamed about his earlier lack of faith. All that he could utter was, "My Lord and my God!" (John 20:28) In response Jesus said that people who are able to believe without seeing are blessed (see John 20:29).

If it ever happens to you that people doubt your testimony, do not be upset about it. God is able to bring about faith in a person's heart, and He too will make sure that the good work that you have begun through your witnessing will one day come to completion.

Lord, I am sorry that I sometimes become despondent when my testimony is disregarded. Help me to persevere in my witnessing for You, because I know that You Yourself will empower my testimony. Amen.

Those Who Proclaim the Gospel

Then the disciples went out and preached everywhere, and the Lord worked with them and confirmed His word by the signs that accompanied it. Mark 16:20

After the resurrection of Jesus He gave His disciples another commission to be His witnesses, "Go into all the world and preach the good news to all creation" (v. 15). Jesus also told them that they would be able to cast out demons in His name, speak in other tongues, heal the sick and do all kinds of other miracles.

After this, Jesus ascended to heaven and the disciples began their task of witnessing on earth. Luke reported that they proclaimed the gospel everywhere and that God worked together with them and empowered their preaching. Because the Lord Himself was with them, many people believed in Jesus. In the book of Acts you can read more about the different ways in which they witnessed wherever they went and how many miracles took place when the disciples proclaimed the gospel over the whole of the then known world.

Today we can still see the results of the disciples' obedience. There are millions of people on earth who believe in Jesus, a direct result of the disciples' obedience to the commission Jesus gave them to be His witnesses. They spread the gospel and it is because of them that you and I now have the privilege of being Christians.

Lord Jesus, make me like Your disciples of old, obedient to Your commission to be Your witnesses. Thank You very much that I know that You will also empower my testimony and will help and support me when I witness. Amen.

Peter Testifies on Pentecost

When the people heard this, they were cut to the heart and said, "Brothers, what shall we do?" Peter replied, "Repent and be baptized, every one of you, in the name of Jesus Christ for the forgiveness of your sins. And you will receive the gift of the Holy Spirit." Acts 2:37-38

On the Day of Pentecost, the very same Peter who denied Jesus three times delivered a powerful testimony of the Jesus who had lived amongst them, who had been crucified and who had ascended to heaven where He is now, seated at the right hand of God, His Father. The people who were listening asked him what they could do to be saved. "Repent and be baptized in the name of Jesus Christ. And you will receive the gift of the Holy Spirit," was Peter's answer. The story of Pentecost is widely known – more than three thousand people repented and received the Holy Spirit that day.

It is probably the dream of every evangelist today to deliver a sermon that causes more than three thousand people to repent. And it was the fearful Peter, who at first did not even want to acknowledge that he knew Jesus, who delivered this sermon! The Spirit of God in Peter's life was the cause of an unbelievable change – it transformed him from a coward into a powerful witness. The Spirit of God can – and will – do the same for you. Ask Him to take your fear away and to help you with your task of witnessing.

Holy Spirit, I pray that You would change me, that You would bring me to the place where I can replace my fear of witnessing with faith in You. Amen.

It Is Impossible to Keep Quiet!

"Which is right in God's eyes: to listen to you, or to Him? You be the judges! As for us, we cannot help speaking about what we have seen and heard." Acts 4:19-20

When Peter and John healed a lame man near the temple, everyone was in an uproar. The people who had seen the miracle were amazed; the man who had been made whole praised God.

Peter used the opportunity to preach to the people in Solomon's colonnade and on hearing his sermon still more people came to salvation. At this, the Jewish Council and the scribes were not happy at all and they brought Peter and John before them to give account of what had happened.

When the two fishermen witnessed before the Jewish Council, a second miracle took place! The council members tried in vain to silence Peter and John because they did not want large numbers of people running after them. But Peter and John did not take any notice of this ban on speaking about Jesus. They would decide for themselves what was right before God, and told the Council that they would rather obey God than them.

God has asked you to be His witness in the world and to proclaim the message of Jesus. If you truly love Jesus, it will be almost impossible for you not to talk about Him.

Lord Jesus, thank You very much that I can love You and talk to people about You. Like Peter and John, may I find it impossible not to talk about You. Amen.

Witness to Everyone

Then Peter began to speak: "I now realize how true it is that God does not show favoritism but accepts from every nation the one who fears Him and does what is right."
Acts 10:34-35

The Jews in Jesus' day did not ever mix with "heathens." But God convinced Peter through a vision of unclean animals that He commanded him to kill and eat, that people should not see things as unclean which God has declared as pure and that His gospel is meant for all people.

Peter obeyed God's command and went with Cornelius, who was not a Jew, and his three servants to his house in Caesarea. When Peter arrived there he told them that God makes no distinction between people, but accepts people from all nations who honor Him. He also testified to them that each one who believes in Jesus would receive forgiveness for their sins. While he was still busy talking to them, the Holy Spirit came upon the people who had gathered together in Cornelius's house to listen to Peter's testimony. Then Peter baptized them.

You too should not decide that there are people you are not prepared to witness to. All people are included in God's invitation to be His children, even those that you might not consider worthy.

Lord, forgive me for sometimes selecting the people that I want to witness to. I realize now that all people are included in Your invitation and that each one should be given a chance to hear the gospel. Amen.

The Spirit Gives Confidence

After they prayed, the place where they were meeting was shaken. And they were all filled with the Holy Spirit and spoke the word of God boldly. Acts 4:31

From the start the chief priests and the Jewish Council did their best to prevent Peter and John from witnessing. They were afraid that too many people would listen to them and they forbade them to speak to anyone else in the name of Jesus.

After Peter and John had been released by the chief priests they went to their fellow Christians and reported back to them. After this they all prayed together that they would be allowed to proclaim the Word with boldness and that signs and wonders would take place as a result of their witnessing. After they had prayed, the place where they had gathered was shaken and all those who were there were filled with the Holy Spirit and they proclaimed the Word of God with boldness. The shaking of the building was more than likely caused by the Holy Spirit who took possession of their lives.

To try to witness without the power of the Holy Spirit is a task that is doomed to fail. It is He who gives you the boldness and the words to talk to others about God. Without Him it is not only impossible to be a witness, but your testimony will also not bear fruit.

Holy Spirit, I pray that You would give me the boldness and the right words to proclaim the Word of God. Amen.

Philip and the Ethiopian

The Spirit told Philip, "Go to that chariot and stay near it." Then Philip ran up to the chariot and heard the man reading Isaiah the prophet. "Do you understand what you are reading?" Philip asked. "How can I," he said, "unless someone explains it to me?" Acts 8:29-31

On a quiet road between Jerusalem and Gaza, an Ethiopian was busy reading the scroll of Isaiah. The section that he was reading happened to be a prophecy about Jesus who would be led like a lamb to the slaughter. Even though the Ethiopian was a heathen, God knew that there was a hunger for Him in his heart. He sent Philip to talk to him.

When Philip asked the man if he understood what he was reading, he answered that he could not understand unless someone explained it to him. This was Philip's chance to tell the man about Jesus. When they drove past a stream of water, the man asked if Philip would baptize him.

God knows when people are seeking Him – and He always gives these people the opportunity to find Him. But God needs us to tell other people about Him. Are you, like Philip, willing to be a witness and to make the way of sanctification clear to those who do not yet understand? As He did for Philip, God will give you the right words and the right point of contact.

Lord, forgive me for being so wary of talking to other people about You. Thank You that You will Yourself give me the right words and will send opportunities across my path so that I can do so. Amen.

Paul, a Diligent Witness

Saul spent several days with the disciples in Damascus. All those who heard him were astonished and asked, "Isn't he the man who raised havoc in Jerusalem among those who call on this name?" Acts 9:19, 21

Paul testified that Jesus had said to him on the road to Damascus: "I have appeared to you to appoint you as a servant and as a witness of what you have seen of Me and will see of Me" (Acts 26:16).

Paul did not allow any grass to grow under his feet. When he regained his sight, he immediately began with the work of testifying, which was received somewhat skeptically by the Christians in Damascus. They realized that he was the same man who had previously tried to get rid of the Christians. He had even, before his conversion, obtained letters from the High Priest that gave him the right to arrest Christians outside the borders of Jerusalem (see Acts 9:2).

The Christians in Damascus wondered if it was not perhaps some kind of trap, but Paul simply preached all the more powerfully and many people believed in Jesus as a result of his testimony. He then returned to Jerusalem where he went around with the Christians and brought about even more conversions.

Lord, I really want to be like Paul – he never allowed any opportunity to pass him by to tell people about You. Make me, too, a diligent and enthusiastic witness so that people will come to salvation through what I say. Amen.

Be an Example of Your Faith

You became imitators of us and of the Lord. The Lord's message rang out from you not only in Macedonia and Achaia – your faith in God has become known everywhere. Therefore we do not need to say anything about it. 1 Thess. 1:6, 8

The first epistle that Paul wrote was directed at the church in Thessalonica. And the Thessalonians followed the example of their mentor – they too became witnesses of the good news of Jesus.

They acquitted themselves so well in this work of witnessing that other people who looked at their lives could see that something dramatic had happened to them. But these new Christians not only lived out their faith, they also testified of it. "The Lord's message rang out from you not only in Macedonia and Achaia. Your faith in God has become known everywhere. Therefore we do not need to say anything about it," Paul writes to them.

There are two things that are needed if you believe in God: that you be willing to speak about your faith and that you live according to the commands of God. Your life ought to be a mirror of your faith. It never helps to preach one thing and then to live another. It also does not help to live like a Christian but to keep quiet about your faith. From now on you need to be prepared to speak and live as God asks of you.

Heavenly Father, I truly want to proclaim Your message and live in such a way that people will be able to see from my actions that I am serious about my faith. Please help me to get this right. Amen.

The Message of Paul and Barnabas

When the Gentiles heard this, they were glad and honored the word of the Lord; and all who were appointed for eternal life believed. The word of the Lord spread through the whole region. Acts 13:48-49

Paul and Barnabas were sent out by the church in Antioch on Paul's first missionary journey. During their visit to Antioch, Paul and Barnabas spoke of how they had told the residents of the cities that Jesus was sent as a light to the nations so that He could bring salvation to the farthest corners of the earth. All those who believed in Him would be set free from their sins, they testified. The heathens listened attentively to them, and many of them believed in Jesus.

The Jews in the city were definitely not happy with the large number of heathens who came to listen to Paul and Barnabas and came to faith in Jesus. But their message was crystal clear: "We had to speak the word of God to you first. Since you reject it and do not consider yourselves worthy of eternal life, we now turn to the Gentiles" (v. 46).

The danger still exists today that you could become so used to the good news of God's salvation that you continually put off accepting it, and that people who hear this message for the first time will go ahead of you in the faith. Make sure that this is never true of you!

Lord, protect me from becoming so used to the message of salvation that I will neglect to accept it for myself. Help me to believe in You and to speak of my faith spontaneously. Amen.

Talk about the Good News!

We are therefore Christ's ambassadors, as though God were making His appeal through us. We implore you on Christ's behalf: Be reconciled to God. 2 Cor. 5:20

Witnessing was a way of life for Paul. He committed his whole life to convincing people through the proclaiming of the gospel that Jesus is the Christ. The reason why he testified was because the love of Jesus in his heart compelled him to do so. God reconciled people to Himself through Jesus and entrusted the ministry of reconciliation to us.

Paul saw himself as an ambassador of God. He told the church in Corinth that God Himself was speaking to them through him. And the message was that anyone who belonged to Christ was a brand-new person. All their previous sins were now something of the past.

God forgives sinners because Jesus paid for them on the cross. The good news that each person ought to hear is that Jesus came to make peace between God and the world through His crucifixion. Because He died for your sins, you can be a child of God.

This is a wonderful message that every person on earth ought to hear. Make sure that you tell other people about it.

Lord Jesus, I praise You because through Your crucifixion You made it possible for me to be reconciled with God. Help me to carry out this message and not to keep it to myself. Amen.

Witnessing among the Heathens

"Now get up and stand on your feet. I have appeared to you to appoint you as a servant and as a witness of what you have seen and will see of Me. Open their eyes and turn them from darkness to light, and from the power of Satan to God." Acts 26:16, 18

P aul's dramatic testimony before King Agrippa still leaves us speechless even after many centuries. When he told the king of his vision on the road to Damascus, he also testified that God Himself appointed him as His witness. God had set him apart to open the eyes of the heathen nations so that they could turn from the darkness to the light and from the power of Satan to God. He brought to them the message that if they believed in Jesus their sins would be forgiven and they would become God's people (see vv. 16-18).

Paul's brilliant reasoning almost convinced the king to become a Christian! "Do you think that in such a short time you can persuade me to be a Christian?" he said to him. "Short time or long – I pray God that not only you but all who are listening to me today may become what I am" (vv. 28-29).

Unfortunately Paul's testimony to King Agrippa did not have the desired result – the king was not prepared to change his life and to turn from the darkness to the light.

Heavenly Father, make me responsible for Your message when I hear it so that I will not be like King Agrippa who turned away from Your grace. Amen.

Testimony about an Unknown God

As I walked around, I even found an altar with this inscription: TO AN UNKNOWN GOD. So you are ignorant of the very thing you worship – and this is what I am going to proclaim to you. Acts 17:23

When Paul was in Athens he looked for a point of contact so that he could tell the learned Athenians about God. He went and stood beside one of the city's many altars – one on which was written: "to an unknown god" and told them that it was precisely this God to whom he wanted to introduce them.

Then Paul proceeded with one of his most compelling sermons: It was this God who made the world and all that is in it, it is He who gives breath to all who live, he told them. God made all people to seek Him – He is never far away from us, because in Him we live and move and have our being (see vv. 24-28). After this Paul told the Athenians about Jesus who rose from the dead.

Unfortunately the Athenians were not receptive to Paul's gripping testimony. Yet Luke says that there were a few of them who became believers and who joined Paul. Here Paul gives us a show-and-tell lesson of how a witness should set about their task. With his striking testimony he connected with the life experiences of the Athenians. When you testify before people it is a good idea to talk about things that they can relate to.

Heavenly Father, help me, like Paul, to witness in such a way about You that people will understand my testimony and that they will open their hearts and lives to You. Amen.

Faith Causes You to Speak

It is written: "I believed; therefore I have spoken." Since we have that same spirit of faith, we also believe and therefore speak. 2 Cor. 4:13

Paul was a zealous witness for Jesus. God Himself said to Ananias, "This man is My chosen instrument to proclaim My name to the Gentiles and their kings and to the people of Israel. I will show him how much he must suffer for My name" (Acts 9:15-16).

Shortly after his conversion Paul began with this command to bring others to repentance. We read that he immediately began preaching in the synagogues, proclaiming that Jesus is the Son of God. The fact that the man who wanted to get rid of Jesus' followers with great zeal now witnessed about Jesus did not put him off. Mark tells us that Paul simply preached with more fervor and brought much confusion among the Jews who lived in Damascus (see Acts 9:20-22).

In his letter to the church in Corinth, Paul quoted from Psalm 116:10 where the psalmist testified that he believed and that was why he spoke. The same Spirit was at work in Paul and helped him not only to believe, but also to speak about his faith so that people would hear him and would believe in God.

The Holy Spirit is still available to you to help you testify of your faith. With his support it is possible for you to be a powerful witness for Jesus.

Holy Spirit, I praise You because You have made it possible for me to be a witness who spreads the Good News of the gospel among people. Amen.

Speak to Your Children

Things we have heard and known, things our ancestors have told us. We will not hide them from their descendants; we will tell the next generation the praiseworthy deeds of the Lord, *His power, and the wonders He has done. Ps. 78:3-4*

Here the psalmist tells his children what God has done for their nation. Then through the rest of the psalm he presents us with a history lesson and tells in minute detail the wonderful things God did for His nation.

As the psalmist did here, it is the duty of us as parents to tell our children about God, to share our faith with them and to ensure that each one of them also comes to the certainty of faith.

Already in Deuteronomy 6:6-7, Moses impressed upon the hearts of the Israelites that they should carry out this work of witnessing to their children: "These commandments that I give you today are to be on your hearts. Impress them on your children. Talk about them when you sit at home and when you walk along the road."

Make sure that your children know that you belong to God and that they also know how they can become His children. Tell your grandchildren of the wonderful things of God from the past so that your children and future generations can also share your faith.

Heavenly Father, thank You very much for the privilege of being able to share my faith with my children and that I can boldly testify of You and Your love. I pray that You would open the hearts and lives of my children. Amen.

The Power to Witness

"You will receive power when the Holy Spirit comes on you; and you will be My witnesses in Jerusalem, and in all Judea and Samaria, and to the ends of the earth." Acts 1:8

Jesus' command to witness is never random. When Jesus requested His disciples to make the people of the world His disciples, He also assured them that He would be with them and that all the authority in heaven and on earth had been given to Him (see Matt. 28:18-20). Also, when He told them that the Holy Spirit would come to the earth, He promised that God would work in Him with all His power and that He would make it possible for them to talk about Him – in Jerusalem, in all of Judea and Samaria, and to the farthest corners of the earth.

Therefore, you need never hold back in your work of witnessing. God promises to equip you through His Holy Spirit. Through the working of His Holy Spirit, God will provide you with the necessary power to witness for Him. All that He asks of you is your willingness to put yourself at His disposal. If you agree, He will send the right opportunities your way, put the right words into your mouth and touch the hearts of the people with whom you speak so that they will not only hear your testimony, but will hear the voice of God speaking through your words.

Lord Jesus, I declare myself willing to be Your witness. Thank You that You equip me through Your Holy Spirit and make me a powerful witness. Please give me the boldness to carry Your message to the farthest parts of the world. Amen.

April

Jesus Suffers for You

Every Easter we have the privilege of walking with Jesus on His way to be crucified; to be surprised by God's love anew and again realize the terrible price Jesus' love for us cost Him.

We are once again overwhelmed by the joy of Jesus' resurrection and the promise that we will also rise from the dead one day to live by His side forever.

"The message of Easter cannot be written in the past tense. It is a message for today and the days to come. It is God's message which must echo through your lives," Frank Getty writes.

It is my prayer that you will make the loving message of Easter and the power of Jesus' resurrection your own this Easter, so that you may be blessed by it for the remainder of the year.

Lord Jesus, in this month I want to walk
the Way of the Cross with You, and
contemplate the meaning of Your suffering.
Once again I want to think about
how much You had to suffer so
that I could be saved.
When I pause to think about
the people surrounding Your cross,
teach me the same lessons that they learned.
Grant that I will never deny You,
that I will always be willing to put myself last,
that I will follow You unconditionally.
Thank You that You were forsaken by God
so that I will never have to live without Him.
This is also the month in which
I want to rejoice over Your resurrection;
in which I want to celebrate, because
You have conquered Satan and death for all eternity
and I can now be a conqueror with You.
Make it possible for me to live as a conqueror
from day to day, because I can do anything
in the strength that You give me.
Amen.

Not Me, Lord!

Peter declared, "Even if I have to die with You, I will never disown You." And all the other disciples said the same.
Matt. 26:35

Jesus was distressed about the suffering that was awaiting Him, and He was upset because He knew that His disciples were all going to forsake Him. The impetuous Peter unequivocally declared his faithfulness to Jesus. After all, he was Peter, the rock upon which Jesus would build His church. Peter was willing to relinquish everything for Jesus' sake. And Peter did truly love Jesus, but Jesus knew him better than he knew himself. He knew all too well that in a crisis Peter's human nature would get the upper hand.

To disown someone means to refuse to accept something or someone as one's own, or to say that one has no connection with something or someone. Peter is the last person who would have admitted that he would disown Jesus. And so he vehemently denies that he, Peter, would do so: "Even if all fall away on account of You, I never will" (v. 33). But the real picture looks very different. Peter denied Jesus three times. Only when he heard the rooster crowing did he remember Jesus' words.

Have you perhaps, like Peter, been denying your culpability, saying, "Not me, Lord!" while knowing all too well that you have failed Jesus in the things you have said and done?

Lord Jesus, I want to confess that I have disowned You so many times through my words and actions. Please forgive me and help me not to do it again. Amen.

Peter in a Corner

He began to call down curses, and he swore to them, "I don't know the man!" Immediately a rooster crowed. Then Peter remembered the word Jesus had spoken. Matt. 26:74-75

Matters take an entirely different course from what Peter imagined. Jesus was arrested, and until the very last moment Peter tried to come to His aid. Peter even cut off the ear of the servant Malchus, but then Jesus actually healed the man!

Despite everything, Peter followed Jesus at a distance, right into the courtyard of the high priest. It was here where his faith finally foundered and where he disowned Jesus. Only when he heard the rooster crow did he remember the words Jesus had spoken earlier. At this moment he was filled with remorse.

Peter collapsed when he was put to the test. He denied being a follower of Christ. How about you? Would you be able to continue following Jesus, even if your decision were to have negative consequences for yourself? It requires self-denial to accomplish this.

Jesus Himself said, "Whoever wants to be My disciple must deny themselves and take up their cross and follow Me" (Matt. 16:24). Following Jesus demands commitment, dedication and complete surrender. Are you up to it?

This Easter you will once again have to choose between yourself and Jesus.

Jesus, I want to renew my commitment to You this Easter, even if it means that I will have to follow You while carrying my cross. Amen.

The New Peter

Peter and John replied, "Which is right in God's eyes: to listen to you, or to Him? We cannot help speaking about what we have seen and heard." Acts 4:19-20

Fortunately Peter's story does not end in the courtyard of the high priest. When we read of Peter again, in the beginning of Acts, we encounter an altogether different Peter. His inspiring sermon on the Day of Pentecost caused three thousand people to come to repentance. Afterwards, when the Sanhedrin commanded Peter and John not to speak of Jesus, he declared in no uncertain terms that they could not keep quiet.

What happened to bring about this profound change in Peter? The Holy Spirit was poured out, and the Holy Spirit always brings about a radical change in people's lives. He transforms a scared disciple into a witness for Christ, filled with conviction.

All Christians have the Holy Spirit in their lives, but the Holy Spirit does not yet possess all Christians. How much of yourself you surrender to the Holy Spirit depends on your personal decision. If your own self is still firmly ensconced on the throne of your life, the Holy Spirit will not be able to accomplish anything with your life. Only when you are willing to entrust the control of your entire life to Him, only when you agree to submit your everything to His sovereignty, can He change you as He changed Peter.

Holy Spirit, I want to fully surrender my life to You. Please change me as You changed Peter, and make me a radiant witness for You. Amen.

The Best Seats, Please!

Then James and John came to Him. "Let one of us sit at Your right and the other at Your left in Your glory."
Mark 10:35, 37

Toward the end of His life on earth Jesus continuously implored His disciples to be humble and subservient. In the passage just preceding this one Jesus predicted His death for the third time. And yet the disciples did not quite yet get it. And to make matters worse, it was James and John, two of Jesus' star disciples, who piously asked Him whether they might have the best places at His right and left when He reigned as King.

Jesus was probably deeply hurt by His disciples' behavior and attitude. It must have been extremely difficult for Him to accept that this group of people, who had lived with Him for three years and received all the in-service training they could possibly have needed, could still be this self-centered.

Self-fulfillment remains an important motivating factor in our lives. All of us want to get ahead in life. But Jesus is still seeking people who are willing to follow in His footsteps. You will only manage to do this if you admit that you can do nothing in your own strength.

Perhaps you should use this Easter time to ponder your own attitude. What are the motivating factors in your life? Are you willing to put your own interests last and others' first?

Lord Jesus, forgive me for living such a self-centered life; for regarding myself as the most important. Make me willing to put my own interests last and others' first. Amen.

Beyond the Cross

This is how we know what love is: Jesus Christ laid down His life for us. And we ought to lay down our lives for our brothers and sisters. If anyone has material possessions and sees his brother in need but has no pity on him, how can the love of God be in him? 1 John 3:16-17

John – the same John who so desperately wanted to sit at the left or right of the Lord in His glory, who was so concerned with his own self-importance – has drastically altered his tune. Christians should be willing to lay down their lives for the benefit of their fellow believers. If we ignore the needs of other people, it can mean that we do not have the love of Christ in our lives.

After Jesus' crucifixion, John made an important discovery: he realized that fulfillment can only come about through self-denial. Self-denial means becoming the person God wants you to be: humble and subservient to others.

If you really want to serve God this Easter, you would do well to take a page from John's book. It means that you will also have to be willing to look around you, notice the needs of the people around you and do something about it.

True love is not merely an attractive idea, but always involves action. You too should be willing to show your love for God in the good deeds you do for others. Will you make a commitment to do so?

Lord Jesus, teach me how to transform my love for You into good deeds, so that I can provide for other people's needs. Amen.

The Triumphal Entry into Jerusalem

The crowds shouted, "Hosanna to the Son of David! Blessed is He who comes in the name of the Lord!" Matt. 21:9

At Easter we are often asked to renew our commitment to Christ. The people who were present when Jesus entered Jerusalem were under tremendous group pressure. They acknowledged Jesus as King, not because they really believed this, but rather because the expectation of the Messiah was part of Jewish history. When Jesus rode into Jerusalem on a donkey, they remembered Zechariah's prophecy that the long-awaited King would enter Jerusalem riding on a donkey.

They were not true believers, but really only a group of people who wanted the Man on the donkey to help them personally. To them Jesus was nothing more than the symbol of a national dream: the Messiah who had come to free them from their Roman oppressors.

Many people today still decide to follow Jesus for entirely the wrong reasons. Singing hosanna does not necessarily mean that this King is truly the Ruler of your life. It is infinitely more difficult to actually walk the road to the cross with Him.

When God becomes a symbol that represents the fulfillment of your self-centered dreams, things are taking a wrong turn. It is all too easy to get caught up in mob excitement, but the Lord expects you to make a personal commitment of faith. Surrender yourself completely to Jesus as the King of your life.

Lord Jesus, I pray that You will truly be the King of my life this Easter, and in all the days to follow. Amen.

Jesus Weeps for Jerusalem

As [Jesus] approached Jerusalem and saw the city, He wept over it and said, "If you, even you, had only known on this day what would bring you peace – but now it is hidden from your eyes." Luke 19:41-42

While riding into Jerusalem, Jesus was all too aware of the fact that the hearts of the cheering people did not belong to Him. When He saw the city lying before Him, He was deeply moved. He wept, and His tears were not tears of joy.

Rather, He was weeping for the people who were thinking only of themselves and the future of their country. He wept for people who were not yet ready for a cross. He wept because they did not really understand that He was the Messiah, but saw Him only as the fulfillment of their religious prophecies. He wept because He knew that soon after, these people would renounce and crucify Him.

Does Jesus perhaps have reason to weep for you? Perhaps not because you haven't yet chosen Him as Lord of your life, but because you still cling to an illusionary concept of Jesus, one in which you regard Him as someone who must answer your prayers and help you.

Jesus wants to offer you the gift of His grace and grant you His peace. But then you have to acknowledge Him as the King of your life. Ask Him to help you completely devote yourself to Him.

Lord Jesus, thank You that You offer me an opportunity to choose You as the Lord of my life. Help me to serve You devoutly. Amen.

Would You Like to Meet Jesus?

There were some Greeks among those who went up to worship at the festival. They came to Philip … with a request. "Sir," they said, "we would like to see Jesus." John 12:20-21

In Jesus' time there was a marked division between Israel and the rest of the world, because the Israelites were God's chosen people. No other nation had such access to God. Jesus' miracles caused the people to wonder whether He wasn't perhaps the Messiah who had been promised to them. However, Jesus had no interest in an earthly kingdom, while the Jews only wanted Him to free them from the yoke of Roman oppression.

The Jews would never have approved of Jesus mingling with gentiles like the Greeks. However, these Greeks had heard of Jesus and approached Philip, saying that they would very much like to meet this exceptional man. When Jesus heard that the gentiles wished to meet Him, He realized that the hour of His glorification had arrived. He had to die so that the harvest of God would become visible in the world and that other peoples who believed in Him could also become children of God.

Because Jesus gave His life on the cross it is possible for you too to meet Him, to believe in Him, and to become a child of God. Have you responded to His offer of grace yet? There is no better time to get to know Jesus than right now.

Lord Jesus, thank You that I can meet You once again during this time when we remember Your crucifixion and resurrection. Make me a witness for You. Amen.

Lose Your Life to Gain It

"Very truly I tell you, unless a kernel of wheat falls to the ground and dies, it remains only a single seed. But if it dies, it produces many seeds." John 12:24

In this Scripture passage Jesus explains to His disciples how important His death is to the world. *The Message* translates this verse as follows: "Unless a grain of wheat is buried in the ground, dead to the world, it is never any more than a grain of wheat. But if it is buried, it sprouts and reproduces itself many times over."

A kernel of wheat must die before it can live, Jesus declares. In the same way He too had to die so that we might live. You must undertake to follow His example. If you are willing to put other people's interests above your own you might also perhaps lose your life, as He did, but ultimately you will gain everything, because God guarantees you eternal life.

You have to die to be able to truly live. You can gain life only by losing it. This doesn't sound very exciting to us. It also held no obvious benefits for Jesus' disciples.

When Jesus includes the Greeks and other heathen peoples in His plan of redemption, He breaks down existing boundaries and unites people who would ordinarily have nothing in common. But in doing so He ensures a bountiful harvest for God's kingdom.

Are you ready to be part of that harvest?

Lord Jesus, help me to walk in Your footsteps, to be willing to let my own self die, so that I may one day have eternal life. Amen.

On the Way with Jesus

"Now learn this lesson from the fig tree: As soon as its twigs get tender and its leaves come out, you know that summer is near. Even so, when you see these things happening, you know that it is near, right at the door." Mark 13:28-29

You can experience the story of the Passion in two ways: you can be a spectator of events, like someone watching a Passion play, or you can decide to put yourself in the midst of the action. The events of the last week before Jesus' crucifixion are clearly recorded in the Bible.

Jesus' triumphal entry into Jerusalem was on the Sunday; on the Monday He cursed the barren fig tree and purified the temple; on the Tuesday the fig tree withered; and Thursday was the day of the Lord's Supper, when Jesus also prayed in Gethsemane and Judas betrayed Him. On the Friday Jesus was accused, condemned, crucified and buried. The whole of Saturday He spent in the tomb, and on the Sunday He rose from the dead and appeared to His disciples.

With every Easter that comes around, we are faced with a new challenge: How are you going to experience the events of Easter this year? As spectator or as participant? You are responsible for making this choice. You can choose the crucified Christ by living for Him and testifying about Him. You can walk the Way of the Cross step by step with Jesus. You can truly realize what suffering Jesus was willing to go through in your place.

Lord Jesus, this Easter I want to walk the Way of the Cross with You, step by step. Amen.

Make Disciples!

"Go and make disciples of all nations, baptizing them in the name of the Father and of the Son and of the Holy Spirit, and teaching them to obey everything I have commanded you."
Matt. 28:19-20

Before His ascension, Jesus' last commission to His disciples was to go into the world and to make disciples of all nations. The disciples fulfilled their commission exceptionally well, contrary to expectations.

According to an old legend, after His ascension to heaven the angels wanted to know from Jesus where His army was. In answer to their question He pointed to the small group of people standing on the Mount of Olives. I am sure that His little band of followers seemed rather feeble to the angels. The Bible also does not paint a very positive picture of the disciples. After all, in Jesus' inner circle one disciple betrayed Him, one disowned Him and the rest … deserted Him and fled (see Matt. 26:56).

It appears as if they weren't really the best team for spreading the gospel. And yet this apparently feeble army – with Jesus' help and support – spread His message to the known world as He asked of them. You too are a member of Jesus' army here in this world. Jesus promises to be with you if you are willing to tell others about Him. With His help and strength your testimony can be just as powerful as the testimony of His first disciples.

Lord Jesus, I want to spread Your gospel and make people Your disciples. Thank You for being with me and helping me. Amen.

From Disciple to Traitor

Then Judas Iscariot, one of the Twelve, went to the chief priests to betray Jesus to them. They were delighted to hear this … So he watched for an opportunity to hand Him over.
Mark 14:10-11

Three times in the Gospel of Mark, Judas is referred to as "one of the Twelve." It was an ordinary person who betrayed Jesus; a disciple, someone who was part of Jesus' inner circle. He was specially chosen by Jesus Himself. For three years He walked with Jesus every day, listened to His words, saw His miracles first hand.

The reason for Judas's betrayal is probably found in the surmise that Jesus failed to live up to Judas's human expectations. Judas wanted Him to end the Roman oppression and reinstate Israel as a sovereign nation. Judas was focused on his immediate material world, and he did not have an inkling of what Jesus' kingdom was really about. Therefore he nurtured completely misplaced expectations of Jesus.

None of us really has any sympathy with Judas, and yet we perhaps condemn him too easily. The story of the Passion always places a choice before people. It was Judas's choice to betray Jesus. Perhaps you should ask yourself whether Jesus always lives up to your expectations. Why do you have faith? Do you have faith for the sake of the expansion of His kingdom or merely for the sake of possible gains for yourself?

Lord Jesus, forgive me for still sometimes cherishing misplaced expectations of You. This Easter, help me to choose You as the Lord of my life. Amen.

Your Testimonial

People will be lovers of themselves, lovers of money, boastful, proud, abusive, disobedient to their parents, ungrateful, unholy … treacherous. 2 Tim. 3:2, 4

In this passage Paul provides Timothy with a rather dismal testimonial of the people who will live in the last days. And what is more, the people Paul is speaking about are people of the church, believers – but yet people who have repudiated the power of Christ as a result of their own selfishness.

This list of characteristics reminds one of Judas. "Are you perhaps like Judas?" is the question that yesterday's devotion posed to you. Perhaps you should take the time to contemplate this matter carefully.

What would your testimonial look like should the Lord have to write one for you? What characteristics do other people see when scrutinizing your life? Would they catch glimpses of the selfishness, avarice, conceit and lovelessness of which Paul speaks? Is your love of pleasure still greater than your love for God? Is Jesus truly your King, or are there other little kings? Do you possibly have the external appearance of faith without the substance and strength of faith?

God must never become an instrument to serve your own interests. Make doubly sure that you are willing to deny yourself, to take up your cross and to follow Jesus every day. Or are you still betraying Him like a Judas?

Father, I must confess that I still notice many of the negative characteristics that Paul describes in my own life. Please forgive me and help me to become more Christlike. Amen.

Jesus and the Women

Some women were watching from a distance. Among them were Mary Magdalene, Mary the mother of James the younger and of Joseph, and Salome. Mark 15:40

Throughout His ministry Jesus had a special relationship with women. We read that a group of women cared for Jesus: "In Galilee these women had followed Him and cared for His needs" (v. 41). It was women like Mary and Martha who invited Jesus to eat with them.

Mary even anointed Him with precious oils, washed His feet with her tears and dried them with her hair. The women sincerely loved Jesus and cared for His needs. This group of faithful women also followed Jesus at a distance on the day of His crucifixion.

These women must have found it extremely difficult to see Jesus dying on the cross. Even in the hour of His bitterest suffering Jesus noticed these women. He asked John to take His mother into his home and care for her.

After Jesus' crucifixion it was once again a group of women who went to the tomb to anoint His body. And the first person to whom Jesus appeared after His resurrection was also a woman, Mary Magdalene.

Jesus did not regard women as inferior beings. He recognized women as people in their own right. In His kingdom women have their own special place.

You too are important to Jesus. He loves you, and has a special place and task for you in His kingdom.

Lord Jesus, thank You for not regarding me as inferior to men. Thank You for loving me and using me in Your service. Amen.

The Centurion at the Cross

When the centurion, who stood there in front of Jesus, saw how He died, he said, "Surely this Man was the Son of God!"
Mark 15:39

Throughout the Bible we find a contrast between Jesus' own people who rejected Him, and the gentiles and foreigners who worshiped Him and acknowledged Him as the Messiah.

The Jewish elders, teachers of the law and the scribes took no notice of Jesus' teachings, while sinners and publicans were converted when He spoke to them. Pilate unequivocally declared that he found no guilt in Jesus, while the Jewish leaders insisted on having Him crucified. While Jesus was hanging on the cross, the Jews mocked Him and told Him to save Himself, yet one of the thieves crucified next to Him begged Him for mercy.

It is not surprising that the Jews completely failed to notice the unusual events that took place during Jesus' crucifixion: the darkness and the tearing of the temple curtain. But an unknown Roman soldier who was in command at the cross noticed these events and testified that Jesus must surely be the Son of God.

Who is Jesus to you? Is He just a historical figure who you read of in your Bible, or can you testify from your heart that He is truly the crucified, resurrected Savior, the Son of God who came to sacrifice His life to atone for your sins?

Lord Jesus, thank You that I may be assured that You are truly the Son of God. Amen.

Only One Sacrifice Is Necessary

Such a high priest truly meets our need – one who is holy, blameless, pure, set apart from sinners, exalted above the heavens. Unlike the other high priests, He does not need to offer sacrifices day after day, first for His own sins, and then for the sins of the people. He sacrificed for their sins once for all when He offered Himself. Heb. 7:26-27

When Jesus died on the cross for our sins, He made the perfect offering. This sacrifice, Jesus Himself, will never have to be repeated. Through Jesus' atoning death, we who believe in Him are redeemed once and for all. Jesus died for the sins that you have already committed as well as the sins that you are still going to commit in the future. No further sacrifice is necessary. God willingly paid a costly price for your sins to be forgiven. You have to do nothing on your part to earn atonement through Jesus' sacrifice.

However, you can and must have an answer to His sacrifice. I recently saw a striking poster of Jesus on the cross. Underneath was written: "It's your move." In dying on the cross Jesus did everything in His power; there is nothing left that He can do.

But what about you? Have you accepted His offering yet? Have you made it your own and asked Him to forgive your sins? It is indeed your move.

This Easter, decide for yourself what you are going to do with the sacrifice that Jesus made for your sake.

Lord Jesus, how could I possibly thank You for such a great sacrifice? I accept it with all my heart. Please forgive all my sins and help me to live as Your child from now on. Amen.

Crucified with Jesus

We know that our old self was crucified with Him so that the body ruled by sin might be done away with, that we should no longer be slaves to sin. Rom. 6:6

Walking the Way of the Cross together with Jesus this Easter makes us part of all that happened to Jesus on the cross. It is once again a demonstration of God's grace and love for us. You can do one of two things with God's grace: you can either underestimate it or overestimate it.

You can try to earn God's grace by keeping His commandments, or you can scorn His grace by continuing to sin, because after all, God will just have to forgive you. Unfortunately there are very few Christians who regard sin as seriously as they ought to.

It is crucial for you to understand God's grace correctly: Jesus died in your place on the cross, but you too must be willing to die with Him. Your sinful human nature should have died with Him on the cross.

You should be willing to get rid of every sin that is still present in your life. Every time when you are tempted to commit a sin, remind yourself that you are dead to your sinful nature, and resist sinning through Jesus' strength!

If your sinful nature has been crucified, it means that you will live for Christ from now on. He has made you a new creation; live as God wants you to live.

Lord Jesus, I am sorry that my old sinful nature resurfaces every now and again. Help me to truly crucify my sinful nature, so that I can live only for You from now on. Amen.

Reconciled to God

If, while we were God's enemies, we were reconciled to Him through the death of His Son, how much more, having been reconciled, shall we be saved through His life! Rom. 5:10

*T*he Message translates this verse as follows: "If, when we were at our worst, we were put on friendly terms with God by the sacrificial death of His Son, now that we're at our best, just think of how our lives will expand and deepen by means of His resurrection life!"

Jesus sacrificed His life so that you could return to God, and so that sinful people and a holy God could be reconciled. When He died, the curtain of the temple was torn in two. Jesus' sacrificial death not only broke down the walls between God and sinful people, but also the walls that people build between one another.

If you are to participate in Jesus' act of reconciliation, you ought to be able to testify that you live in a close relationship with God. Furthermore, your relationship with your neighbor should be indicative of this reconciliation.

If this is not yet the case, confess the sins that are marring your relationship with God, and restore the relationships between you and the people close to you.

Always remember that Christ is one with your fellow believers, regardless of the differences that may exist between you and them.

Lord Jesus, I praise You for enabling me to live in peace with God and my neighbor through Your death on the cross. Amen.

Reconciliation and Redemption

Now that you have been set free from sin and have become slaves of God, the benefit you reap leads to holiness, and the result is eternal life. Rom. 6:22

Reconciliation and redemption go hand in hand. The wages of sin may be death, but God grants us eternal life because Jesus has earned it for us on the cross.

Ever since the Fall, man has been living in a prison – every human being has original sin in their blood. We have all already been condemned to death. But when the shadow of Jesus' cross falls on the door of your prison it is unlocked. Jesus frees you from the power of sin.

The Message puts it like this in Romans 8:1: "Those who enter into Christ's being-here-for-us no longer live under a continuous, low-lying black cloud … The Spirit of life in Christ, like a strong wind, has magnificently cleared the air, freeing you from a fated lifetime of brutal tyranny at the hands of sin and death."

If you profess the belief that Jesus has freed you, the door of your prison cell has been opened, but you might still be trapped in the death cell. You may be a new creation, but you will also have to learn to live like one. If you have been crucified with Christ, you are now in the service of God.

Will you meet this challenge with all your heart?

Lord Jesus, would You please keep sin from ever having a hold over me again? Help me to live only for You from now on. Amen.

Jesus Becomes Human

You must have the same attitude that Christ Jesus had. Though He was God, He did not think of equality with God. He took the humble position of a slave and was born as a human being. Phil. 2:5-7

When we talk of Jesus' suffering on earth we usually refer to the time and events surrounding His crucifixion. We often forget that Jesus' suffering started with His birth. Jesus, the Son of God, left heaven of His own free will and became an ordinary human being, just like us. It must have been a terrible humiliation, and yet He did not recoil from it for even one moment. The Bible tells us that we should have exactly the same attitude as He did.

The Horse Whisperer is based on the true story of Monty Roberts, a legendary American horse-breeder. Monty had the extraordinary ability to become one with his horses, to speak their language, as it were. Because of this gift he was able to tame even the wildest horse.

Jesus became a human being for us, a human being like us. Therefore He understands us completely. He was willing to sacrifice all His rights and to become a servant. And you and I must, in turn, be willing to become like Him. Martin Luther writes that one's attitude is proved only when it is transformed into deeds. What does your attitude look like? Are you able to live, act and serve as Jesus did?

Lord Jesus, You know me inside and out, because You were a human being just like me. Make me humble and willing to be a servant, as You were. Amen.

Prepared to Suffer

It has been granted to you on behalf of Christ not only to believe in Him, but also to suffer for Him. Phil. 1:29

God's children need to keep in mind that suffering is inevitable in the Christian life. It is part and parcel of human life. But because we don't ordinarily regard suffering as a privilege, Paul's choice of words in this passage seems rather odd. Suffering is not something that we would willingly choose and we would definitely not regard it as a privilege. But when your suffering is the consequence of the fact that you are a Christian, you know that God is using you positively by allowing you to suffer for His sake.

The apostles left the Sanhedrin, rejoicing because they had been counted worthy of suffering disgrace for the name, Luke reports in Acts 5:41. This kind of suffering – for the sake of your faith – shows other people that you are faithful to God. There are essentially four positive things about this kind of suffering:

- It provides you with the correct perspective on earthly comforts.
- It brings to light the true colors of those who are Christians in name only.
- It strengthens the faith of those who persevere.
- It serves as a powerful example for potential followers.

Jesus showed His obedience by suffering for your sake. Are you willing to do the same for Him?

Lord Jesus, please make me willing to suffer for Your sake. Amen.

The Meaning of Jesus' Suffering

At about three o'clock, Jesus called out with a loud voice, "Eli, Eli, lema sabachthani?" which means "My God, My God, why have You abandoned Me?" Matt. 27:46

Jesus' suffering must never become commonplace to us. We think of His suffering in human terms, focusing on the physical pain that He suffered.

But Jesus' mental anguish was much worse than the physical punishment that He had to endure. On the cross Jesus bore the full brunt of God's wrath against sin. And He did it without the assistance of His Father.

When you know that God is with you, it is possible to endure suffering and yet to remain hopeful, but without Him it is altogether impossible.

The worst suffering that a Christian can endure is to be forsaken by God. On the cross Jesus experienced the worst conceivable suffering on earth when His Father left Him, particularly because He was used to living close to His Father and being one with God.

The intensity of His suffering culminates in His cry: "My God, My God, why have You forsaken Me?"

Jesus suffered because of God's wrath against sin. He bore it in our place so that you and I would never have to experience that wrath again. Through His suffering Jesus earned God's absolution for you. He lost His life so that yours could be saved; He died so that you may have eternal life.

Lord Jesus, thank You that You bore God's wrath against sin in my place, and in so doing gave me eternal life. Amen.

Obedient unto Death

Even though Jesus was God's Son, He learned obedience from the things He suffered. He became the source of eternal salvation for all those who obey Him. Heb. 5:8-9

During His life on earth, Jesus often endured physical, human suffering. He lived the life of a vagrant, He often experienced discomfort, and had no home or possessions of His own. He also knew that tremendous suffering awaited Him at the end of His life.

In the Garden of Gethsemane He implored His Father to take the cup of suffering from Him, but ultimately He resigned Himself to God's will.

Through His suffering on earth and on the cross Jesus taught us what true obedience to the Father means. Because He was willing to be obedient to this extent, He is now our source of eternal salvation. His obedience makes it possible for us to be God's children.

God asks the same kind of obedience from us. And through His Holy Spirit He enables us to walk in the footsteps of Christ.

Are you prepared to yield your will to the will of God? Are you willing to be truly obedient to all His commands, even if that were to cause you suffering and pain?

If you are not yet absolutely obedient to God, perhaps this Easter is a good time to say *yes* to God's commands.

Lord Jesus, it is so difficult for me to be as obedient as You were, especially when the cost is high. Thank You for helping me to be more obedient every day. Amen.

God Gives His Son

For God so loved the world that He gave His one and only Son, that whoever believes in Him shall not perish but have eternal life. John 3:16

It is no coincidence that John 3:16 is one of the best known verses in the Bible, because it summarizes God's love for His people in a nutshell: He loved us so much that He sacrificed His Son's life so that we may have eternal life.

With each Easter we are amazed once more by the extent of God's love for His sinful human children. We rejoice over the wonder of Jesus' willingness to leave heaven, to come to earth as an ordinary man, and to be crucified so that our sins could be forgiven.

God is love, and we should carefully consider what this means. God loved us so much that He sent His Son to redeem us from our sins.

This is God's most important and salient quality: He is love. You only have to consider Jesus' death on the cross to realize the extent of God's love for you personally. God loves the world so much, God loves *you* so much, that He sacrificed His only Son so that you may have life.

If you are going to accept His offer of grace, it is essential for you to believe in Jesus: "Whoever does not believe stands condemned already because they have not believed in the name of God's one and only Son" (v. 18).

Lord Jesus, I believe in You. Thank You for the assurance that I will not perish, but that I already have eternal life. Amen.

The Meaning of Jesus' Resurrection

If Christ has not been raised, your faith is futile; you are still in your sins. If only for this life we have hope in Christ, we are of all people most to be pitied. 1 Cor. 15:17, 19

Jesus' resurrection confirms everything He told His disciples. It irrevocably establishes the fact that He redeemed us from our sins. It also confirms the fact that we who believe in Him will one day rise from the dead just as He did.

According to the Heidelberg Catechism, Jesus' resurrection means three things:

- It fulfills the promise of Good Friday. Jesus died on the cross so that we could have life. Jesus has paid all the debt of our sins, and we have been justified by faith. Because of Jesus, God forgives your sin. When God looks at you, He sees you through the cross of His Son.
- The resurrection also has a bearing on the way you live. God's children ought to live with the power of the resurrection in them. They are, after all, people who daily experience Jesus' peace in their lives.
- The resurrection compels us to look ahead toward the unknown that awaits us: death is inevitable. But for Christians, Jesus has removed death's sting. Through His crucifixion He conquered death, and you too will one day rise from death into a new life.

Lord Jesus, thank You that You not only died for me, but also rose from the dead so that I will one day have eternal life with You. Amen.

Live in Reverence before God

Since you call on a Father who judges each person's work impartially, live out your time as foreigners here in reverent fear. 1 Pet. 1:17

Although we are here on earth temporarily, God still expects His children to live in a distinctive way, revering God. If you revere your parents you will be obedient to them. The same is true of Christians: we show our reverence for God by obeying His Word.

In the Sermon on the Mount, Jesus gives a detailed description of what the citizens of heaven should be like. They are people who are salt and light, who love their enemies, and who choose God rather than Mammon. The ultimate requirement for people who revere God is contained in Jesus' summary of the commandments: They should love God above all and their neighbor as they love themselves.

Most of us feel at home here on earth. We so easily become accustomed to the fact that the world doesn't really have much reverence for God and His commandments. We try to live like people who hold two passports: one for heaven and one for the world.

Unfortunately, it doesn't work this way. You will have to choose which one is more important to you, and you will have to be willing to live in such a way that the world will hear your testimony loudly and clearly.

Lord Jesus, help me to live my life here on earth in reverence for You, so that other people will be able to see You in my life. Amen.

Love One Another

You know that it was not with perishable things such as silver or gold that you were redeemed … but with the precious blood of Christ. Now that you have purified yourselves by obeying the truth, love one another deeply, from the heart.
1 Pet. 1:18-19, 22

God hates sin and can never leave it unpunished. The wages of sin are always death. But through His death on the cross, Jesus redeemed us of the punishment for sin, and therefore we should love one another in obedience to Him, as Peter writes. Jesus is the power behind our obedience. His death on the cross freed us from the tyranny of our sinful human nature and redeemed us from our sins, so that we could be God's children.

This month we walked the Way of the Cross with Jesus. We contemplated the fact that Jesus was crucified for our sakes, that He rose from the grave and conquered death. And because He did this, heaven is our destiny. His crucifixion and resurrection make eternal life possible for us. God redeemed us from sin through Jesus' death. Jesus earned our heavenly citizenship for us; all we have to do to receive it is to believe in Him.

You can live your earthly life in the assurance that heaven awaits you. This fact bestows on you a different value, makes you different from the rest of the world. From now on you should live and behave in such a way that people notice this difference in you.

Lord Jesus, thank You for earning a place in heaven for me through Your death on the cross. Help me to live as Your child by loving other people. Amen.

What Does God Ask of You?

Now that you have purified yourselves by obeying the truth so that you have sincere love for each other, love one another deeply, from the heart. 1 Pet. 1:22

How should we live? What exactly does God ask of us? What is His purpose with us? The Bible clearly shows us God's purpose and direction: we should purify ourselves by obeying the truth, and love one another sincerely.

God expects us to love one another: "Love one another, for whoever loves others has fulfilled the law" (Rom. 13:8). This commandment sums up all of the other commandments.

When we consider what exactly this biblical love looks like, we always fall far short of the ideal. The love that God requires of us is self-sacrificing and unselfish. It does not seek its own best interests, but always puts the interests of other people first. It does not exist because our fellow human beings deserve it, but rather flourishes despite all the shortcomings and faults of our neighbors. This is the way in which Jesus loved.

And now God asks you to love others in the same way that Jesus loves you. It sounds impossible, and so it is. In your own strength you will never accomplish this, but God can make it possible through His Holy Spirit who lives in you. Ask Him right now to help you.

Lord, when it comes to love I always fall short of Your ideals. You know that I still love myself better than I do others. Please forgive me, and enable me to love my neighbor in the same way that You love me. Amen.

Arise in a New Life!

If we died with Christ, we believe that we will also live with Him. In the same way, count yourselves dead to sin but alive to God in Christ Jesus. Rom. 6:8, 11

To have been crucified with Jesus means to be dead to sin. All the wrong you did before should now be something of the past. Your old nature and love for sin died with Christ. As Paul testifies in Galatians 2:20, "I have been crucified with Christ and I no longer live, but Christ lives in me." That is why you should not get bogged down in the thought of Jesus' death on the cross, but should rather concentrate on the fact that He lives and that you live with Him.

You now share in His resurrection life and have an intimate Father–child relationship with God. As a brand-new person, you should live every day to the utmost, and to the glory of God.

Unfortunately all of this does not mean that you will be completely free of sin from now on. But you are no longer the slave of sin. Sin is no longer your master. When you commit a sin, you know that you are doing wrong and you can immediately make a U-turn back to God. He is willing to forgive your sin every time, and will always accept you with open arms.

Lord Jesus, I praise You for the wonder of being crucified with You and now living my life to the fullest for You. Show me when I do wrong and help me to be willing to leave my sins behind me. Amen.

Eternal Life

Jesus said to her: "I am the resurrection and the life. The one who believes in Me will live, even though they die; and whoever lives by believing in Me will never die." John 11:25-26

None of us likes to talk about death. Besides the fact that such talk spoils our appetite for life, death also remains a largely unknown territory to us. We don't quite know what to make of death. What we are sure of is that it awaits all of us. No one can escape death. Actually, death provides us with irrefutable proof of the reality of the Fall. We carry its seed in us from the day of our birth.

Death also awaits Christians. The Bible says that our lives are brief and transient, like the flowers of the field.

But Jesus also promised Martha that everyone who believes in Him will live, even though they die. Because Jesus died and rose from the dead, He has made eternal life possible for us. It is impossible for us to grasp this fact with our limited understanding, but we can believe it, because Jesus has made it a reality for us through His death on the cross.

At Easter the orthodox Greeks greet each other with a traditional Easter greeting: "Truly, He is risen!" If you do not yet believe this with all your heart, you are standing on the threshold of heaven – but still outside.

Lord Jesus, I praise You as the risen Savior who came to make life after death a reality for me. Amen.

May

On the Road with Peter

When we travel with Peter, we often catch glimpses of ourselves.

Peter is someone we can easily identify with because he demonstrates so many typically human characteristics, such as uncertainty, rashness, doubt and denial.

But Peter was also honest. He was not afraid to ask questions, but he was afraid to acknowledge that he was a follower of Jesus. He was an ordinary, middle-class person like most of us.

There is a very important lesson that we can learn from Peter: to acknowledge Jesus and to get to know Him better.

We also notice a gradual process of growth in Peter himself. He slowly progressed from a scared disciple who did not want to acknowledge that he knew Jesus to a powerful preacher at Pentecost and a miracle-worker who even raised a woman from the dead.

Heavenly Father,
thank You for the precious lessons I learn
this month while walking in Peter's footsteps.
You know that I recognize so many
of my own characteristics in his life:
my impulsiveness and my tendency
to speak before I think; the fact that I, too,
often disappoint and even disown You,
in spite of my good intentions.
I pray that You would work in my life as
You did in the life of Peter,
that You would strengthen my love for You,
that You would make me willing
to follow You unconditionally,
that You would give me a key role
to play in my congregation,
and that You would make me willing
to guide and teach Your children.
I pray that You would change me too,
from being a faint-hearted doubter
to being a fisher of men,
and a powerful witness to Your omnipotence.
Help me to be prepared for the devil's attacks.
Help me to live a holy and godly life and to expect
Your second coming every day, so that
I will not be caught unawares.
I ask this in Your name.
Amen.

A Fisher of Men

As Jesus was walking beside the Sea of Galilee, He saw two brothers, Simon called Peter and his brother Andrew. They were casting a net into the lake, for they were fishermen. "Come, follow Me," Jesus said, "and I will send you out to fish for people." Matt. 4:18-19

Peter and his brother, Andrew, were fishermen at the Sea of Galilee. Andrew was a follower of John the Baptist and when he heard John say that Jesus was the Lamb of God, he investigated the matter further. After meeting Jesus, Andrew told Peter, "We have found the Messiah" (John 1:41).

While Peter and his brother were fishing in the lake, Jesus came past and invited them to follow Him. He promised to make them fishers of people if they followed Him. Peter and Andrew were prepared to follow Jesus immediately. They left their nets and families and followed Him.

When Peter met Jesus, he left his former life behind. He was willing to follow Jesus unconditionally and to be His disciple.

Jesus still calls upon people to follow Him. He wants to make us fishers of people too. One of our most important tasks as Christians is to tell others about Jesus' good news. Are you willing to sacrifice everything and follow Jesus so that you can be a witness for Him?

Lord, like Peter, make me willing to sacrifice all that is dear to me and follow You unconditionally. Help me to expand Your kingdom by winning people for You. Amen.

Peter Walks on Water

"Lord, if it's You," Peter replied, "tell me to come to You on the water." "Come," He said. Then Peter got down out of the boat, walked on the water and came toward Jesus.
Matt. 14:28-29

This account gives us a glimpse of Peter's impulsive nature. He is someone who acts first and then thinks. When he saw someone on the water approaching the boat, he thought that it must be Jesus. However, he was not quite certain. "Lord, if it's You, tell me to come to You on the water," Peter said. "Come!" Jesus invited him.

And then a miracle happened. Peter actually walked toward Jesus on the water – until he saw how strong the wind was. When Peter got scared, he began to sink. In a moment, the brave Peter turned into a scared man who almost drowned. However, he knew where to turn for help and Jesus was close enough to put out His hand and catch hold of him.

"You of little faith, why did you doubt?" (v. 31) Jesus wanted to know when He got into the boat with Peter. Peter would probably never forget this encounter with Jesus. For the other disciples, it confirmed that Jesus was truly the Son of God. "Then those who were in the boat worshiped Him, saying, 'Truly You are the Son of God,'" Matthew reports (v. 33).

Lord, I, too, sometimes become afraid when observing the conditions surrounding me. Help me to continue believing in You and please deliver me from dangerous situations, as You rescued Peter. Amen.

Peter's Credo

"But what about you?" [Jesus] asked. "Who do you say I am?" Simon Peter answered, "You are the Messiah, the Son of the living God." Matt. 16:15-16

When Jesus asked the disciples who the people said He was, they replied that some thought He was John the Baptist and others thought He was Elijah or one of the prophets.

Jesus then asked, "Who do you say I am?" Peter answered, "You are the Christ, the Son of the living God."

Jesus told Peter that His answer was a revelation from God. He then told Peter that he was the rock on which His church would be built, and that He would give him the keys to the kingdom of heaven.

Peter must have been pleased with himself when he heard Jesus' announcement, and that the keys to the kingdom of heaven would be given to him. But Peter's glory was not to last very long. In the verses that follow, he again rushed in where angels fear to tread.

Lord Jesus, thank You that, like Peter, I can confess that You are the Christ, the Son of the living God. Help me to avoid Peter's mistakes in my own life. Amen.

Peter, the Stumbling Block

Peter took Him aside and began to rebuke Him. "Never, Lord!"
he said. "This shall never happen to You!" Jesus turned and
said to Peter, "Get behind Me, Satan! You are a stumbling
block to Me; you do not have in mind the concerns of God, but
merely human concerns." Matt. 16:22-23

Within a few minutes, Peter progressed from being the rock on which Jesus would build His church, to becoming a stumbling block! In his rashness he felt confident enough to rebuke Jesus when He told His disciples that, in Jerusalem, He would suffer many things, that He would be killed and that on the third day He would rise from the dead. Jesus called Peter Satan, shortly after praising him for being open to a revelation from God.

Peter must have been embarrassed by Jesus' response. All he wanted to do was to give Jesus some good advice. Humanly speaking, it was, after all, impossible that the long-awaited Messiah was going to die and be resurrected three days later. But Peter learned a valuable lesson – one of self-denial and taking up your cross if you want to follow Jesus.

Sometimes we are just like Peter. We feel that we are not being treated fairly. But we must remember that Jesus cannot make mistakes. Trust in Him and be prepared to take up your cross and follow Him.

Lord, please forgive me that I, too, have sometimes thought
that You treat me unfairly. Remind me once again that You
know what is best for me and make me willing to take up my
cross and follow You. Amen.

Peter and the Question of Taxes

When Peter came into the house, Jesus was the first to speak. "What do you think, Simon?" He asked. "From whom do the kings of the earth collect duty and taxes – from their own children or from others?" Matt. 17:25

When the temple tax collectors wanted to know from Peter whether Jesus paid tax, Peter said He did. Jesus, however, asked him whether the kings collect tax from their own children or from others. "From others," Peter answered. "Then the children are exempt," Jesus said. "But so that we may not cause offense, go to the lake and throw out your line. Take the first fish you catch; open its mouth and you will find a four-drachma coin. Take it and give it to them for my tax and yours" (vv. 26-27).

Peter experienced another of Jesus' miracles. When he responded to Jesus' command, he caught a fish with sufficient money in its mouth to pay his and Jesus' temple tax. Many people have a problem when it comes to paying tax. Some ignore their conscience by cheating on their tax returns. Jesus expects honesty from His followers. Although, strictly speaking, He owed no temple tax, He still paid it.

When the Pharisees asked Jesus a trick question regarding the payment of taxes, Jesus replied, "Give back to Caesar what is Caesar's, and to God what is God's" (Matt. 22:21). See to it that you are honest when paying your taxes.

Heavenly Father, I pray that You will help me to be honest in my conduct at all times. Amen.

Peter Seeks a Reward

Peter answered Him, "We have left everything to follow You! What then will there be for us?" Matt. 19:27

Today's Scripture verse is Peter's response to Jesus' statement that it is easier for a camel to go through the eye of a needle than for a rich man to enter the kingdom of God. Jesus made it clear that wealth is a stumbling block to eternal life. It seemed that He was suggesting that it is impossible for a rich man to go to heaven.

Naturally, the impetuous Peter wanted to know what the disciples were going to gain because they had left everything to follow Him. Jesus replied that one day the twelve disciples would sit on twelve thrones, judging the twelve tribes of Israel. Then He added, "Everyone who has left houses or brothers or sisters or father or mother or wife or children or fields for My sake will receive a hundred times as much and will inherit eternal life" (v. 29).

But Jesus' words contain a warning: "Many who are first will be last, and many who are last will be first" (v. 30). Jesus wanted to teach Peter that eternal life is a gift of pure grace that no one can earn.

There are no calculations that can measure your merit in the eyes of God. You were redeemed through grace and, purely through grace, God enables you to be His child.

Lord Jesus, thank You for Your great grace in my life. Grant that my possessions will never be more important to me than You. Amen.

Peter's Mountain-top Experience

He received honor and glory from God the Father when the voice came to Him from the Majestic Glory, saying, "This is My Son, whom I love; with Him I am well pleased."
2 Pet. 1:17

Even the glorification of Jesus does not cause Peter to hold his tongue. Once again he speaks out of turn: "Lord, it is good for us to be here. If You wish, I will put up three shelters – one for You, one for Moses and one for Elijah" (Matt. 17:4). The mountain-top experience was a highlight in his life.

We all sometimes experience moments that are almost perfect – times when we experience the presence of God so intensely that we, like Peter, wish we could feel like that for ever. These are moments when God allows us to experience Him in all His glory and majesty. I experience such moments when I walk along the beach, when I watch the sun set in flaming clouds of color, and when I see the world in a new light through the eyes of my granddaughter.

"These moments are given to us so that we can remember them when God seems far away and everything appears empty and worthless. These experiences are true moments of grace," writes Henri Nouwen.

When you next experience mountain-top moments like these, store them in your memory for those days when you are feeling low.

Heavenly Father, thank You for moments when You are especially near to me. I glorify You for enabling us to get a glimpse of Your glory. Amen.

Peter Swears Allegiance

Peter replied, "Even if all fall away on account of You, I never will." Matt. 26:33

Peter is one of three disciples that Jesus drew into His inner circle. He shared the mountain-top experience with them and also invited them to pray with Him in Gethsemane. Peter was one of Jesus' confidants and his love for Jesus was genuine. However, Peter was only human. He just could not succeed in being truly loyal.

When Jesus told His disciples that His followers would be scattered, Peter was the first to swear eternal allegiance to Jesus. Peter promised that even if all deserted Jesus, he never would. But Peter could not keep this promise. Together with all the other disciples, he ran away when Jesus was taken captive in the Garden of Gethsemane by the chief priests and Pharisees.

When we hear about acquaintances who have disappointed the Lord, we think to ourselves that we would never do that. We will remain true to our faith no matter what. But all people are fallible. All of us stumble in many ways, writes James (see James 3:2).

If, on occasion, you have failed to keep your promises to God, you can count on this promise: Even though we are faithless, God remains faithful. He cannot disown Himself (see 2 Tim. 2:13). You can depend on God's faithfulness to you in times of trouble.

Lord Jesus, please forgive me that I condemn people like Peter while I often disown You in the things that I say and do. Thank You for the assurance that You will always remain faithful to me. Amen.

Peter Experiences a Miracle

When [Jesus] arrived at the house of Jairus, He did not let anyone go in with Him except Peter, John and James, and the child's father and mother. Luke 8:51

P eter was present when an important member of the synagogue council knelt before Jesus, pleading with Him to heal his terminally ill daughter. However, on the way to Jairus's house, Jesus first stopped to talk to a woman who had suffered from bleeding, but who was cured from her illness when she touched His cloak. While Jesus was still speaking to her, someone arrived with the news that Jairus's daughter had just died.

Perhaps Peter wondered why Jesus did not go directly to Jairus's house. He had often witnessed Jesus healing sick people. However, a dead person was a different story altogether. He was most probably surprised by Jesus' calm words that Jairus should keep believing.

At Jairus's house, Peter heard Jesus say to the mourners that the little girl was not dead, but only sleeping. They laughed at Him because they knew that she was dead. Jesus sent all the people away. He only allowed Peter, John, James and the girl's parents to enter the room. Then Peter saw how Jesus took the dead little girl by the hand and commanded, "My child, get up!" (v. 54). Peter then knew beyond any doubt that nothing was impossible for Jesus.

Lord Jesus, I know that You can do everything, that to You nothing is impossible. I pray that You would strengthen my faith so that I can see the miracles You perform in my life. Amen.

At Passover

Jesus sent Peter and John, saying, "Go and make preparations for us to eat the Passover." Luke 22:8

Peter and John were singled out again when Jesus asked them to prepare the venue for Passover. This would be the last time that Jesus ate with His disciples before the crucifixion and it was also the meal during which He instituted the sacrament of communion.

Jesus told them exactly where the communion meal was to be held. They had to follow a man carrying a jar of water until they reached a specific house where they were to ask the owner if Jesus could eat the Passover there with His disciples. Jesus also said that the man would show them a large upper room, furnished in readiness for the feast. Everything happened as Jesus had said. Once again Peter must have been surprised at Jesus' knowledge of the events that were still to happen.

At this meal, Jesus used bread and wine to introduce the first communion service. Jesus told His disciples that the bread was His body that would be broken for them, and that the wine was His blood that would be poured out for them. He also announced that one of the disciples would betray Him.

Every time you partake in communion, the sacrament should be a reminder of Jesus' love for you, of His crucifixion that enabled you to have a relationship of trust with God.

Lord Jesus, thank You for being willing to die on my behalf, and for instituting communion so that I can commemorate Your crucifixion with the bread and wine. Amen.

Jesus Washed Peter's Feet

[Jesus] came to Simon Peter, who said to Him, "Lord, are You going to wash my feet?" Jesus replied, "You do not realize now what I am doing, but later you will understand." "No," said Peter, "You shall never wash my feet." John 13:6-8

At Passover, Jesus took it upon Himself to wash the feet of the disciples, even though He was their Teacher. When Jesus started washing their feet, Peter was the first to protest, "You shall never wash my feet" (v. 8). When Jesus said that unless He washed his feet, he would have no part with Him, Peter jumped to the other extreme: "Then, Lord, not just my feet but my hands and my head as well!" he requested (v. 9).

Jesus realized that Peter did not understand what His act of washing the disciples' feet meant. "Those who have had a bath need only to wash their feet; their whole body is clean," Jesus explained to him (v. 10). Jesus used the ceremony of feet washing to demonstrate to His disciples that His love for them lay in service and sacrifice. Just as He was willing to wash their feet, they were to be willing to serve each other, doing the things expected of slaves.

Jesus also expects a willingness on your part to serve other people. Are you ready to demonstrate sacrificial love and service to others – just as He did?

Lord, I do not really enjoy serving other people. Please forgive my selfishness and make me willing to follow Your example and perform sacrificial duties for Your kingdom. Amen.

Peter in Gethsemane

[Jesus] took Peter and the two sons of Zebedee along with him, and He began to be sorrowful and troubled. Then He said to them, "My soul is overwhelmed with sorrow to the point of death. Stay here and keep watch with Me." Then He returned to His disciples and found them sleeping.
Matt. 26:37-38, 40

Time and again, Jesus chose Peter, John and James when He only wanted a few of His disciples with Him. When Jesus went to the Garden of Gethsemane to pray before His crucifixion, Peter was one of those whom He asked to accompany Him.

In Gethsemane, Peter failed Jesus again. He and his fellow disciples could not even succeed in keeping watch with Jesus for a few hours. Jesus told His followers how sorrowful and troubled He was, but even this was not sufficient to motivate them to stand by Him. Although Jesus asked them three times to pray and keep watch with Him, they fell asleep each time.

The three disciples who were closest to Jesus failed Him miserably when He needed them most. To make matters worse, these disciples also ran away when He was taken captive and, a short time later, Peter disowned Jesus three times.

Before you get too indignant with Peter and his companions, consider whether you, too, have not failed Jesus by the things you have said and done.

Lord Jesus, I apologize for all the times in the past when I have failed You. Teach me to watch and pray so that I will not fall into temptation. Amen.

Peter and the High Priest's Servant

*Then Simon Peter, who had a sword, drew it and struck the
high priest's servant, cutting off his right ear. (The servant's
name was Malchus.) John 18:10*

B y now, we are so used to Peter's rashness and impulsiveness that we are not in the least surprised
that he was the one to draw his sword and cut off the
ear of the high priest's slave when Jesus was taken
captive. At least Peter tried to do something to prevent
Jesus from being captured.

I am sure that Peter was quite taken aback by Jesus'
conduct. Instead of thanking him, Jesus said, "Put
your sword away! Shall I not drink the cup the Father
has given Me?" (v. 11). Once again Jesus gave Peter
and the other disciples a demonstration of His divine
omnipotence – He touched Malchus's ear and healed
him.

Although Peter meant well and his deed seemed
heroic, He tried to interfere with God's plan for His Son.
Jesus had to die in order for our sins to be forgiven –
and this is exactly what Peter tried to prevent with his
impulsive actions.

Sometimes, we act on impulse too, without first
ensuring that what we do is in accordance with God's
will. Resolve to pray first and then act.

*Lord, help me to live so close to You that I will always first
check that what I do forms part of Your will for my life.
Amen.*

Peter Disowns Jesus

Immediately the rooster crowed the second time. Then Peter remembered the word Jesus had spoken to him: "Before the rooster crows twice you will disown Me three times." And he broke down and wept. Mark 14:72

W hen Jesus told Peter that he would disown Him three times, he emphatically insisted, "Even if I have to die with You, I will never disown You" (v. 31). Peter, who was so convinced that he would never forsake Jesus, followed at a distance after Jesus had been taken captive. At least Peter risked entering the courtyard of Caiaphas, but there three times he denied that he was a follower of Jesus. Peter even began to call down curses on himself and swore when he was questioned, "I don't know this Man you're talking about" (v. 71).

After Peter had disowned Jesus three times, a rooster crowed. "The Lord turned and looked straight at Peter," Luke reports (Luke 22:61). Peter was devastated. He realized how his actions must have hurt Jesus. Peter went outside and wept bitterly.

It is very easy to condemn Peter for disowning Jesus. But we must think twice before doing so. Don't you sometimes disown Jesus by acting and talking in a way that is not what is expected of a Christian?

Lord Jesus, once again I stand accused before You. You know how often I have disowned You by acting and talking in a way that's contrary to what You expect of Your children. Please help me to lead a life that will testify that I am Your child. Amen.

Peter at the Tomb

Peter, however, got up and ran to the tomb. Bending over, he saw the strips of linen lying by themselves, and he went away, wondering to himself what had happened. Luke 24:12

When they heard from the angels at the empty tomb that Jesus was not there, but that He had risen from the dead, the excited women immediately returned to the village to share the news of Jesus' resurrection with the disciples. But they did not share in the women's excitement. To them, the story sounded too far-fetched to be true. But Peter believed the women. Perhaps he remembered what Jesus had said on the day he had dared to rebuke Him! He would not easily forget that Jesus had called him Satan and a stumbling block.

Although Peter believed the women's account, he wanted to go and see for himself. Once again, he took the lead and ran ahead to the tomb. When he arrived there, he only found the linen burial cloths. Although Peter did not see an angel at the tomb, he knew for certain that Jesus had truly risen from the dead. Luke wrote that he went away wondering to himself what had happened.

Jesus' resurrection and His victory over death fill His children with joy and wonder to this day. His resurrection enables us to have everlasting life.

This promise is for you, too. If you belong to Jesus, you have eternal life.

Lord Jesus, Your resurrection remains a miracle to me. Thank You for the assurance that I, too, will rise from death one day to live with You for all eternity. Amen.

Peter's Second Chance

"But go, tell His disciples and Peter, 'He is going ahead of you into Galilee. There you will see Him, just as He told you.'"
Mark 16:7

Mark reports that the angel instructed the women to go and tell the disciples that Jesus had risen from the dead. He mentioned Peter by name. The angel told them that Jesus had gone to Galilee and would see them there as He had predicted.

Jesus knew that Peter was going to disown Him – He told him so! In Galilee, Jesus gave Peter a chance to repent of his denial. Peter eagerly responded to Jesus' offer of forgiveness. Peter was so eager to be with Jesus, that he jumped straight into the water and swam to shore to reach Him sooner (see John 21:7).

In the competitive world in which we live, people are not really inclined to give each other a second chance. But Jesus is not like other people. Not only does He give His children a second chance, but also a third, tenth and even a 490th (70 times 7) chance to rectify our mistakes. He is willing to forgive us every time we sin.

Have you, like Peter, blundered by disowning Jesus in one way or another? Do not hesitate to respond to Jesus' gift of grace. Ask Him to forgive your sins. He will gladly do so.

Lord Jesus, I apologize for disappointing You so often. Thank You that You are willing to give me another chance to rectify my mistakes. Amen.

The Miraculous Catch of Fish

"I'm going out to fish," Simon Peter told them, and they said, "We'll go with you." So they went out and got into the boat, but that night they caught nothing. John 21:3

Peter and the other disciples had been fishing all night without catching a single fish. Suddenly they saw Jesus standing on the shore. He asked them whether they had caught anything. "Throw your net on the right side of the boat and you will find some," Jesus said (v. 6). Peter probably wondered why Jesus was sending them for a second time to do something that was hopeless – and yet he obeyed Jesus' command. He threw out the net and, this time, there were so many fish that the net almost tore and they were unable to haul it in.

When he saw that the net was filled with fish, Peter knew that this was a miracle. Perhaps he thought about the first time he had met Jesus, when Jesus promised to make him a fisher of men. Jesus' promise was fulfilled when Peter radically changed after this. From being a fisherman filled with fear, who did not want to acknowledge that he was one of Jesus' followers, Peter became a forceful preacher who conveyed his message with so much conviction that about three thousand people repented on that first day of Pentecost.

If you are willing to unconditionally obey Jesus' commands, you will discover that He will also perform miracles in your life.

Lord Jesus, please make me like Peter – willing to obey Your commands unconditionally. Amen.

"Peter, Do You Love Me?"

The third time [Jesus] said to him, "Simon son of John, do you love Me?" Peter was hurt because Jesus asked him the third time, "Do you love Me?" He said, "Lord, You know all things; You know that I love You." John 21:17

Three times Jesus asked Peter whether he truly loved Him – once for each time Peter had denied Him. Peter answered yes every time, and each time Jesus gave him a command, "Feed My lambs", "Take care of My sheep", "Feed My sheep" (vv. 15-17).

When Jesus asked Peter for the third time whether he loved Him, Peter was hurt. "Lord, You know all things; You know that I love You," he answered (v. 17). Each question of Jesus probably reminded Peter anew of his earlier denial of Jesus.

Peter had learned his lesson. There is very little left of the impetuous Peter who acted first and then thought. The new Peter is indeed a rock, as his name indicates. He is someone who Jesus could truly depend on to be a leader in the early church, someone who accepted the responsibility of telling people about Jesus and who guided new converts onto the right path.

Indeed, in his sermon on that first day of Pentecost, Peter did not hesitate to give powerful testimony about Jesus. This "new" Peter was so persuasive that approximately three thousand people were added to the church on that day (see Acts 2:41).

Lord, You know that I love You. Use me in Your kingdom and help me to be willing to take on a leading role in my own congregation and to guide others into the faith. Amen.

Peter's Sermon at Pentecost

Peter stood up with the Eleven, raised his voice and address-
ed the crowd. Those who accepted his message were baptized,
and about three thousand were added to their number that
day. Acts 2:14, 41

The frightened Peter, who forsook Jesus when He was taken captive, and who disowned Him in the court-yard, underwent a complete metamorphosis. He brought such a powerful message on the first day of Pentecost that three thousand people were converted. Peter told those gathered there about Jesus' crucifixion and resurrection. He also told them about the outpouring of the Holy Spirit, which Jesus had promised His disciples.

Peter's testimony touched all who were gathered there. When the people wanted to know from him what they had to do to be saved, Peter had an answer ready: "Repent and be baptized, every one of you, in the name of Jesus Christ for the forgiveness of your sins. And you will receive the gift of the Holy Spirit" (v. 38). Peter went on to explain that this message was not only for the Jews, but for everyone whom God calls.

The Good News of Jesus is also for you today. Have you repented and invited Him into your life? Then you will also receive the Holy Spirit to guide and sustain you.

Lord Jesus, I thank You for dying on my behalf, for rising
from the dead and for ascending into heaven so that I can be
a child of God. Thank You for the gift of the Holy Spirit in
my life. Amen.

A Crippled Beggar Is Healed

*Peter said, "Silver or gold I do not have, but what I do have
I give you. In the name of Jesus Christ of Nazareth, walk."
Taking him by the right hand, he helped him up, and instantly
the man's feet and ankles became strong. Acts 3:6-7*

On their way to the temple, Peter and John met a man
who had been crippled since birth. He earned a
living by begging. In those days, people with disabilities
were totally dependent upon the generosity of others.
When the crippled man saw Peter and John entering
the temple, he asked them for some money.

"Look at us!" (v. 4) Peter said to the crippled man.
When the man looked at them in the hope that they
would give him some money, Peter said to him, "Silver
or gold I do not have, but what I do have I give you. In
the name of Jesus Christ of Nazareth, walk" (v. 6). Peter
helped him up and instantly the man's feet and ankles
became strong so that he could stand upright. Then the
crippled man went with Peter and John to the temple
and praised God. All the people were filled with wonder
and amazement at what had happened to him.

The crippled man received much more than what
he had hoped for. The healing power of Jesus flowed
through Peter and restored his health. The gospel offers
much more than temporary benefits. It offers a brand-
new understanding of God; hope, joy and recovery.

*Lord Jesus, thank You that faith in You is much more precious
than material things, that it guarantees me hope, joy and
peace. Amen.*

Peter's Speech in the Colonnade

All the people were astonished and came running to them. When Peter saw this, he said to them: "Repent, then, and turn to God, so that your sins may be wiped out." Acts 3:11-12, 19

When the people heard about the miraculous healing of the crippled beggar, they ran to the temple to see Peter. They were also curious to see the healed man with their own eyes. They were not disappointed when they saw the wonderful sight of the once crippled man dancing and jumping for joy!

Peter seized this opportunity to fulfill his calling to witness. "Why does this surprise you?" (v. 12) he asked the crowds gathered at the temple. He told them that the healing of the crippled man was not the result of his own powers, but the power of God. He rebuked them again for having crucified Jesus, and also urged them, "Repent, then, and turn to God, so that your sins may be wiped out" (v. 19).

Jesus is still able to perform miracles today. He can heal the sick, as He did when He dwelt on earth, as well as forgive sins. If you want to experience His miraculous power in your own life, simply believe His Word and believe in Him.

Lord Jesus, I know that You have always been able to perform miracles and that You can heal me when I am ill, if it is in accordance with Your will. I pray that You would strengthen my faith in You every day. Amen.

Peter as Witness

Peter and John replied, "Which is right in God's eyes: to listen to you, or to Him? You be the judges! As for us, we cannot help speaking about what we have seen and heard." Acts 4:19-20

P eter was still talking to the crowds in front of the temple when the priests heard about it. They did not like Peter's testimony at all and had him and John seized and put into jail until the following day. Peter and John were then brought before the Sanhedrin. They wanted to know what power Peter had used when he had healed the crippled man.

Once again, Peter did not hesitate. He told them that the miracle had taken place in the name of Jesus whom they had crucified and that there was "no other name under heaven given to mankind by which we must be saved" (v. 12). The Sanhedrin commanded the two apostles not to speak or teach in the name of Jesus.

However, Peter and John did not allow this important group of people to deter them. "Which is right in God's eyes: to listen to you, or to Him? You be the judges! As for us, we cannot help speaking about what we have seen and heard," they replied.

Follow Peter's example and do not allow other people to stop you from testifying about Jesus. You should find it impossible to remain silent about what Jesus has done for You and what He means to you.

Lord Jesus, thank You for Your grace in my life. Make it impossible for me to remain silent about what You have done in my life. Amen.

Peter Performs Miracles

As a result, people brought the sick into the streets and laid them on beds and mats so that at least Peter's shadow might fall on some of them as he passed by. Acts 5:15

Peter's ministry went from strength to strength, as did the miracles he performed. God worked so powerfully through him that more and more people brought their sick to him. "Crowds gathered also from the towns around Jerusalem, bringing their sick and those tormented by impure spirits, and all of them were healed," Luke reports (v. 16). The power that radiated from Peter was so strong that people brought their sick into the streets so that his shadow could fall on them and they could be healed.

Jesus' earlier promise to His disciples, "Very truly I tell you, whoever believes in Me will do the works I have been doing, and they will do even greater things than these" (John 14:12) was indeed realized in the life of Peter. Peter possessed these supernatural powers not because he was so wonderful, but because he lived in close contact with God.

God still brings His miraculous power into the lives of His children today, if we pray for it. If you need strength, you can confidently call on God, asking Him to give you His power. With this strength, you will also succeed in doing great things in God's kingdom. Just be sure to always give the glory to God.

Heavenly Father, please strengthen me with Your power so that I, like Peter, can succeed in doing great things for You. Amen.

Peter Raises Tabitha from the Dead

Peter went with them, and when he arrived he was taken upstairs to the room. Peter sent them all out of the room; then he got down on his knees and prayed. Turning toward the dead woman, he said, "Tabitha, get up." Acts 9:39-40

In the little town of Joppa there lived a faithful woman whose heart went out to those who were less privileged than her. "She was always doing good and helping the poor," Luke reports (v. 36). This woman was herself a widow. Widows had no rights in those times, and were normally dependent on the care of their children. However, Tabitha was a very special woman. She took little notice of her own difficult situation. Instead of complaining, she reached out to the poor. She made clothes for them and did her best to help them.

This good woman fell ill and died. The widows to whom she had been so kind were inconsolable. They sent for Peter. When Peter arrived, they took him upstairs to the room where Tabitha lay. Peter sent them all out of the room and started to pray fervently.

Turning toward the dead woman, he said, "Tabitha, get up." Tabitha opened her eyes and sat up. Her friends were overjoyed to have their benefactor in their midst again. Many people who heard about this miracle believed in Jesus.

Lord, I still do so little for You. Help me, like Tabitha, to look away from my own problems, to notice those with big problems and to offer them assistance. Amen.

Peter Learns a Life Lesson

"Surely not, Lord!" Peter replied. "I have never eaten anything impure or unclean." The voice spoke to him a second time, "Do not call anything impure that God has made clean." Acts 10:14-15

Peter was a Jew through and through. He never even considered eating food that God had declared unclean. But then something happened. While Peter was on the roof praying, he saw a vision of something like a large sheet, filled with unclean animals, and he heard a voice calling to him, "Get up, Peter. Kill and eat" (v. 13). Peter refused point blank. He had never eaten something that was unclean. He heard the voice speaking to him for a second time saying, "Do not call anything impure that God has made clean" (v. 15). After Peter had seen the vision for the third time, the sheet disappeared.

Peter must have been bewildered and he must have wondered what this strange vision meant. But God had already been working in the heart of Cornelius, a centurion in the Italian regiment. Cornelius was a God-fearing Gentile who prayed to God regularly. According to Jewish law, he was unclean and Peter was not allowed to enter his house.

But the vision God sent to Peter made it clear that the barriers between Jews and Gentiles were abolished with the advent of Jesus. All who believe in Jesus have access to heaven, whether Jew or Gentile.

Lord Jesus, I praise You for making no distinction between people, but that all who believe in You will be saved. Amen.

God Does Not Show Favoritism

I now realize how true it is that God does not show favoritism but accepts every nation the one who fears Him and does what is right. Acts 10:34-35

Before Peter had seen the vision of the sheet with the unclean animals, God had commanded Cornelius to fetch Peter from Joppa. Cornelius then sent two of his servants and a soldier to Joppa. "While Peter was still thinking about the vision, the Spirit said to him, 'Simon, three men are looking for you. So get up and go downstairs. Do not hesitate to go with them, for I have sent them'" (vv. 19-20).

The men told Peter that Cornelius wanted to hear what he had to say. After offering them accommodation for the night, he accompanied them to Cornelius's house the next day. He told all the people gathered there that God had shown him that no person is impure or unclean, because God does not show favoritism, but accepts men from every nation who fear Him and do what is right (see vv. 34-35).

While Peter was still talking to the Gentiles about Jesus, the Holy Spirit came on all who were listening to him. Peter instructed them to be baptized in the name of Jesus Christ, and he stayed and taught them for a few days. In the church of Christ, the barriers between different people are being broken down. We are all equal in His eyes and each of us has access to heaven.

Lord Jesus, please teach me the same lesson that You taught Peter: that You do not show favoritism, but accept all who worship You. Amen.

Peter Is Freed from Jail

Peter came to himself and said, "Now I know without a doubt that the Lord has sent His angel and rescued me from Herod's clutches." Acts 12:11

When Herod saw that the Christian persecution pleased the Jews, he decided to take Peter captive. While he was in jail, an angel appeared to him. He ordered Peter to get up, put on his clothes and sandals, and wrap his cloak around him. When he obeyed the angel, the chains fell off Peter's wrists. He followed the angel and saw that the iron gates leading to the city were opening for him. Only then did Peter realize that God had sent an angel to free him from jail. He immediately went to Mary's house, where the Christians were gathered, praying for his release.

Peter's release from jail was not only a miracle but also a clear answer to prayer. Luke says, "The church was earnestly praying to God for him" (v. 5). It is ironic, however, that when the servant girl told the praying believers that Peter was standing at the door, they refused to believe it, and told her that she was out of her mind!

Sometimes we also pray for a miracle, but when it happens, we refuse to accept it. God can still perform miracles in your life. Make sure that your faith is stronger than that of the Christians in Judea!

Heavenly Father, I praise You for being able to do everything – even that which is humanly impossible. Thank You for freeing Your children and protecting them from danger. Amen.

Peter on Suffering

Dear friends, do not be surprised at the fiery ordeal that has come on you to test you, as though something strange were happening to you. But rejoice inasmuch as you participate in the sufferings of Christ, so that you may be overjoyed when His glory is revealed. 1 Pet. 4:12-13

Peter faced much suffering in his own life. He had first-hand knowledge of this topic. Peter said that Christians should not be surprised when they encounter problems and suffering. All Christians face suffering. Even Jesus had to suffer much when He was in this world. Therefore, when we suffer for His sake, we should see it as a privilege, which will result in abundant joy when He returns one day.

There are very few people who succeed in rejoicing in times of suffering. But if you give some thought to the times of suffering in your own life, you will discover that your suffering was to your advantage, because it brought you closer to the Lord. God uses suffering in the lives of His children to draw us closer to Him and to provide us with a new revelation of His love for us and His grace toward us.

Therefore, do not be surprised when crises surface in your life. Remember that Jesus also suffered. You can look forward with joy to His second coming, when He will put an end to all suffering forever.

Lord Jesus, I apologize for complaining when I experience difficulties. Help me to depend on You in times of suffering and to look forward to Your second coming. Amen.

Peter's Warning

Be alert and of sober mind. Your enemy the devil prowls around like a roaring lion looking for someone to devour. Resist him, standing firm in the faith. 1 Pet. 5:8-9

Peter writes that we should be self-controlled and alert, because we face a dangerous enemy who is out to destroy us. The devil never leaves God's children in peace. However, we have God on our side. If the devil attacks us, we should fight back with the strength God gives us.

When Jesus spoke to His disciples about His return to His Father, He said, "I will not say much more to you, for the prince of this world is coming. He has no hold over Me, but he comes so that the world may learn that I love the Father and do exactly what My Father has commanded Me" (John 14:30-31).

With the strength that you get from Jesus, you will be able to ward off the attack of the devil successfully. Then the devil will have no power over you and, like Jesus, you will succeed in diligently obeying the commands of your heavenly Father.

Therefore, follow Peter's advice: Be alert and on your guard, so that you will know when the devil attacks you in an attempt to lure you away from God. Remain steadfast in your faith and resist him. Then he will be defeated.

Lord Jesus, thank You for siding with me in battle because with You, I will always be more than a conqueror. Amen.

Live Holy and Godly Lives

Since everything will be destroyed in this way, what kind of people ought you to be? You ought to live holy and godly lives. 2 Pet. 3:11

In Peter's day, the people expected the Second Coming at any moment and they could not understand why Jesus was delaying His return. We have been waiting for two thousand years for the Second Coming. Peter calls on God's children to live holy and godly lives.

The word "holy" has a negative connotation for some people. They regard it as a synonym for being hypocritical. The Greek word from which "holy" has been translated in today's Scripture verse is *hagios*, which means to be complete and perfect. It refers to a person of integrity. Thus holiness is actually a positive concept.

For someone who is truly holy and godly, nothing is of greater importance than God. "These have come so that the proven genuineness of your faith – of greater worth than gold, which perishes even though refined by fire – may result in praise, glory and honor when Jesus Christ is revealed," Peter writes at the beginning of his letter (1 Pet. 1:7).

Jesus' second coming is as close or as far away as your death. Be prepared for it now and don't waste time calculating when "one day" will be. Are you already leading a holy and godly life? Or are there things in your life that are of greater importance than God?

Lord Jesus, make me holy and completely devoted to You, so that I will be prepared for Your second coming every day. Amen.

Peter and the Second Coming

The Lord is not slow in keeping His promise, as some understand slowness. Instead He is patient with you, not wanting anyone to perish, but everyone to come to repentance. 2 Pet. 3:9

Sometimes we become impatient because Jesus does not seem to be coming soon. Peter gives two interesting reasons why we should not become despondent if Jesus' second coming takes longer than we anticipate.

We cannot apply our concept of time to God. To Him a day is like a thousand years. Secondly, the lapse of time between His first and second coming is not a postponement of a promise, but rather the merciful withholding of such a promise. It is God's will that *all* people should be saved. Therefore, He is mercifully giving people the chance to hear and respond to the gospel message. God knows what He is doing and His timing is perfect.

This time of grace should be a fruitful time of labor for those of us who look forward to Jesus' second coming, a time to testify to others about His redeeming love, a time to encourage those who do not yet know Him.

You can follow John's advice: "Dear children, continue in Him, so that when He appears we may be confident and unashamed before Him at His coming" (1 John 2:28). From now on live your life in such a way that Jesus will be satisfied with your life when He comes.

Lord Jesus, thank You for the promise that You will return one day to fetch Your children. Help me to be fruitful in Your service so that, on that day, You will be satisfied with me. Amen.

June

Honor and Glorify God!

In his book *The Keys to Spiritual Growth*, John MacArthur writes that any Christian's main aim in life is to glorify God.

"Glorifying God is the end result of the Christian life. Spiritual maturity is simply concentrating and focusing on the Person of God until we are caught up in His majesty and His glory."

We ought to glorify God because He is our Creator, and everything we have comes from Him. He made all things to glorify Himself.

All God's qualities can be seen in creation, and if we take notice we will discover that this is precisely what creation does: it glorifies Him.

This month we are going to learn to honor and glorify God in everything we say, do and perceive.

Lord, I want my purpose in life to be to
glorify You in everything I do.
When I see Your creation, I become so
intensely aware of Your glory and majesty.
From now on I want You and Your will
to be my first priority in life.
I want to give You the credit for my achievements.
I want to confess my sins before You,
so that I can be forgiven.
I want to trust You fully
and glorify You by producing much fruit for You.
I am willing to give up my own honor,
to carry out Your command to love and be Your witness.
I want to praise You with everything in me
and glorify You together with the whole of creation.
Lord Jesus, I also want to glorify You
through my suffering because it helps me
to understand Your suffering better and
serves as my guarantee that I will
one day share in Your glory.
I praise You for the promise that
the glory You are preparing for me
will by far surpass my present suffering.
I want to praise You in my prayers,
by leading people to You,
and by avoiding sexual sin,
so that You will also be glorified in my body.
It is wonderful that I may enjoy You,
and experience Your constant joy in my life.
Let me grow in grace and knowledge of You
so that I will bring You the honor due to Your name.
Yours is the kingdom and the power and the glory,
forever and ever,
Amen.

Do Everything for God's Glory

Whether you eat or drink, or whatever you do, do it all for the glory of God. 1 Cor. 10:31

P aul told the church in Corinth that he didn't seek his own good, but the good of many, and that everything he did was done in such a way that his life would glorify Christ. Then he asked the believers to follow his example by doing everything to the glory of God.

We ought to do everything in such a way that people will see how important God is to us, how mighty and magnificent He is. If we manage to do this, God will receive the honor for everything we achieve and He will truly be glorified through our lives.

This command includes all things. When you are doing housework, do it to the glory of God. His glory should top your priority list at work. The upbringing of your children, your marriage relationship and your conduct should be of such a nature that others will see that God is all-important to you.

To glorify God in everything is a decision of the will. It is something only you can decide and only you can put into practice. Try to glorify God in everything from now on, in important as well as unimportant things. Jesus testifies that He also glorified God on earth by completing the work that God sent Him to do (see John 17:3).

Heavenly Father, help me to do all things in such a way that people will be able to tell by my conduct how magnificent and mighty You are. Amen.

The Glory of Jesus

The Word became human and made His home among us. He was full of unfailing love and faithfulness. And we have seen His glory, the glory of the Father's one and only Son.
John 1:14

In Old Testament times no one could see God's glory and live. God sent His Son to the world that people could have a glimpse of that glory. The New International Version says, "The Word became flesh and made His dwelling among us. We have seen His glory, the glory of the one and only Son, who came from the Father, full of grace and truth. No one has ever seen God, but the one and only Son, who is Himself God and is in closest relationship with the Father, has made Him known" (John 1:14, 18). Here glory refers to the importance or impressiveness (among other things) of a person in the eyes of others.

John, James and Peter are directly confronted with Jesus' glory on the Mount of Transfiguration. While He prays, Jesus' outward appearance changes and two men appear to Him in glorious splendor. Then God Himself speaks and confirms that Jesus is His Son (see Luke 9:28-36). The three disciples could never again doubt Jesus' glory. We are no longer privileged to see God's glory through Jesus, yet we can see it every day in His creation.

Lord Jesus, although You are not on earth anymore, I catch a glimpse of Your glory every day when I see the wonders of creation around me. Thank You, Lord! Amen.

Choose God above Everything

I fully expect and hope that I will never be ashamed, but that I will continue to be bold for Christ, as I have been in the past. And I trust that my life will bring honor to Christ, whether I live or die. For to me, living means living for Christ, and dying is even better. Phil. 1:20-21

Today we do not worship idols made of wood and stone, like the Israelites of old. However, this does not mean that we don't have idols. Anything that is more important to you than God is an idol. If you want to make sure you are not nurturing such an idol, make a list of things you spend most of your time and money on. What is the most valuable thing in your life? Is it your family, your security or perhaps your work?

Paul could honestly testify that for him life revolved around Jesus, that He was the most important Person to him and that all other things faded into the background in comparison to Jesus. Throughout his life Paul glorified Jesus in everything he did. Even when he was in prison, he used his circumstances to introduce other people to God's greatness. He lived every day with his eyes focused on heaven.

What about you? Can you testify in all honesty that, for you, life is Christ? That you cannot do without God? If not, you are not yet glorifying God in your life.

Lord Jesus, there are still so many other things that are priorities in my life. I want You to be the most important to me from today onwards, and I want to glorify You with my whole being. Amen.

Put God's Will First

"My soul is deeply troubled. Should I pray, 'Father, save Me from this hour'? But this is the very reason I came!"
John 12:27

Jesus could not glorify His Father's name before He, in spite of His inner turmoil, had asked that God's will be done. The same goes for us. In Gethsemane, Jesus prayed that He might be spared the cup of bitterness, but added that God's will be done.

When our eldest son and his wife were expecting their first baby, the gynecologist found that the hormone count in my daughter-in-law's blood was exceptionally high. She told the parents that it was one of the signs of Down's syndrome. At first I was terribly upset at the news. The first day and night I prayed non-stop that the baby would be normal. However, from the second day I prayed that God's will be done – that we would accept the little girl and love her very much, even if she wasn't normal. And immediately I experienced a strange peace. I just knew this baby was normal and this was confirmed a week later by means of an amniocentesis test. Yet it was clear that I first had to be prepared to put God's will first.

Are you prepared to obey God's will for you at all costs, even if it should result in great unhappiness? Then you will discover that God's will is always best for you.

Lord Jesus, make me willing to obey Your will in everything, even if it runs directly counter to my own will. Amen.

Share in God's Glory

Since we are His children, we are His heirs. But if we are to share His glory, we must also share His suffering. Yet what we suffer now is nothing compared to the glory He will reveal to us later. Rom. 8:17-18

Sometimes God's children wonder why, if He loves them, He allows them to suffer. Paul tries to answer this question for the church in Rome. Both suffering and glory are part of our heritage on earth. Fortunately the glory outweighs and outlasts the suffering. When we suffer ourselves, we understand a little better what it cost Jesus to carry the sins of all of humankind on the cross without the support of His heavenly Father. The more we suffer, the better we understand Jesus' suffering when He was on earth. John of the Cross rightly says that the purest suffering produces the purest understanding.

If you want to share in Jesus' glory one day, you will have to be prepared to suffer for Him here on earth. It is precisely this suffering that results in glory in the end. Paul promises the church in Corinth, "That is why we never give up. Though our bodies are dying, our spirits are being renewed every day. For our present troubles are small and won't last very long. Yet they produce for us a glory that far outweighs them and will last forever!" (2 Cor. 4:16-17).

Lord Jesus, thank You that I can understand Your suffering better through my own suffering. Thank You for the promise that I will one day share in Your glory. Amen.

The Glory Is the Lord's

Yours, O LORD, is the greatness, the power, the glory, the victory, and the majesty. Everything in the heavens and on earth is Yours, O LORD, and this is Your kingdom. We adore You as the One who is over all things. Wealth and honor come from You alone, for You rule over everything. Power and might are in Your hand, and at Your discretion people are made great and given strength. 1 Chron. 29:11-12

In Deuteronomy 10:12, Moses tells Israel what God requires of them: "He requires only that you fear the LORD your God, and live in a way that pleases Him, and love Him and serve Him with all your heart and soul." It is of the utmost importance to God that His children give Him the honor due to Him. This is one of the ways in which we glorify Him.

King David obeyed this precept: When the people brought their abundant contributions toward the building of the temple, David thanked God. He took no credit himself (it was, after all, David who organized the collection campaign and contributed more than anybody else), but He gave God all the credit. He admitted frankly that wealth and honor are from God only, and that He rules over everything.

This is the attitude God wants from you, too. If you received many talents and achieved great things, the honor is the Lord's, not yours. Make sure that every time people admire or praise you, you make it very clear that the honor for your achievements goes to God.

Lord, I want to honor You for everything I have achieved, because You make my accomplishments possible. Amen.

Confess Your Sins

Joshua said to Achan, "My son, give glory to the LORD, the God of Israel, by telling the truth. Make your confession and tell me what you have done." Josh. 7:19

Another way of glorifying God is to admit and confess your sins. If you go on sinning, you can't share in God's glory. Paul writes to the Romans, "Everyone has sinned; we fall short of God's glorious standard" (Rom. 3:23). If you want to share in God's glory, you will first have to confess your sins.

When Achan was disobedient and kept back some of the spoils of war for himself – something that God explicitly forbade – all of Israel was punished for his sin. Only when Joshua asked him to give God the honor due to Him, did he admit that he had done wrong. At that, he and his whole family were killed. Achan's punishment may sound excessive, but God wants to show us how strongly He feels about sin.

John MacArthur writes, "Confession of sin glorifies God because if you excuse your sin, you impugn God." God knows about each and every one of your sins in any case. It is pointless to try to hide them from Him. Thus, confessing your sins is one of the ways to glorify God, because it actually means that you agree with God that you were wrong. If you confess your sins, you can rest assured that God is faithful and just, and that He will forgive your sins every time.

Father, I stand before You with my guilt because I have been sinful from birth. I want to glorify You now by confessing my sins. Please forgive them. Amen.

Don't Blame Others for Your Sins

The man replied, "It was the woman You gave me who gave me the fruit, and I ate it." Gen. 3:12

T he opposite of yesterday's devotion is also true. If you keep thinking up excuses for doing wrong, you dishonor God, and consequently don't succeed in glorifying Him.

When God admonished Adam for allowing Eve to tempt him into eating the fruit of the tree God forbade them to eat, he was ready with an excuse: "The woman You gave me brought me the fruit and I ate it." What Adam is in effect saying is that his sin was actually God's fault because the woman God gave him was the reason why he ate the fruit. MacArthur writes that, "Implying that He is somehow responsible maligns His holiness. So those who try to sneak out from under the absolute responsibility for their own sin commit a grievous sin against the glory of God."

It is never God who is responsible for your sins, but always you yourself. After all, you were born sinful. When you confess your sin, no "buts" are allowed at all. It is much better for you to recognize, admit and sincerely confess it before God, and to undertake not to sin again in future.

Lord, I am sorry, because I have also shifted the blame for my sins onto others. Help me to be aware of my sins, to confess every one of them before You and keep me from sinning again, so that I can glorify You. Amen.

Pagans Can Honor God

Make models of the tumors and of the rats that are destroying the country, and give glory to Israel's god. Perhaps He will lift His hand from you and your gods and your land.
1 Sam. 6:5

This is a very interesting, yet not so well-known story where we are told how a pagan nation glorified God. The Israelites (who had not paid any attention to their Covenant God for years) brought the ark of the covenant to the battleground, thinking that God would give them the victory. Just the opposite happened. They lost the war and the Philistines captured the ark and placed it in the temple of their god, Dagon.

God struck the Philistines with an outbreak of tumors and a plague of rats. When the Philistines consulted their priests and diviners, they were advised to make gold models of the tumors and mice and send these back to Israel with the ark. And strangely enough, God accepted this homage paid to Him by a pagan nation!

Because they confessed their guilt with this offering, the Philistines glorified Him with it, although they didn't know Him at all. By means of these offerings and confession of guilt they also admitted that God's punishment was just.

If you suffer at times because of your own sin, know that Jesus has already earned God's forgiveness for that sin of yours on the cross.

Lord Jesus, I praise You that You have already earned God's forgiveness for me on the cross, so that I no longer have to bear the punishment for my sin. Amen.

Trust God!

*Abraham never wavered in believing God's promise. In fact,
his faith grew stronger, and in this he brought glory to God.
He was fully convinced that God is able to do whatever He
promises. Rom. 4:20-21*

A braham continued trusting God. He knew that the
promise of a great number of descendants would
come true for him, and God rewarded Abraham's faith
in Him. Abraham reacted precisely the opposite way
that we would. We read that his faith became stronger.
If we feel that the things we trust God for have become
impossible, we easily throw in the towel and in the
process forget that God is almighty and can do anything.

When things aren't going your way, have faith in
God's promises in His Word. In the end, things work out
for those who trust in Him. Also hold onto Philippians
4:19 if God's promises have not been realized in your
life: "This same God who takes care of me will supply
all your needs from His glorious riches, which have
been given to us in Christ Jesus."

If you can trust God for today and for the future, He
will meet every one of your needs. Nobody who has
trusted God has ever been disappointed. Just remember
that God does not place a time limit on His promises.
He will fulfill them in His own time – and this might
mean that you will have to be prepared to trust Him,
like Abraham did, even if it takes a long time.

*Heavenly Father, I want to glorify You and keep on trusting
You, even if Your promises for me have not come true yet.
Amen.*

Glorify God by Bearing Fruit

"I am the vine; you are the branches. Those who remain in Me, and I in them, will produce much fruit. For apart from Me you can do nothing. When you produce much fruit, you are My true disciples. This brings great glory to My Father." John 15:5, 8

Jesus Himself says that His Father is glorified when His children produce much fruit for Him. However, we can only produce fruit when we remain in Jesus and He in us. A branch that is not attached to the grapevine cannot bear fruit. This means that we are to stay in an intimate relationship with Jesus if we want to produce fruit for Him. And the purpose of this fruit is to glorify God. A warning is included in Jesus' image of the owner of the vineyard; the Father allows only the shoots that bear fruit to remain on the vine. The others are cut off and burned.

In Colossians 1:10, Peter explains what this fruit means: "The way you live will always honor and please the Lord, and your lives will produce every kind of good fruit. All the while, you will grow as you learn to know God better and better." The fruit that God wants you to produce is obedience to Him and that you will do the things He created you for. Paul writes to the Ephesians, "He has created us anew in Christ Jesus, so we can do the good things He planned for us long ago" (Eph. 2:10). If you do this, you glorify God!

Heavenly Father, I want to glorify You by doing the good things You planned for me a long time ago. Amen.

Set Apart for God

You are not like that, for you are a chosen people. You are royal priests, a holy nation, God's very own possession. As a result, you can show others the goodness of God, for He called you out of the darkness into His wonderful light.
1 Pet. 2:9

We also glorify God by being set apart for Him, by living a holy life, as He is holy.

In the Old Testament God chose Israel from all the other nations to be His people of the Covenant. He promised to be their God, to stand by them and help them if they would be willing to obey Him. In the New Testament everyone who believes in Jesus can now be part of God's people and glorify Him. Each of God's children is especially chosen by Him; someone who must be set apart for Him, tell others about Him and His role as our Savior.

The Message says, "You are the ones chosen by God, chosen for the high calling of priestly work, chosen to be a holy people, God's instruments to do His work and speak out for Him, to tell others of the night-and-day difference He made for you – from nothing to something, from rejected to accepted."

You ought to glorify God with your life – and it is a very big responsibility that you will never be able to manage on your own. Tomorrow you will hear how it can become possible.

Heavenly Father, I praise You for calling me out of the darkness of sin to be Your child and to live in Your light, so that people who look at me will see You. Amen.

Jesus Shows How to Glorify God

I want you to understand what really matters, so that you may live pure and blameless lives until the day of Christ's return. May you always be filled with the fruit of your salvation – the righteous character produced in your life by Jesus Christ – for this will bring much glory and praise to God.
Phil. 1:10-11

O nly Jesus can make it possible for a human being to be set free from their sins. Only Jesus can make it possible for them to produce fruit that will glorify God, because only Jesus can put us in the right relationship with God by delivering us from our sin. When you are in the right relationship with God, you will automatically strive to become more like Jesus every day.

Peter writes, "He never sinned, nor ever deceived anyone. He personally carried our sins in His body on the cross so that we can be dead to sin and live for what is right" (1 Pet. 2:22, 24). Thus, because Jesus suffered for you, you don't have to pay for your sins before God. No, just live your life to the full for God!

Because Jesus has already paid for every one of your sins on the cross, He shows you how to live to the full for God; you simply need to follow His example, and that will bring glory to God.

Lord Jesus, as from today, I undertake to live to the full for You, to follow Your example, so that I may be in the right relationship with God and glorify Him. Amen.

Turn the Spotlight on Jesus

"If any of you wants to be My follower, you must turn from your selfish ways, take up your cross daily, and follow Me. If you try to hang on to your life, you will lose it. But if you give up your life for My sake, you will save it." Luke 9:23-24

It is impossible to glorify God if you glorify yourself; if your own desires, wants and will are still more important to you than God's will. When you do good things so that people will take notice of you, then you do not understand the meaning of the glorification of God at all.

Jesus warns in Matthew 6:2, "When you give to someone in need, don't do as the hypocrites do – blowing trumpets in the synagogues and streets to call attention to their acts of charity!" Always guard against trying to make the glory of God yours by your egotistical conduct; wanting to turn the spotlight on yourself instead of on Him. Jesus sets great store by humility, and He condemns pride in people.

If you want to be serious about glorifying God with your life and with your deeds, you will have to be willing to forget about your own glory and take second place, so that God is Number One in your life.

In today's Scripture reading Jesus explains exactly what you must do if you want to glorify God: put aside your own selfish interests, shoulder your cross and follow Him; watch out for vainglory and glorify Him!

Heavenly Father, I discover daily how important my own ego is to me. Help me to get my priorities straight so that You would be first in my life. Amen.

Carry Out Jesus' Command to Love

Most important of all, continue to show deep love for each other, for love covers a multitude of sins. Do you have the gift of speaking? Then speak as though God Himself were speaking through you. Do you have the gift of helping others? Do it with all the strength and energy that God supplies.
1 Pet. 4:8, 11

One of the best ways to glorify God is to obey His command to love each other, to really care for others and love them like God loves you. Why not refresh your memory and read 1 Corinthians 13 again? This is the love you need if you want to glorify God. The love God is talking about is patient and kind toward others; it is not jealous or boastful or proud or rude. It does not insist on its own way, is not irritable and it keeps no record of wrongs. This love is never glad about injustice, but wants the truth at all times. It never gives up, never loses faith, is always hopeful and endures everything. It is a love that lasts forever.

Peter highlights a few other things that match this command to love. He states that, apart from loving each other, Christians should also be hospitable without complaining, be willing to serve one another with their gifts and also be of service in the congregation with the strength that God gives.

If you can follow all the above-mentioned directives, you are indeed busy glorifying God "in everything."

Heavenly Father, I am sorely lacking in my efforts to obey Your command to love. Please help me to love other people with the same unconditional love You show to me. Amen.

Proclaim the Gospel

Let the whole earth sing to the LORD! Each day proclaim the good news that He saves. Publish His glorious deeds among the nations. Tell everyone about the amazing things He does. Honor and majesty surround Him; strength and joy fill His dwelling. 1 Chron. 16:23-24, 27

When the ark of the covenant was brought to Jerusalem, and the Levites placed it in the tent that David had prepared for it, David wrote a beautiful song of praise. In this song God is glorified and a request is made that all the nations must be told about His might; that all the nations should hear of His glorious deeds. The twenty-seventh verse is a lovely summary of what the glory of God means: He radiates honor and majesty; strength and beauty fill the place where He is.

We glorify God every time we testify about Him. When we talk to other people about God, who He is, the things He does for us, the wonders that happen in our lives, the intensely personal way in which God talks to us in His Word, they gain insight into our faith and also into the way we think about God. Paul writes in his epistle to the Romans that when we confess with our mouth that Jesus is Lord, and believe with our heart that God raised Him from the dead, we will be saved (see Rom. 10:9). Then we also glorify God because we are spreading His gospel.

Heavenly Father, sometimes I have a problem with being Your witness. I am sorry that I find it so difficult to talk to other people about You. Help me to glorify You by spreading Your gospel. Amen.

The Holy Spirit Glorifies Jesus

"He will bring Me glory by telling you whatever He receives from Me. All that belongs to the Father is Mine; this is why I said, 'The Spirit will tell you whatever He receives from Me.'" John 16:14-15

When Jesus told His disciples that He was going away, He promised to send the Holy Spirit to the world in His place. The Holy Spirit would do three important things: He would convict the world of its sin, He would let the people realize that righteousness is on His side, and thirdly, He would proclaim to them that no one can stop the final judgment. But the most important task of the Holy Spirit was to glorify God and to pass on to the disciples the things that were to come.

To glorify someone means to highlight the importance of that person to others. In God's case it means that you will acknowledge Him as the Lord of your life, that you will endorse His kingship, and support Him in everything. This is what the Holy Spirit wants to teach you! He will even make it possible for you to reflect God's glory in your own life. Paul testifies in 2 Corinthians 3:18, "All of us … can see and reflect the glory of the Lord. And the Lord – who is the Spirit – makes us more and more like Him as we are changed into His glorious image." Make sure it will be true of you!

Holy Spirit, make it possible for me to understand how important Jesus is, and help me to reflect the glory of God. Amen.

Praise God and Glorify Him

Let all that I am praise the LORD; with my whole heart, I will praise His holy name. Let all that I am praise the LORD; may I never forget the good things He does for me. He forgives all my sins and heals all my diseases. He redeems me from death and crowns me with love and tender mercies. Ps. 103:1-4

When we praise God, we glorify Him, because praise glorifies God.

C. M. Hanson writes, "Praise is like a plow set to go deep into the soil of believers' hearts. It lets the glory of God into the details of daily living." You ought to praise God even when you are going through troubled times. In this case the Bible talks about a sacrifice of praise. An offering is always accompanied by sacrifice.

We read in Psalm 50:14 and 23, "Make thankfulness your sacrifice to God … giving thanks is a sacrifice that truly honors Me." It is in particular the songs of praise you to sing God while you are surrounded by darkness that are the most precious to Him.

You can really try putting your praise into words when you pray as a way of glorifying God. And if you don't know how, start by praying through the psalms. The old psalmists mastered the art of glorifying God by bringing Him the praises of their hearts.

Lord, I want to praise You with everything in me. I want to sing along with the mighty chorus of believers whose songs of praise go up to You. Please give me the right words to glorify You. Amen.

Creation Glorifies God

Ever since the world was created, people have seen the earth and sky. Through everything God made, they can clearly see His invisible qualities – His eternal power and divine nature.
Rom. 1:20

No one can see God or His glory, but there is a way that we can conclude without a doubt that He has eternal power, that He is truly God and Lord. We come to this conclusion by looking at creation. It is impossible to see the miracle of birth, the glittering of the first stars, a delicate spider's web dotted with dew diamonds or the kaleidoscope of colors in a sunset, without becoming aware of God's glory.

In Revelation 5:13, John hears the angels call out, "Then I heard every creature in heaven and on earth and under the earth and in the sea. They sang: 'Blessing and honor and glory and power belong to the One sitting on the throne and to the Lamb forever and ever.'"

All things in creation glorify God; it is only mankind that is not by nature part of this spontaneous glorification. Although we know about God, we don't honor and thank Him as we should and we stay in the dark as a result of a lack of insight. Whenever you doubt God's glory again, just take a good look at nature around you and delight in the wonder of it all.

Lord God, together with creation I want to praise You and admit that all the praise and honor and glory belong to You forever and ever. Amen.

Glorify God through Suffering

Be happy when you are insulted for being a Christian, for then the glorious Spirit of God rests upon you. But it is no shame to suffer for being a Christian. Praise God for the privilege of being called by His name! 1 Pet. 4:14, 16

MacArthur writes that you glorify God when you suffer for His sake.

Peter impressed on the heart of his readers that all Christians would be subjected to suffering. Jesus Himself suffered much when He was on earth; therefore we should be glad when we suffer like He did, because it means that we will be filled with joy one day at His second coming (see 1 Pet. 4:13). The type of suffering Peter talks about here is suffering on account of our faith.

When you are going through a tough time or people are prejudiced against you or insult you simply because you love Jesus, it is proof that the Holy Spirit of God is at work in your life. Suffering should not catch you unawares, make you despondent or cause you to doubt. It should rather serve as proof that you are done with sin.

If you ever suffer because you are a Christian, you should actually be glad and glorify God by your suffering, because that suffering proves that you will one day share in Jesus' glory at His second coming.

Lord Jesus, make it possible for me to rejoice when I suffer on Your account, because it is the guarantee that Your Spirit lives in me and that I will glorify You with that suffering. Amen.

Glorify God When You Pray

"You can ask for anything in My name, and I will do it, so that the Son can bring glory to the Father. Yes, ask Me for anything in My name, and I will do it!" John 14:13-14

Jesus is not referring to a general prayer that makes all our requests known to God, but a prayer that the work of God will be done on earth. This prayer is in accordance with God's will, and that is why He will answer it.

Through prayer the believer makes sure that he or she is in step with God. You must always make sure that what you ask is in accordance with the will of God. You can only ask for something "in the name of Jesus" if you know that Jesus Himself also asks it of the Father. For this reason both Father and Son will be glorified by such a prayer.

Jesus' name indicates His very being. Praying in Jesus' name means that you pray in accordance with Jesus' will and character.

And it is God's will that we pray like this, so that when He answers our prayers He is glorified. John MacArthur says, "God delights to reveal His glory in answered prayer. That is why He commands us to pray – so that He can show us His greatness and we can give Him the praise He's worthy to receive. People who never pray miss one of the most effective ways to glorify God."

Heavenly Father, thank You for the privilege of being able to pray. I pray that Your work and Your will be done on earth. Amen.

Spreading the Good News

[Jesus] said to His disciples, "The harvest is great, but the workers are few. So pray to the Lord who is in charge of the harvest; ask Him to send more workers into His fields."
Matt. 9:37-38

When people give their hearts to the Lord, He is glorified. But this can't happen if there aren't people to tell them about Him. The reason Jesus was sent to the world was to deliver God's message so that people would believe. He chose twelve disciples to help Him with this task. In today's Scripture, Jesus said to His disciples, "The harvest is great, but the workers are few. So pray to the Lord ... ask Him to send out more workers into His fields." He repeated this command after His resurrection, "As the Father has sent Me, so I am sending you" (John 20:21).

Paul was very serious about his calling to gather people for the heavenly harvest. He wrote to the church in Rome, "How can they call on Him to save them unless they believe in Him? And how can they believe in Him if they have never heard about Him? And how can they hear about Him unless someone tells them?" (Rom. 10:14). It is every Christian's task to be a witness of God's Good News so that as many people as possible can become God's children. Are you answering God's call for you to be a witness?

Lord Jesus, please forgive me for neglecting my task of glorifying You by leading people to You. Make me a bearer of Your Good News. Amen.

Avoid Sexual Sin

Run from sexual sin! No other sin so clearly affects the body as this one does. For sexual immorality is a sin against your own body. God bought you with a high price. So you must honor God with your body. 1 Cor. 6:18, 20

P aul implored the church of Corinth to glorify God with their bodies, because the body is God's temple.

We glorify God with our bodies when we obey His rules about sexual behavior. In the world today, sexual sin is no longer sin in the eyes of most people. The media promotes sexual practices that the Bible condemns, and people accept this sexual behavior with enthusiasm. Everybody takes part in it – even some self-declared Christians. When a Christian commits sexual sins, they violate God's temple and do damage to His holiness – no matter how they try to justify it.

Paul gives three reasons why a Christian must not allow sexual sin in their life: it is a sin against your own body; the believer's body is God's temple and does not belong to you; and you must honor God with your body. This is not possible if you are living a sexually immoral life. The fact that there are so many sexually transmitted diseases that people die from today is undeniable proof that people's lifestyle is not in line with God's will.

Lord, please make it possible for me to obey the sexual directives You give me in Your Word so that I can glorify You with my body. Amen.

Unity among Christians

"I pray that they will all be one, just as You and I are one – as you are in Me, Father, and I am in You. And may they be in Us so that the world will believe You sent Me. I have given them the glory You gave Me, so they may be one as We are one." John. 17:21-22

God desires that His children be united, because this is one of the ways in which God is glorified in our lives. I always remember a certain man who said that instead of Christians using their ammunition against the devil, they use it to destroy one another. Instead of firing complaints and grievances at other Christians and other denominations, we ought to celebrate the unity among us – after all, we are God's children and our main aim in life is to glorify Him. But God cannot be glorified if there is discord or strife among His children.

There is a place for different churches and different opinions, but if you don't acknowledge that Christ is God, that's a different matter. As Christians we may not deny fundamental truths of our faith (like the virgin birth of Jesus or His resurrection from the dead), like many present-day theologians are doing. John MacArthur says that, "We glorify God only when with one mind and one mouth we declare the message of Christ clearly and accurately to an unsaved world."

Lord Jesus, I pray for unity among Your children. Grant that we will be one and in this way glorify You together. Amen.

The Glory Far Exceeds the Suffering

What we suffer now is nothing compared to the glory God will reveal to us later. Rom. 8:18

One day God's children will share in His glory. Not one of us can escape suffering on earth. Each one gets their burden of troubles that they have to carry themselves. Fortunately, the glory that God will give His children in the future exceeds this suffering by far.

In any case, earthly suffering lasts only a short while, while the glory that waits for us in heaven will last forever and ever, "That is why we never give up. Though our bodies are dying, our spirits are being renewed every day. For our present troubles are quite small and won't last very long. Yet they produce for us a glory that vastly outweighs them and will last forever!" says Paul (2 Cor. 4:16-17).

God would not have allowed suffering in your life if it could not make a positive contribution to His grace: "Those He predestined, He also called; those He called, He also justified; those He justified, He also glorified" (Rom. 8:30).

This promise holds good for you as well, to this day! God has already predestined you as His child; He called you and has justified you. Now glorification awaits you. Take heart, one day your earthly suffering will end in glorify.

Heavenly Father, I am sorry that I complain so much about my problems. Please teach me again that they are nothing compared to the glory that You are preparing for me in heaven. Amen.

Enjoy God!

You have given me greater joy than those who have abundant harvests of grain and new wine. In peace I will lie down and sleep, for You alone, O LORD, will keep me safe. Ps. 4:7-8

In Westminster's shorter Catechisms the question is asked: "What is the chief end of man?" The answer to this question is: "Man's chief end is to glorify God, and to enjoy Him forever." I think it's wonderful that God made it my main aim in life to enjoy Him forever; in other words, to find joy in my relationship with Him!

MacArthur writes, "When we live to glorify God, He responds by giving us overwhelming joy. I sometimes think that if I were any happier and had more joy, I would not be able to stand it. Life becomes thrilling in response to glorifying God."

In Acts 13:52, we read that the first believers were filled with joy and with the Holy Spirit. Nobody and nothing can take away this inner joy that ought to be part of any Christian.

If you are going through a particularly difficult time, take God at His word – claim His joy for yourself, start glorifying Him; praise Him even if you feel that there isn't really anything to praise Him for. If you live in honor of God and glorify Him, the joy will inevitably follow, even amidst hurt, pain and suffering. Why not try it?

Heavenly Father, I praise You for the bubbling joy that You make a part of me, because You make it possible for me to glorify and enjoy You forever! Amen.

You May Share in God's Glory

*He called you to salvation when we told you the Good News;
now you can share in the glory of our Lord Jesus Christ.
2 Thess. 2:14*

The sun's light is reflected by the planets. They do not produce light themselves, although it might look like that to us. You manage to glorify God as soon as people see His glory reflected in your life. And you do this by living in such a way that people will see your good works and glorify God for them (see Matt. 5:16). This means that you will let others realize precisely what God's glory means, by demonstrating it to them personally.

When Moses was in God's presence for forty days, his face shone to such an extent that the Israelites couldn't look at him (see Exod. 34:30-35). You also won't be able to hide that you love God – other people will see His glory reflected in your eyes and your smile. And the more difficult your life is on earth, the better you are able to radiate this glory.

Colossians 3:4 promises, "When Christ, who is your real life, is revealed to the whole world, you will share in all His glory."

Each child of God has God's glory in them. And the only glimpse that the world gets of God's glory is in the life and conduct of God's children. Live in such a way that it will be true of you!

Lord, I would like my life to reflect Your glory. Help me to live in such a way that it will become a reality. Amen.

Suffering Often Goes before Glory

Be very glad – for these trials make you partners with Christ in His suffering, so that you will have the wonderful joy of seeing His glory when it is revealed to all the world. 1 Pet. 4:13

Suffering on earth is sometimes a Christian's guarantee that we will one day share His glory. All of us can expect suffering on earth. Sometimes God lets us suffer, not only so that we will understand His glory better, but also may share it to a greater extent.

It is true that we are never as thankful for our health as after a long illness; that we treasure our marriage for the rest of our lives after it has been on the rocks; that our faith is tremendously strengthened when disaster strikes and God guides us through it.

It is only when you have gone through the depths of suffering yourself that you are able to experience God's glory in depth. God promises to give you this glory after a time of suffering. Peter writes in 1 Peter 5:10, "In His kindness God called you to His eternal glory by means of Jesus Christ. After you have suffered a little while, He will restore, support and strengthen you, and He will place you on a firm foundation."

When you are going through an extremely bad patch, remember that God is just preparing you for that glory that you will one day share at Jesus' second coming.

Heavenly Father, I praise You for the promise that I will experience heavenly glory after my earthly suffering. I know now that my suffering at the moment will prepare me better for that glory. Amen.

All Glory to God

Oh, how great are God's riches and wisdom and knowledge! How impossible it is for us to understand His decisions and His ways! For everything comes from Him and exists by His power and is intended for His glory. Rom. 11:33, 36

Everlasting glory belongs to God alone. In Matthew 6:9-13, the Lord teaches His disciples how to pray. In the New King James version of the Bible, the Lord's Prayer ends with the words, "For Yours is the kingdom and the power and the glory forever." Unfortunately this conclusion is not included in later translations of the Bible because it is not in the original text. If you work for God's kingdom, He will give you all the other things as well. His power is inexhaustible and always available for you, and His glory should be reflected by you so that everybody will notice it.

John MacArthur writes, "God's intrinsic glory is part of His being. It is not something that was given to Him. If men and angels have never been created, God would still possess His intrinsic glory. If no one ever gave Him any glory, any honor or any praise, He would still be the glorious God that He is. That is intrinsic glory – the glory of God's nature. It is the manifestation and combination of all His attributes."

Is God the Lord of your life yet? Do you bring Him the honor and glory that is due to Him?

Heavenly Father, I worship You as the Lord of my life; may the kingdom, the power and the glory be Yours forever and ever. Amen.

God Deserves Our Praise

"You are worthy, O Lord our God, to receive glory and honor and power. For You created all things, and they exist because You created what You pleased." Rev. 4:11

In Revelation 4, John has a vision of God sitting on a throne, while everybody glorifies and praises Him. The four living beings (that symbolize creation) and the twenty-four elders (a symbol of the believers) celebrate God's glory. This vision illustrates that we must continuously bring God the praise and honor that are due to Him; that we ought to join in the symphony that praises God.

In Revelation 5:12-13, Jesus is included in this praise. Now the four living beings and the twenty-four elders sing a new song in a mighty chorus, "Worthy is the Lamb who was slaughtered – to receive power and riches and wisdom and strength and honor and glory and blessing" (Rev. 5:12).

God and Jesus are worthy to be glorified. It would be a good idea to follow Peter's recommendation in 2 Peter 3:18, "You must grow in the grace and knowledge of our Lord and Savior Jesus Christ. All glory to Him, both now and forever!" The better you know God, the better you will be able to honor and praise Him for His creation as well as for His omnipotence and glory. Don't you feel like writing a personal song of praise in which you glorify God? Why not do it right now?

Lord God, I want to get to know You better, so that I can honor and glorify You better. Yours is the praise and the honor and the glory forever and ever. Amen.

July

Suffering

Suffering and pain form part of human existence. Life is not always pleasant, nor is it always easy. But God uses suffering to bring about good in our lives.

In times of suffering, God is the only One to whom you can turn.

Many people struggle with God's goodness because He does not relieve their suffering.

"You need to exchange your soft religion for a hard cornerstone on which you can stand firm under all circumstances.

"If everything goes wrong and it feels as though God has forsaken you, your faith must be strong enough to keep you steadfast in the knowledge that your Helper is actively with you. Then you must savor the knowledge that you belong to God, your "only consolation in life and death".

"God has placed you in this world and He provides you with a faith that is strong enough for this life.

"With Him, you will find shelter against the bitterest cold and the deepest darkness," writes Willem Nicol.

I pray that this will become your testimony too.

Father, how good it is to know that,
even though You do allow pain and suffering into my life,
You will never forsake me in my distress.
Thank You for the assurance that You counsel me when I
am at the end of my tether; that You are the answer to all
my "why" questions; that I need not understand You, but
nevertheless can steadfastly trust in You.
I know that You only want what is best for me, that You
give me light in times of darkness, that You listen to my
prayers and answer every one of them,
even though sometimes it does not feel that way to me.
Lord, I want to glorify You,
because Your kindness toward me lasts for ever.
I have begun to understand the benefits of suffering:
I now know that You are in complete control of my life,
that tribulation teaches me to steadfastly believe in You, to
persevere and to fix my hope on You, that You are with me
in times of suffering, that You take care of me and that You
will ensure that everything ends well for me.
Amen.

At the End of Your Tether

What strength do I have, that I should still hope? What prospects, that I should be patient? Do I have any power to help myself, now that success has been driven from me?
Job 6:11, 13

I n this chapter, Job has reached the end of his tether. "If only my anguish could be weighed and all my misery be placed on the scales! It would surely outweigh the sand of the seas," he laments in verses 2 and 3. Eventually he realizes that his own strength is spent and that he can do nothing about his desperate situation – he is at the end of his tether.

Perhaps you, like Job, have sometimes felt that you could no longer carry on. If you have reached the end of your tether, remember that God is always there for you. When you have no idea how to continue you will find wisdom and counsel with Him. He offers you His wonderful strength when your strength is spent.

God is offering you His counsel and love today so you can banish your despondency. Allow Him to do this for you!

Heavenly Father, You know just how despondent I feel today. Thank You that I can rest assured in the knowledge that You are always there for me, that Your strength carries me when my own is spent, and that I can depend on Your counsel when I reach the end of my tether. Surround me now with Your love. Amen.

Please Answer Me!

If only I knew where to find Him; if only I could go to His dwelling! I would state my case before Him and fill my mouth with arguments. I would find out what He would answer me, and consider what He would say. Job 23:3-5

Job himself provides the answers to his despondent questions of chapter 6: If only he knew where to find God, he would have gone to His dwelling and tried to obtain an answer from Him, tried to understand what God was saying to him in this period of suffering.

Job lived before Jesus died on the cross. He could not find his way to God on his own. God seemed far away and inaccessible to him. Unlike Job, we know exactly where to find God. To us He is but a prayer away. Jesus opened the way into the Holiest of Holies so we could draw near to His throne and lay claim to His grace.

I am sure that, on occasion, you have also sought answers from God. There are thousands of things in our lives that we fail to understand and to which we have no answer. Even though God does not always provide you with every answer that you seek, you can always rest assured in the knowledge that He loves you. That, in the end, He Himself is the Answer to each one of your "why" questions.

Heavenly Father, thank You that You are there for me, every moment of the day, should I wish to talk to You. Please teach me once again that I do not need answers to all my "why" questions, and help me to become still in Your presence. Amen.

God Is Eager to Help You

So justice is far from us, and righteousness does not reach us. We look for light, but all is darkness; for brightness, but we walk in deep shadows. Surely the arm of the LORD is not too short to save, nor His ear too dull to hear. Isa. 59:9, 1

The prophet Isaiah lived during a time of great darkness in the lives of God's people. They were often disobedient to God, and so He caused many enemies to rise up against them. He also warned them that their country would be overrun and they would be sent into exile. But He would eventually have compassion on them and show them mercy by allowing them to return to their own country.

There are two ways in which you can respond when you are faced with difficulties. You can turn your back on God and try coping on your own. But we find, time and again, that God is the only One who can really help us in our crises.

God's people know that they do not need to turn to things such as alcohol or drugs to alleviate their anxiety. Only God can come to your rescue when you are faced with a crisis. And He *wants* to do it for you!

His arm is never too short to save, nor His ear too dull to hear your complaints. Even though you are surrounded by darkness, He will eventually bring the light back into your life.

Lord, my life is filled with darkness and I can see no light. Thank You for the promise to which I can cling: that Your arm is never too short to save me, nor Your ear too dull to hear me. Amen.

To Advance the Kingdom

I want you to know, brothers, that what has happened to me has actually served to advance the gospel. As a result, it has become clear throughout the whole palace guard and to everyone else that I am in chains for Christ. Phil. 1:12-13

Paul was often unjustly tortured and imprisoned. Yet his attitude was remarkable: He testifies that his unjust treatment has led to the advancement of God's kingdom. He regards his imprisonment as an opportunity to preach the Word of God. "What has happened to me has really served to advance the gospel," he writes to the Christians in Philippi.

Precisely because Paul was imprisoned, the palace guard and everyone else who came into contact with him had the opportunity to hear about Jesus. When they saw the unusual way in which Paul responded to his unjust treatment, their own faith was strengthened. Paul realized that it was not his circumstances but what he made of them that helped to spread the gospel.

How you respond to negative events speaks volumes about your faith. None of us can choose our circumstances, but we can all choose to remain positive.

Do you manage to not become bitter when things go wrong? Do you use your negative circumstances in a positive way for the kingdom of God?

Heavenly Father, forgive me that, unlike Paul, I have so much to say when I am unjustly treated. Teach me to handle injustice like a child of Yours, so that the faith of others may be strengthened by my actions. Amen.

Can God Refuse to Listen?

"I will deal with them in anger; I will not look on them with pity or spare them. Although they shout in My ears, I will not listen to them." Ezek. 8:18

God had finally reached the end of His patience with His disobedient people. Speaking through the prophet Ezekiel, He declares that He will no longer look on them with pity. Although they may shout in His ears, He will not listen to them. The people themselves brought about this apparent callousness on the side of God. They refused to accept His love and constantly turned their backs on Him to worship pagan idols.

Have you prayed when faced with a crisis, only to feel as though God was not listening to you? As though He no longer heard what you wanted to tell Him, nor thought about the things you requested of Him?

In times like these, you should do some soul-searching and take a good look at your own sins and shortcomings. If God does not respond, it is probably your own fault. But He loves you too much to forsake you. As soon as you confess your sins He will forgive them and accept your prayers once again.

"He fulfills the desires of those who fear Him; He hears their cry and saves them," declares the psalmist (Ps. 145:19). Do not hesitate to receive God's love and grace for you!

Lord, I praise You because You listen, and You are always ready to help me. Help me never to try Your patience like Israel did, but to identify and confess my sins. Amen.

In Times of Suffering

Do not hide Your face from me when I am in distress. In my distress I groan aloud and am reduced to skin and bones.
Ps. 102:2, 5

T his psalm is the "prayer of an afflicted man. When he is faint and pours out his lament before the LORD" (introduction to Psalm 102). The psalmist is going through extremely difficult times. He pleads with the Lord not to hide His face from him, to listen to him and to hear his prayers. He has been reduced to skin and bones and feels that the end of his life is near. But what causes him the most suffering is the feeling that the Lord has forsaken him.

We do not know what had happened to the author of this psalm. But in spite of his perilous situation he clings to the fact that the Lord remains forever constant, that He will reign forever and that He responds to the prayers of the destitute (v. 17). Therefore, he has faith that the Lord will help him in his time of suffering just as He has always done in the past.

If you are going through a difficult time you might also feel that God is far away. Although you may feel this way, remember that this is not the case. God loves you and stays close by your side. Through His Spirit, He dwells in you. God always remains constant. He listens to your prayers and is always ready to help.

Heavenly Father, thank You that You are constant, that You are never far away from Your children, and are always willing to listen to their prayers and to help them. Please hear my prayers today. Amen.

Darkness Turning into Light

"I will lead the blind by ways they have not known, along unfamiliar paths I will guide them; I will turn the darkness into light before them and make the rough places smooth."
Isa. 42:16

God promises that He will turn the darkness into light and make the rough places smooth for His people. Throughout the Bible, times of suffering are likened to darkness. When Jeremiah is at his most despondent, he laments, "He has driven me away and made me walk in darkness rather than light" (Lam. 3:2).

When you face difficulties, it might feel at times as though you are surrounded by darkness and that the sun will never shine again. But even if you cannot see the sun on dark and cloudy days, it is still there. In the same way, God is your Light in times of darkness and He promises to turn the darkness into light again.

"Though I have fallen, I will rise. Though I sit in darkness, the LORD will be my light," says the prophet Micah. "I will bear the LORD's wrath, until He pleads my case and upholds my cause. He will bring me out into the light; I will see His righteousness" (Mic. 7:8-9).

You can gladly hold onto God in times of darkness. He can change your situation or help you to work through it so that it works out for your good in the end.

Heavenly Father, thank You that even when I am surrounded by darkness, I can know that You are still by my side and that You can turn my darkness into light once again. Amen.

God's Favor Lasts a Lifetime

His anger lasts only a moment, but His favor lasts a lifetime; weeping may stay for the night, but rejoicing comes in the morning. Ps. 30:5

T he suffering the psalmist experiences is the result of God's anger at sinfulness. But he knows that God's anger lasts only for a short while, and that God's favor lasts a lifetime.

God can turn our tears into joy. Praise and glorify Him! People who belong to God can hold onto this promise during times of suffering. God's grace and love for them lasts a lifetime. Although the night of suffering may endure for a short while, they can rest assured that joy will await them in the morning.

This psalm contains a beautiful message of comfort for all who are suffering: the God in whom we believe can change a dismal situation into a joyful one.

Remember, when darkness descends on you, then God is working in your life. You might feel the tremor of God's wrath, but His grace will soon transform life into a song of joy. "Do not fear the night, for it is in the night that the Lord comes to us," writes Heinrich Jung-Schilling.

If you are facing relentless difficulties, begin thinking of how God can be glorified in your circumstances.

Heavenly Father, I glorify You for Your love and grace that lasts a lifetime. Help me to hold onto this love when darkness descends on my life – and thank You that I can rest assured in the knowledge that joy awaits me in the morning. Amen.

Pray During Times of Suffering

Hear my prayer, LORD; listen to my cry for mercy. When I am in distress, I call to You, because You answer me. You, Lord, are forgiving and good, abounding in love to all who call to You. Ps. 86:6-7, 5

I n this psalm, the psalmist pleads for God's help because he finds himself in great distress. He calls to God, confident in the knowledge that God will hear his prayer and help him because He abounds in love for those who call on Him. God inspires trust in His children because He has shown Himself to be a God who is able to deliver and help His children.

You too can call on the Lord for help in times of trouble. He will hear your prayer and answer it; He will demonstrate His abundant love for you and help you.

You can confidently ask God to help you in times of trial. If you stay close to God, He will ensure that you are not tempted beyond your ability to withstand it, and He will deliver you from every tribulation.

In closing, the psalmist testifies to others about what the Lord has done for him. You too should testify to others about the goodness of the Lord in your life.

Heavenly Father, I praise You for always helping me when temptation and tribulation come against me. Thank You that I can pray to You, secure in the knowledge that You will listen to me and will answer my prayers. Amen.

Suffering Puts You to the Test

In this you greatly rejoice, though now for a little while you may have had to suffer grief in all kinds of trials. These have come so that the proven genuineness of your faith – of greater worth than gold, which perishes even though refined by fire – may result in praise, glory and honor when Jesus Christ is revealed. 1 Pet. 1:6-7

Nobody enjoys suffering, but none of us can escape it. Believers are able to endure their suffering gladly, because we know that God is with us when we go through difficult times. The Lord can use suffering to put our faith in Him to the test. God purifies us so that our faith may be proved genuine, resulting in praise and honor when Jesus Christ is revealed.

Through our trials God teaches us to persevere in the faith. Before gold can be extracted from gold ore, it must first be purified. Tribulation forms part of God's process of purification for His children. Therefore, try to remain cheerful during times of suffering.

If you keep focusing on your own misery, your view will remain clouded. Rather look toward God. Think of all the times that He has helped you in the past. He is omnipotent and can do all things. He is able to help you with whatever problems you face. He will provide for your need at just the right time.

Heavenly Father, thank You for this new insight that You use my suffering to test my level of faith. Please help me to pass this test of faith with flying colors! Amen.

Suffering Has an Added Advantage

See what this godly sorrow has produced in you: what earnestness, what eagerness to clear yourselves, what indignation, what alarm, what longing, what concern, what readiness to see justice done. 2 Cor. 7:11

The godly sorrow of the Corinthian Christians resulted in positive things: It made them aware of the indignation, alarm, longing, concern and readiness to see justice done.

The Message clarifies it even further:

And now, isn't it wonderful all the ways in which this distress has goaded you closer to God? You're more alive, more concerned, more sensitive, more reverent, more human, more passionate, more responsible. Looked at from any angle, you've come out of this with purity of heart.

This proves that sorrow and suffering bring about positive results in the life of a Christian. Therefore, when you experience pain and suffering in your own life, reflect on the advantages that the pain has brought into your life. You may even succeed in thanking God for it!

Heavenly Father, none of us enjoys pain and suffering. You know that I find this time of sorrow extremely difficult. However, I have discovered that it is beneficial for me – and for that I wish to thank You. Amen.

The World Suffers from Birth Pains

"Nation will rise against nation, and kingdom against kingdom. There will be famines and earthquakes in various places. All these are the beginning of birth pains." Matt. 24:7-8

Jesus told His disciples that they would suffer trials and tribulations. And this suffering, He explained, would prepare them for the things awaiting them in the future. These things occur because the world is suffering from birth pains.

No one will deny that the world we live in is a mess. Violence, crime and fraud have become so commonplace that they no longer move us. When we listen to the news or read the newspapers, we cannot but wonder whether these evil things will ever come to an end.

Even though the world is imperfect, life is not meaningless for God's children. The promise of God's new world where everything will be good and whole again shines brightly in our imperfect world.

If your courage threatens to fail when you observe the current state of affairs in the world, go and read the beautiful picture of God's new world in Isaiah 11 and 65, and Revelation 21. Then go and live in such a way that you will be ready when this new world dawns.

Lord Jesus, thank You for the promise that a new heaven and a new earth are waiting for me, where all suffering will end. Help me to keep this promise in mind when my own little world suffers from birth pains. Amen.

Do Not Lose Heart!

We do not lose heart. Though outwardly we are wasting away, yet inwardly we are being renewed day by day. For our light and momentary troubles are achieving for us an eternal glory that far outweighs them all. 2 Cor. 4:16-17

P aul had firsthand experience of suffering. Yet even in the most difficult of circumstances he did not lose heart, because he knew the secret that motivates millions of Christians to persevere, regardless of their dreadful circumstances. We can endure suffering because we have the promise that it will pass, and that it will achieve an eternal glory for us.

The Message translates today's text wonderfully: "So we're not giving up. How could we! Even though on the outside it often looks like things are falling apart on us, on the inside, where God is making new life, not a day goes by without His unfolding grace."

You can hold on to this promise during troublesome times. No suffering is completely unbearable if you know that God is with you. On your sickbed, beside an open grave, when you're retrenched or when people leave you in the lurch, He never forsakes you. And He wants to surround you with His loving presence – especially during troubled times.

Heavenly Father, I praise You that I can know that You are with me, even when things are very bad. Thank You that I can hold on to my hope, because I believe that today's suffering will, in the end, bring me eternal joy. Amen.

You Have a Future!

We fix our eyes not on what is seen, but on what is unseen,
since what is seen is temporary, but what is unseen is eternal.
2 Cor. 4:18

There is a second reason why Christians do not allow suffering to get the better of them: They know they have an eternal future in heaven in the presence of God. They can fix their eyes on the unseen glory that awaits them. Our earthly abode is like a tent, compared to the eternal house that God is building for us in heaven, writes Paul (see 2 Cor. 5:1).

Therefore, you do not need to be obsessed about your tribulations. With God's help you can look past your suffering and see heaven waiting for you. When we know that a reward awaits us, we can remain positive through times of suffering. It is not difficult to study very hard for a while if you know that you will get good grades on your tests.

Even though things might be hard right now, you can focus on the eternal glory that awaits you in heaven – for God has promised this to all who believe in His Son (see 2 Cor. 5:8). Although you cannot yet see the new world that God has prepared for us, you know that your final destination will be with God in heaven. And knowing this helps you to make the best of things right now.

Heavenly Father, I glorify You for the promise that I have
an eternal future with You. Help me to persevere for a little
while, until I reach my true destination. Amen.

In Times of Wakefulness

When I was in distress, I sought the Lord; at night I stretched out untiring hands, and I would not be comforted. You kept my eyes from closing; I was too troubled to speak. Ps. 77:2, 4

This psalmist suffered from insomnia. Through the wakeful nights he prayed and called on the Lord for help, but God remained silent. He felt more and more dejected. What worried him most was that God seemed to be responding differently from how He had in the past (see v. 10).

Perhaps you can identify with this cry of distress. Even though you might succeed in falling asleep while wrestling with major issues, if you wake up during the night, it is often almost impossible to go back to sleep again. In these wakeful times it sometimes feels as though God is not answering your prayers in the same way as He did in the past.

But remember, God never changes. Sometimes He makes us wait for an answer, but He will answer each one of His children's prayers. In times of suffering you can hold on to this promise: God will deliver you once again. Perhaps He wants you to learn something about your life through your suffering. Therefore, try to look past your problem toward God and implicitly trust Him to deliver you.

Heavenly Father, at the moment I am finding it hard to recognize that You are the same merciful God You have always been. Forgive me and teach me to keep believing that You will deliver me. Amen.

God Holds the Reins!

I lie down and sleep; I wake again, because the LORD sustains me. Ps. 3:5

When he wrote this psalm, David was in a perilous situation: He was fleeing for his life and, to make matters worse, his own son wanted to kill him. His enemies were thrilled by this turn of events. They declared that the Lord had forsaken him. And to all intents and purposes, it seemed that they were right.

David, however, knew better. Even though things were going so badly for him, he remained calm and slept peacefully at night. Under these difficult circumstances, David prayed to God and believed that the Lord would help him. He trusted in God implicitly. He knew that the Lord would help him once again, as He had always done in the past.

You, too, might feel as though the Lord does not hear you, as though He is delaying helping you, just when you need His help the most. Like David, you can trust steadfastly in the Lord and sleep peacefully, even though everything might seem to be going wrong.

If you love God, He holds the reins of your life firmly. He can use your suffering for His glory. Regardless of what may happen to you, the Lord is always in complete control of your circumstances.

Heavenly Father, thank You for the assurance that You will take care of me, that nothing will happen to me that You cannot use for Your glory. Help me to sleep peacefully, knowing that You are in control. Amen.

All's Well that Ends Well

We know that in all things God works for the good of those who love Him, who have been called according to His purpose. What, then, shall we say in response to these things? If God is for us, who can be against us? Rom. 8:28, 31

God uses suffering to mold the lives of His children. It is never the will of God that His children should suffer, but sometimes He allows it in order for us to grow closer to Him. Even suffering can be used by God for your good in His perfect plan for your life. If you belong to God you can be sure that He is on your side and therefore there is nothing at all that can come against you and harm you.

When things go very badly for you, if you lose your job or fall seriously ill, you probably tend to pray more than you usually do and so the negative circumstances in your life bring you closer to God. God is always in complete control of your life. "God is not the Author of all events, but the Master of all events," the old saying goes.

God does not cause your suffering, but He does control it so that, in the end, it can be for your own good. If you are facing a crisis at the moment, you can gladly hold on to the promise in Psalm 138:8, "The LORD will vindicate me; Your love, LORD, endures forever."

Father, how wonderful is Your master plan! Thank You for the promise that You do not cause my suffering, but that You control it and use it to bring me closer to You. Amen.

Surrounded by Darkness

*Who among you fears the L*ORD *and obeys the word of His servant? Let the one who walks in the dark, who has no light, trust in the name of the L*ORD *and rely on their God. Isa. 50:10*

Things were going very badly for God's people. They thought that God had forgotten about them. Everything around them was pitch black. But Isaiah's words comforted them: "Let the one who walks in the dark, who has no light, trust in the name of the LORD."

In the Bible, darkness is often used to describe suffering. Even children of the Lord have to contend with dark clouds obscuring their path through life. And in this darkness it is easy to bump your toe against a stone, to get lost or even to go completely astray at times. God promises to be with you when darkness descends: "Even though I walk through the darkest valley, I will fear no evil, for You are with me; Your rod and Your staff, they comfort me," David testifies in Psalm 23:4.

If your life is filled with darkness, allow God to be your light. "You, LORD, keep my lamp burning; my God turns my darkness into light," proclaims the psalmist (Ps. 18:28).

Trust Him to do the same for you!

Heavenly Father, I praise You for being a Light to me, that You are always by my side to guide me safely through the times of darkness in my life. Thank You that I can rest assured in the knowledge that You will never forsake me in that darkness. Amen.

Steadfast in Temptation

Blessed is the one who perseveres under trial because, having stood the test, that person will receive the crown of life that God has promised to those who love Him. James 1:12

God is good and just – and He will never lead anyone into temptation. "When tempted, no one should say, 'God is tempting me.' For God cannot be tempted by evil, nor does He tempt anyone," James warns in verse 13. It is usually our own sinful desires that cause us to succumb to temptation.

However, God can reverse the consequences of sin. He can turn the negative circumstances in your life around so that they will benefit you eventually.

During a youth sermon, one of my husband's colleagues asked a group of young people what event in their lives they were the most grateful for. One girl replied that her father's illness had brought her so much closer to the Lord and that she had praised Him for it many a time.

When temptation confronts you on the path of life, take God at His Word. Persevere under trial and trust in Him, so that you will receive the crown of life that God has promised.

Heavenly Father, I pray that You will help me to persevere under trial, that You will turn my negative circumstances around so that they will be for my good. Thank You that I can trust in You to help me. Amen.

Rejoice in Your Problems

If I must boast, I will boast of the things that show my weakness. The God and Father of the Lord Jesus, who is to be praised for ever, knows that I am not lying. 2 Cor. 11:30-31

P aul knew full well what it was to suffer because he had endured much of it in his own life. The list of disasters that he had to brave while he worked for the Lord reads like a nightmare: He was often in deadly peril, he was beaten and stoned, he was shipwrecked, on many a journey he feared for his life, and he was often hungry, thirsty and cold. But through all these things, he cared for his congregations (see vv. 23-28).

These negative experiences reminded Paul that in himself he had nothing to boast about. He glorifies God for his achievements.

In Romans 5:3-5, Paul outlines the positive results of suffering in his own life: "We also glory in our sufferings, because we know that suffering produces perseverance; perseverance, character; and character, hope. And hope does not put us to shame, because God's love has been poured out into our hearts through the Holy Spirit, who has been given to us."

Like Paul, with God's help you can rejoice in suffering, because it will guarantee you perseverance, character and hope.

Heavenly Father, help me, like Paul, to rejoice in those things that I would have preferred to be different because, in the end, these trials teach me to persevere, to believe in You and to place my hope in You. Amen.

Where Is God When
You Are in Trouble?

The Egyptians came to dread the Israelites and worked them ruthlessly. They made their lives bitter with harsh labor; in all their harsh labor the Egyptians worked them ruthlessly. Exod. 1:12-14

A t first, all went well with God's people in Egypt. The pharaoh was kind toward them and they prospered in this foreign country. However, four hundred years on, the picture changed completely. The new pharaoh did not know the story of Joseph. Besides, the Israelites increased in number to such an extent that they became a threat to the Egyptians.

Pharaoh's solution was to kill all newborn Israelite boys and to use the people for slave labor. The people suffered greatly. It seemed to them as though God had forgotten them. But God never forgets His children. He was already working to bring about their deliverance. He was preparing Moses to set them free from bondage in Egypt and to lead them to a land of great abundance.

While the Israelites thought that God had forgotten them, He was already bringing about their salvation. Consider that while you doubt God's love for you.

Heavenly Father, forgive me for feeling as though You have forgotten me. Thank You for the assurance that this could never happen – and that You are already in the process of bringing about my deliverance. Amen.

God Knows Your Situation

The Israelites groaned in their slavery and cried out, and their cry for help because of their slavery went up to God. God heard their groaning. So God looked on the Israelites and was concerned about them. Exod. 2:23-25

B ecause the Israelites suffered as much as they did, they called on God for help. And God heard their groaning. He looked on them and was concerned for them. Although they could not see Him in their difficult circumstances, He was close to them, ready to help and to change their situation.

When circumstances turn against you, you might feel as though God has forgotten about you, as though He does not care what happens to you. Biblical figures like David, Job and Jeremiah all at times questioned God's love for them. But they all discovered eventually that God was there for them and that He would deliver them, as He had always done.

Even in your times of deepest despair, the Lord is by your side. He knows about your situation and He is already working on the solution. He is able to use even the most inexplicable things to fulfill His master plan for your life. As a matter of fact, these inexplicable things often form a very important part of God's plan for you. God wants to use you – even in times of crisis.

Trust in Him to bring about your deliverance.

Heavenly Father, I glorify You for the assurance that You are by my side, that You are aware of my situation and that You co-ordinate the inexplicable disasters in my life in such a way that they form part of Your perfect plan. Amen.

Do Not Be Afraid

Moses answered the people, "Do not be afraid. Stand firm and you will see the deliverance the LORD will bring you today. The Egyptians you see today you will never see again. The LORD will fight for you; you need only to be still."
Exod. 14:13-14

God chose Moses to set His people free from slavery in Egypt. But they had hardly left when they faced their first crisis. The Egyptians pursued them so that, almost literally, they found themselves "between the devil and the deep blue sea." Before them lay the Red Sea and behind them, Pharaoh and his army. The people were terrified and unhappy. They reacted typically by blaming Moses. It would have been better for them to serve the Egyptians than to die in the desert, they muttered.

But Moses calmed them down and assured them that they had no reason to fear, because the Lord would fight for them. And God saved His people by creating a path for them through the waters of the sea and by causing the Egyptians to drown.

This promise – that God fights for His children – is still valid today. When you find yourself in a crisis, remember the two things that Moses said to the people: "Do not be afraid ... you need only to be still."

Heavenly Father, I glorify You because You are able to save me from dangerous situations. Please help me to exchange my fear for trust and to remain calm, because I rest assured in the knowledge that You will help me. Amen.

A Caring God

Remember how the LORD your God led you all the way in the wilderness these forty years, to humble and test you in order to know what was in your heart, whether or not you would keep His commands. Deut. 8:2

In today's Scripture passage, Moses requests the people to be obedient to God and to always remember how He took care of them. God was with His people every day as they wandered through the desert, during the day as a pillar of cloud and at night as a pillar of fire. When their water was finished, He caused water to flow from a rock, and when their food was finished, He fed them with manna and quail.

God's people quickly learned that the God whom they worshipped was a God of miracles, a God who never leaves His people in the lurch, a God who can be trusted completely.

God is still the same today. When your road through life leads you into deserts, He will be there to take care of you. You can fully trust in Him to help you, as He helped His people so many years ago. "In the wilderness … you saw how the LORD your God carried you, as a father carries his son, all the way you went until you reached this place" (Deut. 1:31).

God still wants to carry you today – on that you can depend!

Heavenly Father, I glorify You for being a God who takes care of me, a God who carries me every day and a God who will always look after me. Thank You that I can trust in You completely. Amen.

Things That Are Inexplicable

"My thoughts are not your thoughts, neither are your ways My ways," declares the LORD. *"As the heavens are higher than the earth, so are My ways higher than your ways and My thoughts than your thoughts." Isa. 55:8-9*

God does not think in the same way that we do. There are events in our lives that we will never be able to understand. When your friend dies in a car accident, when your father falls seriously ill – all these things make no sense to you at the time. You cannot understand why the Lord allows such pain. But after some time has passed and you look back, you may discover that this specific period of darkness was necessary so that the miracle of God's salvation could become clearer.

When a child is born, the birth goes hand in hand with pain. "A woman giving birth to a child has pain because her time has come; but when her baby is born she forgets the anguish because of her joy that a child is born," Jesus explained to His disciples, assuring them that their sorrow would turn to joy (John 16:21).

Sometimes pain and suffering are necessary for a new birth to take place – a new revelation of God's plan for your life to come forth. God uses the suffering in your life to establish a new, more profound relationship with Him.

Heavenly Father, I know that, sometimes, Your plan for my life includes inexplicable events. Thank You for the assurance that You use the suffering in my life to strengthen my relationship with You. Amen.

God Keeps You Safe

"Since you have kept My command to endure patiently, I will also keep you from the hour of trial." Rev. 3:10

T he Lord warns the church in Philadelphia that a time of suffering will come upon them. Only those people who submit to God will be able to keep going during this oppression. God also gives the congregation a beautiful promise: Because they have kept God's command to endure patiently, He will keep them safe in times of trouble.

To be held safely when you get hurt is a wonderful comfort. Just look at the toddler who hurts his knee in a fall, crying pitifully because of the pain. The moment his mother gathers him tightly in her arms, the hurt is eased.

God's children cannot avoid the pain of suffering. It is inevitable for all of us. Christians can be assured that they will never be alone in their suffering, because God promises to keep them safe in times of trouble.

This promise applies to you, too. God will always be by your side in times of suffering, even though it may not seem like it. God will never forsake you. He promises to keep you safe and to help you in times of trouble, provided that you promise to keep His command to endure. Are you prepared to do so?

Father, how comforting Your promise is – that You will keep me safe in times of suffering. Thank You that I can know that You will never forsake me in times of crisis. Amen.

God Jealously Guards over You

*The LORD is a jealous and avenging God ... The LORD is slow
to anger but great in power. Nah. 1:2-3*

The prophet Nahum emphasizes various facets of
the nature of God. He jealously watches over His
people; He loves them deeply and sincerely cares about
them. The best explanation of the word *jealous*, as it is
used in this context, is that God is like a mother who
is constantly concerned about her children, who prays
for them every moment of the day and who loves them
unconditionally, regardless of what they may do.

Not only does God jealously watch over His children,
He is also a God who takes revenge on His enemies.
God is always angered by sin. But He is a God who is
slow to anger – He is patient toward us and is willing
to forgive us time and again. Moreover, He is great in
power – and He wants to put this miraculous power at
your disposal when you find yourself in a crisis.

When you are facing a crisis, remember that you
worship a God who truly cares about you – just as
a mother cares for her child, God is able to help and
support you.

*Heavenly Father, thank You that You, the great and mighty
God, jealously watch over me. Thank You that I can know
that You truly care about me and that You will come to my
aid. Amen.*

A Refuge in Times of Trouble

The LORD is good, a refuge in times of trouble. He cares for those who trust in Him. Nah. 1:7

Nahum brought the people of Judah a message of hope when the Assyrians reigned over them. He focuses on God and the assurance that He jealously watches over His children. Right at the beginning the prophet proclaims that God is good, that He is a refuge for His children in times of trouble, and that He cares for those who trust in Him.

These promises still hold true for God's children today. Therefore, you can take Nahum's promise for yourself. God is good to His children, even when it does not feel like it. You can find refuge in Him when you are in a crisis, and He will help you.

David agrees with Nahum's words: "The LORD is a refuge for the oppressed, a stronghold in times of trouble. Those who know Your name trust in You, for You, LORD, have never forsaken those who seek You" (Ps. 9:9-10).

If ever you find yourself in a crisis situation, you can confidently find refuge in God. God promises to care for you. "He cares for those who trust in Him," writes Nahum. If you belong to Him, He will give you everything you need.

Heavenly Father, I glorify You as my refuge and secure stronghold. Thank You that I can seek shelter with You when I find myself in a crisis situation, and that I may trust in Your promise that You will care for me. Amen.

When God Does Not Intervene

You cannot tolerate wrongdoing. Why then do You tolerate the treacherous? Why are You silent while the wicked swallow up those more righteous than themselves? Hab. 1:13

Like many people before and after him, the prophet Habakkuk cannot understand why the Lord looks on while His people are in distress, and seems to do nothing about it. We find it hard to understand why the Lord does not immediately intervene and solve our problems.

By the end of the book of Habakkuk, however, the same prophet has learned a very valuable lesson: God does not have to change our circumstances in order to change our disposition. Although our circumstances may remain unchanged, He can help us to rejoice in Him, whatever those circumstances.

God can help you too to praise Him in your crisis. Then your focus will shift from the intensity of your problems to God. You will be reassured by His presence and His love. Like Habakkuk, you can testify, "Though the fig tree does not bud and there are no grapes on the vines, though the olive crop fails and the fields produce no food, though there are no sheep in the pen, yet I will rejoice in the LORD, I will be joyful in God my Savior" (Hab. 3:17-18).

Choose to praise God during your crisis, and to thank Him for those things that you wish were different.

Lord, please teach me to glorify You, even though my circumstances are not to my liking. Amen.

Habakkuk's Testimony

LORD, I have heard of Your fame; I stand in awe of Your deeds, LORD. Repeat them in our day. Hab. 3:2

The prophet Habakkuk inundates God with "why" questions. "How long, O Lord? Why has this happened to me? Why don't You hear me when I call?" Many Christians ask the same questions when bad things happen to them and it seems as though God does not hear their prayers, or that He does not want to intervene to help.

However, after the prophet Habakkuk has become silent before God (see Hab. 2:20), his prayer changes. Instead of "why" questions, he listens to everything that God says about what He has planned. Habakkuk begins with questions of faith, but ends with a confession of faith. He is amazed at the deeds of God, and wants to show us what it means to truly trust Him.

Perhaps you are wrestling today with as many "why" questions as Habakkuk did. If so, follow the prophet's example. Become silent in the presence of the Lord. Tell Him about your problems. And reflect on how great and powerful He really is. Then you too will stand in awe of God's great deeds. And if He does intervene in your crisis situation, make sure that you glorify Him for it.

Heavenly Father, You are aware of all the "why" questions in my heart. You also know that I cannot understand why You don't always intervene to help me. I now choose to become silent in Your presence, and focus anew on how great and glorious You are. Glory be to You. Amen.

God's Great Love

So I say, "My splendor is gone and all that I had hoped from the LORD." Yet this I call to mind and therefore I have hope: Because of the LORD's great love we are not consumed.
Lam. 3:18, 21-22

When Jeremiah's hope dwindles, he remembers that God's compassion toward His children never fails, that His faithfulness is great and that He is good to those whose hope is in Him. This helps Jeremiah to keep his hopes up.

God's children can confidently hold on to their hope. God is omnipotent and fully in control, even though things in your life may sometimes get out of hand. Though you may not have any hope left, you can always hold on to God, and find hope in Him. He promises you eternal glory in heaven where all suffering and pain will pass away.

"If hope didn't whisper to us that tomorrow will be a better day, how would we have the courage to get through today?" writes Robert Burns. As Christians we know that heaven awaits us one day.

If your hope is ebbing, I would like to offer you Paul's beautiful prayer for the church in Rome: "May the God of hope fill you with all joy and peace as you trust in Him, so that you may overflow with hope by the power of the Holy Spirit" (Rom. 15:13).

Heavenly Father, I praise You because I can hope in You, even though my situation seems hopeless. Please help me to be filled with hope by the power of the Holy Spirit. Amen.

August

A Letter of Hope

Paul's letter to the Ephesians is still relevant to both Christians and the church today. In this letter Paul discusses the battle against sin and the evil one, but emphasizes victory over sin through the power of the Holy Spirit that is available to every child of God.

The world in which we live has never been as much in need of hope as now.

Therefore, in the coming month, we are going to walk through Ephesians together. It is my prayer that you will grow spiritually stronger in your faith during this month so that your hope and faith in Jesus will reach new heights.

Father,
I praise You for Your love and grace; for the fact
that You chose me especially to be Your child.
Give me the necessary insight and strength
so that I will get to know You better each day.
Thank You for delivering me from sin,
for loving me dearly and saving me by Your grace
so that I may be a member of Your family and Your church.
Show me how to be of one mind with my fellow believers,
so that Your church can be in perfect union.
Give me Your resurrection power so that I
can spread Your Good News.
I give You the honor for what I achieve in that power.
Thank You that You, through Your power that works in me,
do much more than I could ever think of or pray for.
Please help me to accept my fellow believers and
be patient with them; to grow spiritually and break
with sin until I am as perfect and mature as Jesus.
Thank You for gifts I receive from You.
From now on I want to make the most
of my opportunities and my time.
Please bless my marriage and help me to accept
my husband's authority in our family;
to raise our children for You; to do my
work as if for You and to treat my colleagues fairly.
I now want to put on Your armor prayerfully
so that I will be victorious in the battle against the evil one.
Amen.

Praise God!

Praise be to the God and Father of our Lord Jesus Christ, who has blessed us in the heavenly realms with every spiritual blessing in Christ. Eph. 1:3

Paul's letter is addressed to all the Christians in Ephesus. He starts the letter by wishing the church two things that no Christian can function without, namely grace and peace (see Eph. 1:2). Grace is God's smile for a dependent, sinful person. It is being surprised by God's generous love without us deserving it.

God's grace is still freely available for each of us, but His peace has become extremely scarce in our world today. We are confronted with discord and unrest every day. Biblical peace means being whole; it refers to someone who has achieved their goal in life, has tasted fulfillment of life. Most people today struggle to merely exist.

In Ephesians 1:4, Paul tells the church in Ephesus that God has chosen them especially to live holy and blameless lives, and that they were already destined to be His children in Christ a long time ago.

Today this promise is also addressed to you personally. If you love Jesus, God has already chosen you to honor Him with your life. His grace is yours and His peace will become a reality in your life. For this you can praise Him every day of your life!

Heavenly Father, I want to praise You for Your grace and peace that You make available to me. Thank You that You have already chosen me to belong to You. Amen.

What We Receive in Christ

In Him we have redemption through His blood, the forgiveness of sins, in accordance with the riches of God's grace that He lavished on us. Eph. 1:7-8

Paul tells the church in Ephesus that there are four things in particular that we receive if we belong to Christ:

• We are set free from the power and punishment of sin.

• We learn to know God's will. He makes His will known to us through His Word, but in particular through the Word that became flesh.

• We are united as one body through the church with Jesus as Head.

• We are sealed by the Holy Spirit as God's property.

In grace, the Father chooses us, and this takes place through the Son, but is confirmed in our lives by the Holy Spirit.

God wants to offer you these four things in Christ. By Jesus' atonement you are redeemed from sin; you learn how to know God's will; you do not only become part of God's body on earth, but also part of God's people, and the Holy Spirit is your personal guarantee that each one of God's promises will come true for you.

The grace that God granted you cost the life of His Son. Don't wait any longer to accept the wonderful things that God offers you.

Heavenly Father, I now want to accept everything You offer me in Jesus. Thank You very much. Amen.

To Know God

I have not stopped giving thanks for you, remembering you in my prayers. I keep asking that the God of our Lord Jesus Christ, the glorious Father, may give you the Spirit of wisdom and revelation, so that you may know Him better.
Eph. 1:16-17

P aul starts his letter with a good testimonial for the church of Ephesus. He writes that people are talking about their faith and love. Faith in God and love for other people can never be separated. They are the two sides of a coin. The faith that Paul is praising the Ephesians for is demonstrated in the love they show others.

Paul prays a beautiful prayer for the Ephesians: He asks that God will give the people wisdom through His Holy Spirit and that He will reveal Himself to them in such a way that they will truly know Him.

Shortly before His crucifixion Jesus promised His disciples that He would send them the Holy Spirit when He left, and that this Spirit would testify about Him (see John 15:26).

Without the Spirit of God in your life, spiritual growth and insight into God's will is impossible. You will never know God fully without the wisdom that the Holy Spirit can give you. Ask the Lord to give you His wisdom in your own life and in your congregation, so that you will also be able to grow spiritually and become stronger, and that you will indeed get to know Him better each day and love Him more.

Lord, I pray that you would give me Your wisdom so that I may grow spiritually and truly get to know You. Amen.

To See the Unseen

I pray that the eyes of your heart may be enlightened in order that you may know the hope to which He has called you, the riches of His glorious inheritance in His holy people.
Eph. 1:18

In these Scripture verses Paul is still busy praying for the Ephesians. He asks that the Lord would open their spiritual eyes so that they would know what wonderful things His call includes, and also become aware of the riches of the inheritance that God promised them. He also prays that the church in Ephesus will truly know God. To know God they must have eyes that can see the Unseen.

Faith, however, is a matter of trusting, rather than seeing. The writer of Hebrews agrees: "Faith is the confidence that what we hope for will actually happen; it gives us assurance about things we cannot see" (Heb. 11:1).

God also wants to give you spiritual eyes so that you can see Him, as well as wisdom to really get to know Him. You will discover firsthand what wonderful hope there is for those who believe in God. You will also discover how great the power is that works through you if you trust God for everything. He would like to get this miraculous power working in your life. With this power available to you, it will be possible to gain victory over the evil one.

Heavenly Father, please give me the eyes of faith to see Your heavenly inheritance, and also power to defeat the evil one. Amen.

Called for Service

I pray that the eyes of your heart may be enlightened in order that you may know the hope to which He has called you, the riches of His glorious inheritance, and His incomparably great power for us who believe. Eph. 1:18-19

The more you get to know God and the more wisdom He gives you to discover and use the gifts that you personally receive from Him, the more you realize that you should use those gifts for God's kingdom. He has called you for service in His kingdom.

Peter writes, "Each of you should use whatever gift you have received to serve others, as faithful stewards of God's grace in its various forms" (1 Pet. 4:10). If you are willing to do this, God's power will be at your disposal to put these gifts to use.

Paul explains to the Ephesians what power he is talking about – none other than the resurrection power by which Jesus was raised from the dead! This power makes you a conqueror; *more* than a conqueror.

You will also discover how God increases and blesses the gifts you were born with so that you would be a blessing to other people.

You don't have to accomplish great things in God's kingdom with your own strength. Just trust in God's strength and claim it for yourself. You already know that you can do everything with the help of Christ who gives you the strength you need (see Phil. 4:13).

Heavenly Father, it is a privilege that You call me for service in Your kingdom. I want to use my gifts to expand Your kingdom and to tackle everything in Your strength. Amen.

Death as a Result of Sin

Once you were dead because of your disobedience and your many sins. You used to live in sin, just like the rest of the world, obeying the devil – the commander of the powers in the unseen world. Eph. 2:1-2

Each human being is sinful from the moment they are born, except if God intervenes in their lives. People are dead as a result of their sins, because the wages of sin is always death.

This was also true of the church in Ephesus before they came to know God. And sinners are always in the service of the devil. You, too, worship either the prince of darkness or the Prince of light. With your inherent sinfulness you deserve God's punishment because He doesn't tolerate sin – He always punishes it with death. You are also spiritually dead because you were born in sin, even if you feel you don't commit such wicked sins that deserve death. It is necessary that you admit your sin and ask God's forgiveness.

Fortunately there is hope for you. You don't have to die as a result of your sin anymore. Jesus already paid the price for your sin in full on the cross. You are now free! You can be dead to sin by believing in Jesus. Just as He was raised from the dead after His death on the cross and lives, you can live fully for Him from now on.

Lord Jesus, I praise You for delivering me from my sins, so that I am no longer dead as a result of my sins, but can live wholly for You. Amen.

God Loves Us So Much

God is so rich in mercy, and He loved us so much, that even though we were dead because of our sins, He gave us life when He raised Christ from the dead. (It is only by God's grace that you have been saved!) For He raised us from the dead along with Christ and seated us with Him in the heavenly realms. Eph. 2:4-6

You and I were born sinners, but Paul says God is rich in mercy and He loves us, in spite of our sin. Because He loves us, He gave us life when He raised Christ from the dead, so that if we believe in Him, we can live for Him.

God intervened in your sinful life and made a huge difference by sending His sinless Son to the world to pay the full price for your sin on the cross. Jesus died in your place to pay the wages of your sin in full. But He did not remain in the tomb – He was raised from the dead after three days. Because He was resurrected, He made it possible for all who believe in Him to rise from the death that is caused by sin, to overcome death and live in heaven forever.

You were not only resurrected with Jesus. He has also made it possible for you to go to heaven after your death where He has reserved a place for you – a place that He is already busy preparing.

Heavenly Father, how can I ever thank You enough for Your great love for me that raised me from the dead together with Jesus, and that promises me a place in heaven. Amen.

Saved by Grace

God saved you by His grace when you believed. And you can't take credit for this; it is a gift from God. He has created us anew in Christ Jesus, so we can do the good things He planned for us long ago. Eph. 2:8, 10

We cannot bring about our own salvation or earn it with good works. Salvation is always the result of God's unfathomable grace. It is a gift, a present from God. We have nothing to offer in exchange for it – we can only accept it with outstretched hands, free of charge.

We are so used to being rewarded according to what we deserve, that we don't really know what to do with God's grace. All we have to do is express our gratitude and emphasize our thankfulness through our lives.

You are saved by grace, but there is something more – faith. Faith in Jesus is necessary before His salvation can be realized in your life. Thus faith is the hand with which you accept God's grace.

You have not been saved because you did good works, but so that you can do good works in future. God saves you so that you can live the rest of your life devoted to Him; from now on you can dedicate your life to the good works He has destined you for. Discover God's personal instruction for you and obey it!

Heavenly Father, I now want to take the gift of my salvation. Help me to dedicate my life to the good things You created me for. Amen.

Jesus, the Creator of Unity

Now you have been united with Christ Jesus. Once you were far away from God, but now you have been brought near to Him through the blood of Christ. Christ Himself has brought peace to us. He united Jews and Gentiles into one people.
Eph. 2:13-14

The people of Ephesus used to be heathens on the grounds of their birth. They were far away from God and without hope. They were not part of God's chosen people and His promises did not apply to them. But then, by having faith in Jesus, salvation became possible for them. They became one with Jesus and close to God through the blood of Jesus.

Jesus' death on the cross brought about reconciliation between all who were distanced from God and from one another, and worked peace among all the different parties – peace among believers, and even peace between Christians and heathens. Jesus was willing to give His body so that the wall of enmity between Christians and unbelievers could be torn down.

When Jesus has made you new, the "walls" separating believers, like ethnic differences, should not bother you anymore. In Christ *all* believers are one, despite their differences. We belong to one body of Christ and therefore should be in perfect union and honor Him with our lives.

Lord Jesus, I praise You for making it possible for me to be of one mind with other Christians, in spite of our differences, and that Your blood washes me clean of sin and makes me new. Amen.

A Family and a Building

So now you Gentiles are no longer strangers and foreigners. You are citizens along with all of God's holy people. You are members of God's family. Together, we are His house. And the cornerstone is Christ Jesus Himself. Eph. 2:19-20

Paul uses two images that are still applicable to all believers today. Now that they believe in Jesus, the Ephesians are members of God's family. They are also a building of which Jesus Himself is the cornerstone. If you believe in Jesus you automatically become God's child. He is your Father and Jesus is your brother. You automatically share in all the privileges of being His child. In Romans 8:17 Paul says we are also heirs with Jesus. If we share in His suffering, we will also share in His glory.

You are also part of a building: the church. Jesus is the cornerstone of the building that brings believers together. By means of His mediation, sinners now have free access to a holy God. Personal backgrounds and differences are no longer important.

Your life before you met Jesus doesn't matter to Him, because all who believe in Him are now citizens of the kingdom, members of His family, people who belong together, relatives who are united by the blood of Jesus. They are as close together as the bricks in a wall. Together all believers form one building in which God lives. Therefore the church must be one and members may not be divided.

Lord Jesus, it is wonderful that You make it possible for me to be part of God's family, to be a brick in Your church. Amen.

God's Secret Plan

This mystery is that through the gospel the Gentiles are heirs together with Israel, members together of one body, and sharers together in the promise in Christ Jesus. Eph. 3:6

P aul reveals this mystery to the Ephesians: God chooses people for His kingdom from all nations and languages. In the Old Testament only the Israelites enjoyed this privilege. They were God's chosen people and they were the only people with whom He made a covenant. But Jesus changed all of this: In Him everyone who believed in Him could become part of God's kingdom and a member of God's body.

Paul highlights three facets of this Kingdom:
- All people are welcome.
- The church is assigned the task of sharing this mystery with the world.
- All believers should proclaim Jesus' message.

You also belong to God's people, His church, and His body. You ought to put your calling into practice in your church. It is important that you believe in Jesus and remain in Him. God also gives you the task of proclaiming Jesus' Good News to everybody, so that even more people can know this mystery and join His kingdom!

Heavenly Father, thank You that by faith in Jesus I can be part of Your body on earth. Help me to spread the gospel. Amen.

Paul's Calling

By God's grace and mighty power, I have been given the privilege of serving Him by spreading this Good News. He graciously gave me the privilege of telling the Gentiles about the endless treasures available to them in Christ. Eph. 3:7-8

Paul explains his personal calling to the Ephesians. He is a minister of the gospel who was appointed by God Himself to take the message to the Gentiles. He is only able to do this because the power of God works through him.

Paul's starting point is that the God He proclaims is the Creator God. He made everything and still maintains it. Jesus is Lord and Savior. Only in Him and in alliance with Him do we have the confidence to seek the presence of God. Paul had to suffer in fulfilling His calling, but He saw it as an honor to be able to do so. He remained humble. Although he reached practically the whole world of his time with the gospel of Jesus, he still called himself "the least" of the believers.

Christians today have the same calling as Paul: to proclaim the Good News to the world. Each one of us should be a missionary, and we should accept this task like Paul did – as a privilege. We will never be able to do it in our own strength. Therefore, rely on God's miraculous power every time you proclaim His message.

Heavenly Father, I am willing to be Your messenger and to spread the gospel. Give me Your resurrection power so that I will manage to accomplish this. Amen.

Strength, Faith and Love

I pray that from His glorious, unlimited resources He will empower you with inner strength through His Spirit. Then Christ will make His home in your hearts as you trust in Him. Your roots will grow down into God's love and keep you strong. Eph. 3:16-17

In Paul's second prayer for the Ephesians he asks that God, from His glorious, unlimited resources, will equip them through His Spirit with everything they need to honor Him with their lives. He also asks that God will give them the strength to do it. Every Christian lacks a powerful faith at times. Paul prays that the church in Ephesus will receive inner strength through the Holy Spirit in their lives. He also asks that Christ will live in their hearts through faith, so that He would become an inseparable part of their lives. He then prays that their roots would grow down into God's love.

Make Paul's prayer part of your own life. Your faith is often tested in your daily life. Only when Jesus' immeasurable power is revealed in your life, when His faith is evident and His unconditional love forms the foundation of your life, will God be able to make optimal use of you in His Kingdom.

This strength, faith and love that Paul prays God will grant the Ephesians should also find expression in your church. If it cannot be seen in your congregation, you should pray that it becomes a reality.

Holy Spirit, please give me inner strength so that Jesus will be present in my life and I can spread Your love. Amen.

Knowledge of Love

May you have the power to understand, as all God's people should, how wide, how long, how high, and how deep His love is. May you experience the love of Christ, though it is too great to understand fully. Then you will be made complete with all the fullness of life and power that comes from God. Eph. 3:18-19

We all know the kind of love Paul is talking about here – the incomprehensible, unconditional love that God has for His children. Paul uses every known dimension to describe God's love: We must know how wide, far, high and deep that love goes. Paul's prayer is that the church in Ephesus will get to know this kind of love.

If you want to understand this love of God and make it part of your own life, you will have to work on your relationship with Him every day. Knowledge of God's love comes only when you are in a relationship with Him. In-depth Bible study and regular prayer are necessary for this. Only when you are filled with this love yourself, will you be filled with the fullness of God. Then the Holy Spirit lives in your heart and reveals God's love to you more and more.

Through faith in Jesus, God makes His home in your life, and this is only possible if you hand control of your life over to the Holy Spirit. You are also not to keep God's love for yourself, but share it with all people.

Lord God, Your love for me often leaves me speechless. Help me to gain firsthand knowledge of Your love and share it with other people. Amen.

More Than You Might Ask or Think

*Now all glory to God, who is able, through His mighty power
at work within us, to accomplish infinitely more than we might
ask or think. Glory to Him in the church and in Christ Jesus.
Eph. 3:20-21*

Paul testifies that God works in and through us, and
the things He does for us are far more than we could
ask or think. His power is mighty, and if we have access
to it we can do wonders with it.

People who believe in Him never have to try to do
things in their own strength again – they know from
experience that they will not be able to do it. All the
glory is God's and we give Him that glory through our
bond with Christ, by becoming and acting more and
more like Jesus.

God wants to make His immeasurable strength available to you personally. Don't rely on your own abilities
any longer – He can do much more in your life than
you ever expected. Boldly claim God's miraculous
power for yourself in everything that is expected of you
each day – for all the challenges and problems on your
path of life. But when you achieve great things in that
power, you must guard against pride. Always give God
the glory due to Him. The aim of the church is to exalt
the name of the Lord so that the world can get to know
God's glory.

*Heavenly Father, I want to honor You for all the things I have
been able to achieve in the strength You have made available
to me. Amen.*

Unity among Believers

As a prisoner for the Lord, then, I urge you to live a life worthy of the calling you have received. Be completely humble and gentle; be patient, bearing with one another in love. Make every effort to keep the unity of the Spirit through the bond of peace. Eph. 4:1-3

Paul impresses upon the Ephesians that their way of life should be in accordance with their godly calling. God's people have always been expected to live in line with His guidelines. This means that your lifestyle should serve as proof that you love God and obey His commandments. To be called by Christ means that you will be actively devoted to God and the task for which He has called you. As Christians, each one of us is called to demonstrate the unity of the church in our relationships with other Christians.

The unity that God wants from you doesn't just happen. It must be practiced purposefully – something that can't happen when selfishness and self-interest are still dominant in your life.

Christians are called to be humble and gentle and to treat each other in a friendly and patient way. Because this goes against your selfish nature, you will never manage it on your own, but the working of the Holy Spirit in your life makes it possible for you. Christians also ought to live in peace with each other, be willing to forgive each other and accept each other unconditionally, in spite of their differences.

Lord, I struggle to accept my fellow Christians, to treat them patiently and tolerantly. Please help me to do this. Amen.

The Unity of the Church

There is one body and one Spirit, just as you have been called to one glorious hope for the future. There is one Lord, one faith, one baptism, and one God and Father, who is over all and in all and living through all. Eph. 4:4-6

The unity of the church is not an artificial matter – it is from God Himself. It is a bond of unity that is formed by the Holy Spirit.

Paul talks about different aspects of this unity: Christians are filled with one Spirit, therefore they may not be divided amongst themselves. They are filled with one hope – the hope of the heavenly glory that God promises His children. The fact that Christians share one faith and worship one Triune God creates an even stronger bond between them.

The sacrament of baptism further emphasizes this unity. By means of baptism all believers are cleansed by the blood of Jesus. This unity of the church, as well as the unity among believers, is essential for the church as Jesus' body to continue on earth.

Accordingly, it is necessary for you to let go of your differences with other Christians and your complaints against your church. Allow the Holy Spirit to let the members of the church you belong to be in agreement, where all will serve God and have one common aim: to spread the gospel of Jesus and glorify God.

Lord, I am sorry that I am so often dissatisfied with fellow believers and also with members of my congregation. From now on I want to be as one with other believers so that Your church can be united. Amen.

Each Person Has a Gift

He has given each one of us a special gift. These are the gifts Christ gave to the church: the apostles, the prophets, the evangelists, and the pastors and teachers. Their responsibility is to equip God's people to do His work and build up the church, the body of Christ. Eph. 4:7, 11-12

The church is a unit, although believers differ from each other because each member has received a distinctive gift from God. Each of us should learn to discover and develop our own gift and not compare it to those of other Christians, however attractive their gifts might seem. We should rather use our gift in God's service and to benefit our fellow believers.

Paul writes to the church in Ephesus about the different positions in the church. The gifts mentioned here exist specifically to equip the church and develop it to be of service, and to work together in building up the body of Christ. Each member has their own specific function in this building-up process and they should apply their own personal gift to this cause. If the whole team works together in love, the church will be built up and fortified.

Always remember that you have received a personal gift from God. Make sure you use your gift in such a way that your congregation will be built up and God glorified.

Heavenly Father, thank You for the gifts You have entrusted to me. I want to use mine to glorify You and build up my congregation. Amen.

Spiritual Maturity

This will continue until we all come to such unity in our faith and knowledge of God's Son that we will be mature in the Lord, measuring up to the full and complete standard of Christ. Eph. 4:13

Unity in faith and knowledge of Christ are essential qualities of spiritual maturity. Only when all the members in the church work together to develop the different positions, will they achieve true unity in their faith and knowledge of God's Son.

It is necessary for church members to support and complement each other so that the unity that God asks of the church will prevail. Only then will we, and the church, be as perfect and mature as Christ. If we remain spiritually immature, we are easily thrown off course by all kinds of wrong ideas and teachings. But we can protect ourselves against this by having knowledge of God and the continued support of fellow believers who are members of the same church.

Spiritual maturity always requires a growth process. Each Christian should continue growing in faith by becoming and acting more like Jesus. You can do this by "speaking the truth in love," Paul writes to the believers in Ephesus (Eph. 4:15). Then the body of the congregation will build itself up by functioning in unison, where the different members support one another by applying their gifts.

Lord Jesus, I would like to grow spiritually until my church and I are as perfect and mature as You. Please make it possible for me. Amen.

Break with the Old Person!

Throw off your old sinful nature and your former way of life, which is corrupted by lust and deception. Instead, let the Spirit renew your thoughts and attitudes. Put on your new nature, created to be like God – truly righteous and holy. Eph. 4:22-24

Paul writes to the church in Ephesus, telling them that faith in Christ not only makes a difference in their eternal destination, but also to their lives here on earth. All who believe in Christ are new people who must live and think in a new way.

When you are in Christ, you also need to bid your old lifestyle farewell and adopt a whole new way of life. It is difficult to change your lifestyle radically when you become converted. There will be certain habits you will struggle with because they have become a part of your life. Yet, there should be a big difference between your life before and after your conversion.

This difference will not take place suddenly or easily – you will have to make an effort to achieve it by living the way God wants you to. You have to break with the old person and become renewed in God's image.

Study your Bible so that you know exactly what the life of a new person should look like. From now on you need to live according to God's will as it is outlined for you in His Word and be holy. God will help you.

Lord Jesus, You make it possible for me to become a new person because Your blood has cleansed me of my sins. Help me to break with my sinful habits. Amen.

Do's and Don'ts for Christians

Do not bring sorrow to God's Holy Spirit by the way you live. Remember, He has identified you as His own, guaranteeing that you will be saved on the day of redemption. Be kind to each other, tenderhearted, forgiving one another, just as God through Christ has forgiven you. Eph. 4:30, 32

Although new believers are new people, the old person is not going to go down without a struggle. You will still have to guard against your old habits rearing their ugly heads.

Paul gives the Ephesians a number of practical, positive guidelines for their new life in Christ and He also warns them against a number of sins. New people speak the truth; they are honest with other believers; they are kind and tender-hearted to one another and forgive each other. They do not end their day angry and they don't give the devil a foothold in their lives.

Remember, the devil will leave no stone unturned to undermine your new life as a Christian. Therefore, be alert so that you will realize his plans and sidestep them.

Furthermore, Christians are honest; they don't steal or use bad language, and they don't bring sorrow to the Holy Spirit. You hurt the Holy Spirit when you refuse to listen to His voice in your life.

Go through Paul's lists of do's and don'ts again and mark those that you need to pay more attention to.

Lord, please help me to take off my old person with its old habits and put on the new person. Amen.

Live a Life of Love

Follow God's example, therefore, as dearly loved children and walk in the way of love, just as Christ loved us and gave Himself up for us as a fragrant offering and sacrifice to God. Eph. 5:1-2

Paul asks the church in Ephesus to follow his example by responding to God's love with their lives. The motive for obedience should never be fear of punishment; we ought to be willing to follow God's precepts because we love Him. The only way to respond to God's love is by living a life of love ourselves.

If you love like Jesus, you will try your best to love other people just as much as Jesus loves you – with the same unconditional love that He demonstrated on the cross. Then you will have the kind of love for others that God has for you that inspired Him to sacrifice His Son's life for yours. A life lived in His love means that you will follow a specific lifestyle from now on. You will obey the King because you love Him.

Paul mentions a few things in Ephesians 4 that God's children should stay away from, like sexual immorality, greed and bad language. Those who are guilty of these things can't respond to God's love, because their lifestyle doesn't correspond with their calling. Such people have no place in God's kingdom. Try to live like Paul by setting an example that is worth following.

Lord, make it possible for me to live a life of love, and to obey Your precepts with love. Amen.

People of the Light

Once you were full of darkness, but now you have light from the Lord. So live as people of light! For this light within you produces only what is good and right and true. Eph. 5:8-9

Your old life formed part of the darkness of sin, while new believers are people of light who live in the light. You have now crossed over from the night-time of sin to a life in Jesus' light. When you belong to Jesus, you should also live like a person of the light by doing things that are good and right and true.

Think carefully whether your life has really changed for the better. Ask yourself whether the things you do and think when no one sees you are acceptable to God. And what do other people hear and see when they listen to what you say and watch the things you do? Your yardstick should no longer be your own will, but God's will. A person of the light may no longer live for themselves only, but they should seek God's will and honor in everything they do.

You have a responsibility toward other Christians. Help protect your fellow believers against evil practices, pray for them and set them an example worth following. People of the light refuse to take part in the sinful practices of the darkness, but denounce them instead. Are you ready to speak up when your friends swear in front of you or drink too much?

Lord, it is not always easy to behave like a person of the light. Make me willing to live according to Your standards, and condemn what is wrong. Amen.

Make the Most of
Your Opportunities

Be careful how you live. Don't live like fools, but like those who are wise. Make the most of every opportunity.
Eph. 5:15-16

In order to live life to the full, God's children must learn to make good use of every opportunity that comes their way and make the most of the time at their disposal. Paul urges the believers in Ephesus to be careful how they live and to live like wise people.

Paul's precepts are meant for you too. If you don't abide by God's rules, your life will not honor Him. So make the most of your opportunities. Place a high premium on the time at your disposal so that you don't waste your time or your opportunities.

Many people today pay no heed to the Lord and the precepts in His Word, living exactly as they like. Therefore you must be serious about living according to God's will. You will only be able to do this if you are filled with the Holy Spirit and leave the control of your life to Him. If the whole congregation is prepared to obey these precepts, the church will indeed glorify God's name.

Lord, thank You for opportunities and for the time I have at my disposal. Grant that I will work carefully with my time and my opportunities so that I can honor Your name.
Amen.

Guidelines for Marriage

Submit to one another out of reverence for Christ. For wives, this means submit to your husbands as to the Lord. For husbands, this means love your wives, just as Christ loved the church. Eph. 5:21-22, 25

B eing a Christian affects your whole life and all your relationships – including your marriage. Paul asks that married couples in Ephesus submit to one another out of reverence for God. And this command is still relevant for us today. Putting your faith into practice in your marriage is not always easy. If you can't manage to put your marriage partner first, you are unfortunately going to fall short.

Wives are told to submit to their husbands in love and to acknowledge the leading role that God assigned men in the marriage relationship. This is a voluntary submissiveness like that of the church to Christ. Men are given an even more difficult command – they are expected to love their wives like Christ loves the church.

In today's Scripture reading Paul talks about selfless, self-sacrificing love. In a marriage relationship, respect and love for each other should be founded on your love for God. If you and your spouse follow these guidelines in your marriage, and if Christ is the Lord of your marriage, then your marriage cannot be anything but happy.

Heavenly Father, I want to honor You for my happy marriage. Thank You that You are indeed the most important Person in our marriage. Amen.

A Great Mystery

As the Scriptures say, "A man leaves his father and mother and is joined to his wife, and the two are united into one." This is a great mystery, but it is an illustration of the way Christ and the church are one. Eph. 5:31-32

Paul has more to say about marriage. The unity of the Christian marriage is based on the unity between Christ and the church. Men must love their wives as they love their own bodies. Paul writes that the man who rejects his wife without reason, actually rejects his own body. Every man who follows Jesus should be faithful to his wife like Jesus is to the church. He should treat her like his own body and take loving care of her. It was God's decision that man and wife be one in marriage. Paul calls this relationship a great mystery.

In summary: Every man should love his wife, and every wife should honor her husband in a relationship based on the relationship between Christ and His church.

What about your marriage? Can you honestly say that the relationship between you and your spouse is based on the same relationship as between Jesus and His church? Are you managing to love your spouse unselfishly and to put them first in everything? If your marriage is unhappy, it can be fixed. Go and see a Christian counselor and pray together that the Lord will bless your marriage.

Lord, thank You for the mystery of love in marriage that is based on Your love for Your church. Please bless our marriage. Amen.

Children and Parents

Children, obey your parents because you belong to the Lord, for this is the right thing to do. Fathers, do not provoke your children to anger by the way you treat them. Rather, bring them up with the discipline and instruction that comes from the Lord. Eph. 6:1, 4

In today's Scripture reading Paul talks about family relationships. The family is the first place where children should be taught to submit to authority. Paul wants children to obey their parents. And he expects parents to treat their children fairly and reasonably.

He links the instructions he gives children and parents directly to their Christian faith. Parents are God's representatives in the family. The family is the place where children must learn to submit to authority so that they will be able to do it later on in the community as adults. Paul advises fathers to treat their children fairly and not to force authority on them. It is necessary for children to be disciplined, but in the right way – "instruction that comes from the Lord," Paul explains.

If you and your spouse can succeed in following these directives in educating your children – raising them firmly, reasonably and in line with God's will – their upbringing will take place in an atmosphere of love, even if it is accompanied by discipline and admonishment.

Lord, we thank You for the children You have entrusted to us. Help us to raise them with love and authority, the way You want us to. Amen.

Relationships in the Workplace

Slaves, obey your earthly masters with deep respect and fear. Serve them sincerely as you would serve Christ. Masters, treat your slaves in the same way. Don't threaten them; remember, you both have the same Master in heaven, and He has no favorites. Eph. 6:5, 9

We might not be so familiar with slavery today, but we are still in a relationship with people who work for us or people we work for. Paul asks that Christian slaves work for their owners as if they are working for God Himself, and that they honor and respect their owners. The Lord will reward them at the right time if they always do their work to the best of their ability, and not only work with a profit motive in mind.

There is also a message for the owners (employers) of slaves: They should treat their employees with a positive attitude and always bear in mind that they are under God's authority. They should realize that God does not discriminate between people – in His eyes employer and employee are equal. Employers are not to exploit their employees by paying them too little or forcing them to work too hard. Employees should always be treated fairly and responsibly.

See to it that you treat your employer with due respect, and your employee justly, and always give your best in the workplace.

Lord, help me to do my work as if I am doing it for You. Help me to always treat my employees fairly. Amen.

Ready for Battle!

Put on the full armor of God, so that you can take your stand against the devil's schemes. For our struggle is not against flesh and blood, but against the rulers, against the authorities, against the powers of this dark world and against the spiritual forces of evil in the heavenly realms. Eph. 6:11-12

Paul compares the Christian with a soldier at war. As children of God, we are involved in the battle between light and darkness. The devil is an invisible enemy who will never stop attacking the church of God. In our battle with him we will always be defeated unless we wear the armor that God offers His children. This armor is essential for us to resist the devil in the time of evil.

The armor that Paul describes here corresponds with what the Roman soldiers wore. Paul says we must wear the belt of truth and the breastplate of righteousness. For shoes we should wear the willingness to spread the gospel. We are to have the shield of faith to shield us from the fiery arrows of the enemy, and the helmet of salvation to protect us. God also gives us the Bible, the sword of the Spirit, as a weapon of attack.

If you use this armor in your battle against the devil, you will emerge victorious every time.

Lord, I want to put on Your full armor so that I may emerge as victor from the battle between light and darkness. Amen.

The Necessity and Power of Prayer

Pray in the Spirit at all times and on every occasion. Stay alert and be persistent in your prayers for all believers everywhere. And pray for me, too. Eph. 6:18-19

God's armor is only effective if you make prayer a part of it. The battle against the evil one can never be won without prayer.

Paul knows the power of prayer from experience and can therefore talk about it firsthand. He asks that the people of Ephesus do everything prayerfully, and plead with God through the Holy Spirit on every occasion. The Bible also assures us that the Holy Spirit will not only teach us to pray the correct way, but that He already intercedes for us with God and pleads with God to answer our prayers.

Paul also asks the Ephesians to pray for each other. Prayer for fellow believers is imperative. Lastly, he asks the congregation to also lift him up in prayer.

Ask God every day to help you in your battle against the evil one. Be faithful in praying for other believers. The very best thing you can do for other people is to pray for them. Pray also for missionaries and ministers on a regular basis so that the gospel of God's love will be made known to all people. There is incredible power in the prayers of Christians. When people pray, God answers.

Lord, I praise You that You hear our prayers. Help me to do everything prayerfully from now on and to also pray for other people. Amen.

A Visit from Tychicus

Tychicus will give you a full report about what I am doing and how I am getting along. He is a beloved brother and faithful helper in the Lord's work. Peace be with you, and may God the Father and the Lord Jesus Christ give you love with faithfulness. May God's grace be eternally upon all who love our Lord Jesus Christ. Eph. 6:21, 23-24

Paul concludes his letter to the church in Ephesus by telling them that Tychicus will visit them shortly to tell them how Paul is doing. Tychicus was to deliver the letters to the churches in Ephesus, Colosse and Philemon. Paul gives Tychicus a beautiful testimonial: he describes him as a "beloved brother and faithful helper in the Lord's work" and adds that he loves Tychicus very much.

Tychicus was with Paul on his third missionary journey and he also spent four years with him in Rome while he was in prison. Every time Tychicus is mentioned, he was busy expanding God's kingdom and therefore he was the right person to deliver Paul's letters and give his greetings.

We can see from the things Paul writes about Tychicus that he was a sincere believer who supported other believers. What kind of testimonial would Paul have written had it been you who was to deliver the letter to the Ephesians?

Heavenly Father, help me to live in such a way that my fellow Christians will be able to give me a good testimonial, like Paul gave Tychicus. Amen.

September

People Who Care

Most people today are very busy. We do not even have time for ourselves and for those things that we would like to do, let alone time for others.

In the everyday rat race we forget to really notice one another, to really care for others.

And yet, that is what God expects from His children – that we carry each other's burdens and so fulfill the law of Christ (see Gal. 6:2).

"Care is being with, crying with, suffering with, feeling with," writes Henri Nouwen. "Care is compassion, grace and mercy. It is claiming the truth that the other person is my brother or sister, human, mortal, vulnerable, like I am. To care is to be human."

This month, we are going to spend time with men and women from the Bible who really cared about others and from whose lives we can learn lessons in caring, even today.

I pray that You will give me a caring heart for others,
that I may notice the distress of
the people around me and satisfy their needs.
Help me to have compassion on others, to open my purse,
home and heart to them, to be willing to offer my help,
even though it may be at my own expense.
Grant that I will be willing to support my
friends and family by word and deed,
that I will not show the least of Yours the door –
that I will help even strangers.
Make me obedient and willing
to put myself at Your disposal, to forgive others
unconditionally, as You forgive me.
Teach me to demonstrate my caring love to You through my
way of life, to be unselfish in my marriage,
and make me willing to comfort others
as You comfort me every time I am despondent.
I know that I will never succeed by myself –
please enable me to do so through Your Holy Spirit.
Amen.

Abraham, an Example of Hospitality

He said, "If I have found favor in your eyes, my lord, do not pass your servant by. Let me get you something to eat, so you can be refreshed and then go on your way – now that you have come to your servant". Gen. 18:3, 5

A braham was a very wealthy and important man. And yet his heart went out to others. When three strangers passed by his tent one day, he immediately invited them to join him for a meal. Abraham's "something to eat" became a feast. Three seahs of fine flour were used to bake bread and a calf was roasted. And all of that for strangers! Once the food had been prepared, Abraham served his guests in person.

It is a modern-day tendency for people to be far less hospitable than in the past. Because we are so busy, and perhaps because entertaining has become so expensive, we do not invite friends to dine with us as often as we used to – let alone strangers.

Perhaps you should remember Abraham's example when someone knocks on your door for food, or when you consider inviting a few friends for a meal. Joyfully follow the advice of the writer of Hebrews: "Do not forget to entertain strangers, for by so doing some people have shown hospitality to angels without knowing it" (Heb. 13:2). This was indeed the case with Abraham!

Lord, I apologize for not being more hospitable. Help me to care more about acquaintances, as well as about those people who come knocking on my door for food. Amen.

Lot and His Two Visitors

Lot went outside to meet them and shut the door behind him and said, "No, my friends. Don't do this wicked thing. Look, I have two daughters who have never slept with a man. Let me bring them out to you and you can do what you like with them. But don't do anything to these men, for they have come under the protection of my roof." Gen. 19:6-8

When two strangers arrived on Lot's doorstep, he offered them a place for the night. However, the sinful residents of Sodom demanded that Lot turn his visitors over to them so that they could have sex with them. Lot refused; he was even willing to give his two unmarried daughters to the men, if the people would leave his visitors alone.

When you read this, you tend to think that Lot was taking hospitality a bit too far. The Lord saw what Lot did and rewarded him for it. The strangers saved Lot by striking the residents of Sodom with blindness. When all the residents of Sodom and Gomorrah were later destroyed by fire, Lot and his family were spared.

The story of Lot holds both a lesson and a warning. God requires His children to care about others – including strangers. However, He warns us at the same time that we cannot live among infidels, taking no heed of God's standards, and expect to come off scot-free.

Lord, I pray that You would help me to really care about the people who I come into contact with – including those I do not know. Teach me to obey You and not to seek my friends among infidels. Amen.

Rahab

She had taken them up to the roof and hidden them under the stalks of flax she had laid out on the roof. Josh. 2:6

Rahab, a woman of loose morals, endangered her own life to save the lives of two Israeli spies who she did not even know. She lied to the king and hid them on her roof. When the king's men had gone, she let them down the city wall by a rope. In return, the spies promised to spare the lives of Rahab and her family when they attacked the city.

Rahab knew that these spies worshiped the real God. "The LORD your God is God in heaven above and on the earth below," she testifies (Josh. 2:11).

The spies kept their word and the lives of Rahab and her family were spared. The name of this pagan prostitute was later included in the Hebrews gallery of faith. "By faith the prostitute Rahab, because she welcomed the spies, was not killed with those who were disobedient" (Heb. 11:31).

Because she was willing to help the two strangers, Rahab saved her own life, as well as the lives of her whole family. Even though her life was not perfect, God used her in His plans. Sometimes the Lord requires a caring disposition and courage from you so that His kingdom can be expanded here on earth. And you do not have to be perfect either in order to be used by Him.

Heavenly Father, thank You for using even sinful people in Your kingdom. Make me willing to help others, even though it may endanger me. Amen.

Ruth

Ruth replied, "Don't urge me to leave you or to turn back from you. Where you go I will go, and where you stay I will stay. Your people will be my people and your God my God." Ruth 1:16

Following the death of her husband and two sons, Naomi decides to return to Israel. She requests her two daughters-in-law to return to their families, but Ruth refuses. She will go where her mother-in-law goes.

The young Moabite woman is willing to leave her familiar surroundings and her family behind to travel to an unfamiliar country with her mother-in-law. She does this because she has learned to love Naomi's God, and also because she realizes that without her, her mother-in-law stands no real chance of survival.

When they arrive in Israel, she immediately starts looking for work in order to take care of Naomi and herself. God sends Boaz across her path, they get married and, to Naomi's great delight, a son is born.

Ruth's new husband is impressed with the unselfish way in which she tends to her mother-in-law. "I've been told all about what you have done for your mother-in-law. May the LORD repay you for what you have done," he says (Ruth 2:11-12).

Are you, like Ruth, willing to put your own interests aside to help your family? Ask the Lord to open your heart to them.

Lord, I apologize for not always being willing to extend a helping hand to my family. Make me unselfish, like Ruth, so that I will always be willing to help. Amen.

The Widow of Zarephath

Elijah said to her, "Don't be afraid. For this is what the LORD, *the God of Israel says: 'The jar of flour will not be used up and the jug of oil will not run dry until the day the* LORD *sends rain on the land.'" 1 Kings 17:13-14*

During a famine in Israel, the Lord instructed the prophet Elijah to go to a widow in Zarephath so that she could take care of him. When he asked the widow for water and bread, she told him that she had only a handful of flour and a little oil left with which to prepare a final meal for herself and her son. However, Elijah assured the widow that her flour and oil would last till the famine was over.

Everything happened as Elijah foretold. The flour and the oil never ran out, but, in the meantime, the widow's son fell ill and died. When his distraught mother cried to Elijah, he brought her son back to life. The widow then testified, "Now I know that you are a man of God and that the word of the LORD from your mouth is the truth" (1 Kings 17:24).

If you are willing to obey God, if you are willing to share your possessions with others, you will also discover that He can perform miracles in your life.

Heavenly Father, thank You for the assurance that You will take care of me, should I be willing to be charitable and obedient. Teach me to trust in You to perform wonders for me as well. Amen.

Elisha's Hostess

One day Elisha went to the town of Shunem. A wealthy woman lived there, and she urged him to come to her home for a meal. After that, whenever he passed that way, he would stop there for something to eat. 2 Kings 4:8

This Shunammite woman was a well-to-do woman who noticed the need of a simple prophet and did something to alleviate it. Every time Elisha passed by her house, she invited him to join her for a meal. And it did not end there either. Later on, she urged her husband to build a small room on the roof of their house so that Elisha could stay there when he visited them.

The meals and the room where he could rest must have been a great luxury for Elisha. He rewarded his hospitable friend for her good deeds by promising her a son. And indeed, a year later she gave birth to a baby boy!

Many years later, when a famine broke out in Israel, the woman and her son traveled to the land of the Philistines (see 2 Kings 8). When she returned after seven years, Elisha requested the king to return her possessions to her, which he did. The hospitable woman was richly rewarded for being willing to share her food and her home with Elisha.

How hospitable are you? Make it a priority from now on to notice the needs of others and to share your privileges with those who have less than you.

Heavenly Father, thank You for providing so abundantly for each of my needs. Make me willing to share my abundance with those who are less privileged than I. Amen.

Naaman's Servant Girl

Bands from Aram had gone out and had taken captive a young girl from Israel, and she served Naaman's wife. She said to her mistress, "If only my master would see the prophet who is in Samaria! He would cure him of his leprosy."
2 Kings 5:2-3

Despite the fact that the Arameans had taken the young girl captive and she had to work as a slave, she held no grudge against Naaman. When her employer fell ill with leprosy, she immediately wanted to help him. She told her mistress that the prophet from Samaria could cure her husband. Naaman was willing to listen to the young girl and he left for Samaria where, indeed, he was cured when he washed seven times in the Jordan River, as Elisha had instructed him to do.

The fact that the young girl really cared about the people for whom she worked not only led to Naaman's cure, but he also embraced the faith of his young servant girl. "Now I know that there is no God in all the world except in Israel," he testified after being cured (v. 15).

Because a young girl was willing to ignore her own pain and reach out to her employers, an entire Assyrian family made contact with the God of Israel. From this young girl's example, you can learn not to become embittered when things do not turn out all that well for you, but rather to reach out to others and to remain a witness to the God in whom you trust.

Heavenly Father, help me to retain my faith in You, even though things do not always go well with me. Teach me to be a witness to You wherever I find myself. Amen.

A Queen Risks Her Life

Esther sent this reply to Mordecai: "Go, gather together all the Jews who are in Susa, and fast for me. When this is done, I will go to the king, even though it is against the law. And if I perish, I perish." Esther 4:15-16

When Queen Esther's uncle, Mordecai, heard of evil Haman's plot to destroy all the Jews in Susa, he asked Hathatch, one of the king's eunuchs, to plead with her to ask the king to have mercy on her people. Esther agreed, although she had not been sent for by the king in thirty days, and this brave decision could cost her her life. She asked the Jews to pray for her for three days. Then she went to see the king, although she had not been invited.

The king received her kindly. When he heard about Haman's plot against the Jews, he ordered that Haman himself be hanged on the gallows that he had erected for Mordecai. Unfortunately, the king's decree, ordering the annihilation of the Jewish people, could not be revoked, but the king allowed the Jews to defend themselves against the Persians. With God's help, they succeeded in defeating the Persians. The result of Esther's courage was that her entire nation was saved.

Esther was willing to put her life at stake for her people, because she really cared about them. She was willing to risk her life for the sake of others. What would you have done had you been in her place?

Lord, thank You for using people in Your master plan. Make me willing to be used by You, even though it may mean that I myself may be put at risk. Amen.

Mary, the Obedient

The angel said to Mary, "Do not be afraid, Mary; you have found favor with God. You will conceive and give birth to a son." "I am the Lord's servant," Mary answered. "May your word to me be fulfilled." Luke 1:30-31, 38

When an angel appeared to the young, engaged Mary, telling her that she would fall pregnant and give birth to a son who would be the Son of the Most High, she must have been immensely frightened. She also knew for certain that not one of the residents of her little town (nor her betrothed, Joseph) would believe this story. And yet Mary did not hesitate for a moment – she immediately put herself at God's disposal.

Mary's obedience eventually resulted in all those believing in her Son being able to become children of God. If it were not for her courage, you and I would never have known God. Jesus made it possible for our sins to be forgiven and for us to have eternal life.

God is still looking for women who will unconditionally obey Him and trust in Him. Usually we first think about our own comfort and convenience when we are asked to do things for the Lord. We usually put ourselves first, and then we think of other people.

Are you prepared to put yourself at God's disposal as did young Mary? Then He will fulfill His master plan through your life.

Lord, I pray for the courage to put myself unconditionally at Your disposal, even though this decision could cost me dearly in future. Amen.

Jesus Shows Compassion

Jesus had compassion on them and touched their eyes.
Immediately they received their sight and followed Him.
Matt. 20:34

When two blind men seated next to the road asked Jesus to have mercy on them, He listened immediately, although the crowd tried to keep the blind men quiet. "What do you want Me to do for you?" Jesus wanted to know. "Lord, we want our sight," was the request of the two blind men. Jesus had compassion on them and touched their eyes. They received their sight immediately and followed Him.

Jesus showed true sympathy toward others and helped them. The more one reads about Jesus' life here on earth, the more one realizes that all people can receive Jesus' caring love. This includes those (such as tax collectors and sinners) the rest of the world looks down at. When His disciples, on occasion, complained about this, He said: "I have not come to call the righteous, but sinners to repentance" (Luke 5:32).

Jesus still cares about you. He intercedes for you with His Father!

Lord Jesus, thank You that You showed so much empathy toward people while You walked this earth. It is wonderful to know that You have sympathy and understanding with all my problems and want to help me solve them. I praise You for interceding for me. Amen.

Jesus at the Wedding Feast

The master of the banquet tasted the water that had been turned into wine. Then he called the bridegroom aside and said, "You have saved the best till now." What Jesus did here in Cana of Galilee was the first of the signs through which He revealed His glory; and His disciples believed in Him.
John 2:9-11

The very first miracle that Jesus performed to demonstrate His loving care for people took place at a wedding feast. When the wine ran out, Jesus' mother went to tell Him about it. But Jesus seemed unperturbed: "Woman, why do you involve Me? My hour has not yet come" (v. 4). However, His mother knew her Son. "Do whatever He tells you," (v. 5) she told the servants.

Jesus asked the servants to fill six stone water jars (each holding approximately a hundred liters) with water and to draw some of it and take it to the master of the banquet. When the master tasted the water that had been turned into wine, he called the bridegroom aside and said to him: "Everyone brings out the choice wine first; but you have saved the best till now" (v. 10).

The time was not yet ripe for Jesus to perform miracles in public. However, He listened to His mother's request and turned water into wine because He knew how embarrassing it would have been for the bridegroom if there had not been enough wine. Although it seemed to us like an unnecessary miracle, Jesus did not hesitate to help.

Lord Jesus, thank You for performing miracles in our lives even today. Amen.

"You Feed Them"

Late in the afternoon His disciples came to Him and said,
"This is a remote place, and it's already getting late. Send the
crowds away so they can go to the nearby farms and villages
and buy something to eat." But Jesus said, "You feed them."
Mark 6:35-37

When Jesus addressed the crowds in a remote place, the disciples became concerned that the people would not have anything to eat. They asked Jesus to send the people away to go and buy food. Jesus also cared about the hungry people, but He had something else in mind. "You feed them," He said. The disciples replied that it would take eight months' wages to buy food for so many people. "How many bread do you have?" Jesus wanted to know (v. 38). "Five loaves of bread and two fish," was their reply (v. 39).

Jesus told them to have all the people sit down in groups and, taking the five loaves and the two fish, He gave thanks. Then He broke the loaves and gave them to His disciples to give to the people. After everyone had had enough to eat, there were still twelve basketfuls of broken pieces left.

We often expect others to extend a helping hand to people in need. This is not how Jesus operates. He expects you to help. You should take note of the need of others and do something about it. How many loaves do you have to hand out?

Lord Jesus, thank You for caring about people, for noticing
their hunger and feeding them. Please help me to do the same.
Amen.

Five Loaves and Two Fish

*Another of His disciples, Andrew, Simon Peter's brother,
spoke up, "Here is a boy with five small barley loaves and
two small fish, but how far will they go among so many?"
Jesus said, "Have the people sit down." John 6:8-10*

In John's account of the miracle of the five loaves, he
focuses on the young boy who was willing to give up
his lunch for others. Young boys are normally very fond
of eating! It is unusual that this little boy was so willing
to offer his lunch to Jesus.

Then the day turned into one that he would probably never ever forget in his life. With his own eyes he
saw Jesus praying, breaking his small loaves of bread
and fish, and feeding thousands of people. To crown it
all, there were twelve baskets left over after everyone
had had enough to eat. The excited young boy definitely
would have enjoyed telling this story at home.

If you truly care about others and, like the young boy
in our story, are willing to part with your possessions
so that the kingdom of Jesus may be expanded, He can
still perform miracles with your contributions today.
The important point is that you should be willing to dig
your hand into your pocket. Are you willing to share
your possessions with those who really need them?

*Lord, I pray that you would give me a caring heart so that I
may be willing to share what I have with others. Thank You
that I may know that, with my small contribution, You can
do great things in Your kingdom. Amen.*

Jesus and the Canaanite Woman

A Canaanite woman came to Him, crying out, "Lord, Son of David, have mercy on me! My daughter is demon-possessed." Matt. 15:22

We have seen how Jesus really cared about people and had compassion on them. Therefore, when the Canaanite woman, who was in such need, came to Jesus we would expect Him to help her immediately. Strangely enough, this does not happen. Jesus acts differently to the way He usually does. First, He does not answer her at all, then His words seem rather heartless: "I was sent only to the lost sheep of Israel" (v. 24).

However, the distraught mother refuses to give up, although she must have thought that Jesus did not care about her. When she once again asks Him to help, Jesus tells her it is not right to take children's bread and toss it to their dogs. Her answer totally disarms Jesus: "Yes, Lord," she says. "Even the dogs eat the crumbs that fall from their master's table" (v. 27). Now Jesus knows that the woman truly believes in Him and He heals her daughter with these words, "Woman, you have great faith! Your request is granted" (v. 28).

Sometimes, God does not answer your prayers the first – or even the tenth – time that you pray. However, if you persevere in faith and prayer, He will eventually grant you the desires of your heart, in accordance with His will.

Lord Jesus, I sometimes wonder whether You really care about me, because my prayers are not answered immediately. Please help me to persevere in praying and believing. Amen.

The Little Daughter of Jairus

A leader of the local synagogue, whose name was Jairus, arrived. When he saw Jesus, he fell at His feet, pleading fervently with Him. "My little daughter is dying," he said. "Please come and lay Your hands on her; heal her so she can live." Mark 5:22-23

A very important man named Jairus knelt in front of Jesus and pleaded with Him to come and lay His hands on his terminally ill little daughter. Jesus accompanied him immediately, but on the way to his house there was a delay. While Jesus was talking to a woman who suffered from bleeding, someone from Jairus's house arrived with the news that the girl had died.

Jairus probably thought that Jesus could not care much for either him or his little girl, because He had wasted so much time with a woman that He could just as well have healed later. But Jesus knew Jairus's thoughts, and He did care about him and his little daughter. "Don't be afraid; just believe," (v. 36) were His words to the distressed father. Jesus told the mourners that the girl was only sleeping. They laughed at Him, because they had seen for themselves that she was dead. When He took the girl's hand, she came to life again.

Jesus cares enough about you to save you from sin and to offer you eternal life.

Jesus, thank You that I can rest assured in the knowledge that You love me, even though circumstances sometimes cause me to doubt Your love. I glorify You because I have everlasting life, because You sacrificed Your life for me. Amen.

Healed by His Touch

A woman was there who had been subject to bleeding for twelve years. When she heard about Jesus, she came up behind Him in the crowd and touched His cloak. Immediately her bleeding stopped and she felt in her body that she was freed from her suffering. Mark 5:25, 27, 29

On the way to Jairus's house, the people crowded around Jesus as usual. Among them was a woman who had been suffering from an illness that had been a source of great embarrassment to her for twelve years. She firmly believed that if she could just touch His clothes, she would be healed. And indeed, when she touched Jesus, a miracle happened. She could feel in her body that she had been freed from her suffering.

And Jesus? Even though there were dozens of people rubbing against Him and touching Him, He knew immediately when the woman touched Him. "Who touched My clothes?" He asked (v. 30). Then the woman fell down at His feet and told Him the whole truth.

Although He was in a great hurry, Jesus found time for her. He listened to her and told her that her faith had healed her, and that she had been freed from her illness.

You can take your personal problems to Jesus with the utmost confidence. He cares about you, He already knows about your crises and, should you reach out to Him in faith, He will grant you the wisdom to work through your problems.

Lord Jesus, thank You that I can come to You with all my problems, my anxieties and my doubts. I know for sure that You will listen to me and help me. Amen.

Four Men Bring Their Friend to Jesus

Some men came, bringing to Him a paralyzed man, carried by four of them. Since they could not get him to Jesus because of the crowd, they made an opening in the roof above Jesus by digging through it and then lowered the mat the man was lying on. Mark 2:3-4

These four men really cared about their paralyzed friend. They carried him to the house where Jesus was teaching, but when they could not reach Him because of the crowds of people, they made an opening in the flat roof and lowered their paralyzed friend in front of Jesus' feet.

When Jesus saw the faith of the four friends, He said to the paralyzed man, "Son, your sins are forgiven" (v. 5). When the teachers of the law who were sitting there rebuked Him because He seemed to be blaspheming, Jesus proved to them that He indeed had the authority to forgive sins. He said to the paralyzed man, "I tell you, get up, take your mat and go home" (v. 11).

Right before the eyes of the astounded onlookers, the paralyzed man got up, took his mat and walked out. The people were amazed. They praised God, saying, "We have never seen anything like this!" (v. 12).

The caring attitude of the four friends toward their paralyzed friend resulted in his healing. True faith does not mind sacrifice, especially not where others who could be helped in this way are concerned. Always be willing to help those who need it.

Heavenly Father, help me to help others who are in need and to spare no pains to bring them to You. Amen.

Jesus and the Little Children

People were bringing little children to Jesus for Him to place His hands on them, but the disciples rebuked them. When Jesus saw this, He was indignant. He said to them, "Let the little children come to Me, and do not hinder them, for the kingdom of God belongs to such as these." And He took the children in His arms, placed His hands on them and blessed them. Mark 10:13-14, 16

When Jesus was on earth, society did not regard children as important. For this reason, the disciples tried to prevent the mothers from bringing their children to Jesus. They probably felt that the children would waste Jesus' time. However, Jesus was indignant about the actions of the disciples and passionately declared, "Let the little children come to me, and do not hinder them, for the kingdom of God belongs to such as these" (v. 14).

Jesus demonstrated His caring love for children (and other people who were unimportant in the eyes of the world), by taking them in His arms and touching them. Remember that you should accept God's guidance and sovereignty like a child, and that you must believe in Him unconditionally if you want to be assured of a place in heaven.

Lord Jesus, thank You that You love children and that they are the most important people in Your kingdom. I pray that You would grant me the disposition of a child, so that I will accept Your guidance and sovereignty unconditionally in my own life. Amen.

"Go and Do Likewise"

"Which of these three do you think was a neighbor to the man who fell into the hands of robbers?" The expert in the law replied, "The one who had mercy on him." Jesus told him, "Go and do likewise." Luke 10:36-37

One of the most beautiful parables that Jesus told was that of the good Samaritan who found an injured man next to the road. Although a priest and a Levite walked past the man, neither was willing to help him.

However, a Samaritan came along and bandaged the man's wounds, put him onto his own donkey and took him to an inn. When he had to continue on his journey the next day, he left money with the innkeeper so that the man could receive further care.

We would have expected the priest and the Levite to help the injured man, but they walked past. The Samaritan, who was actually an enemy of the Jews, was the one who cared about the injured man and helped him. In those days, it was totally unacceptable for a Jew to be touched by a Samaritan, because they looked down on Samaritans. It is the person we least expect who demonstrates compassion for his neighbor.

Jesus wants to teach you that you cannot choose your neighbor. Every person is your neighbor. Jesus expects you to follow the Samaritan's example and reach out to others – even though they may belong to a race or faith different from your own.

Lord Jesus, please teach me to truly care for other people. Help me not to hesitate in offering my help, but to reach out to those people who need it. Amen.

Mary Anoints Jesus' Feet

Then Mary took about a pint of pure nard, an expensive perfume; she poured it on Jesus' feet and wiped His feet with her hair. And the house was filled with the fragrance of the perfume. John 12:3

Shortly before His crucifixion, Jesus had dinner with Simon the leper. While the guests were eating, Mary took out a jar of very expensive perfume and poured it on Jesus' feet. With her unselfish, but rather extravagant deed, Mary gave her all to Jesus. She demonstrated her love for Him in a way that left no doubt.

Judas was the first to condemn her. He was of the opinion that the nard could have been sold and the money given to the poor. But Jesus disagreed. He knew that Mary's love for Him was sincere and that her offering came from her heart. "Leave her alone," He said to the disciples. "It was intended that she should save this perfume for the day of my burial. You will always have the poor among you, but you will not always have Me" (John 12:7-8).

Mary demonstrated her care for Jesus in the form of a very expensive perfume that she poured on His feet. What do you do to assure Him of your love? Are you, like Mary, willing to be extravagant, or are you still calculating the cost?

Lord Jesus, thank You that You did not calculate the cost of Your love for me, but were willing to be crucified for me. Help me, like Mary, to offer You my all. Amen.

The Criminal on the Cross

Then he said, "Jesus, remember me when you come into Your kingdom." Jesus answered him, "Truly I tell you, today you will be with Me in paradise." Luke 23:42-43

When Jesus was taken away to be crucified, there were two criminals with Him. One was crucified on His right, the other on His left.

One of the criminals ridiculed Jesus and asked Him, "Aren't You the Messiah? Save Yourself and us!" (v. 39) However, the other criminal rebuked him, saying: "Don't you fear God. We are punished justly. But this Man has done nothing wrong" (v. 40-41). Then he turned to Jesus with a request: "Jesus, remember me when You come into Your kingdom."

Although Jesus was suffering great physical and spiritual pain, He heard this request and granted it without delay. The criminal deserved the death penalty, but Jesus promised him heaven itself.

Grace is something that no one can earn, but it is freely given by God to people who believe in Him. The condemned criminal did not deserve Jesus' sympathy, but Jesus truly cared for him, irrespective of His own pain and suffering. On the cross, the criminal received God's gift of grace that opened the way to heaven.

You too do not deserve God's grace. However, Jesus offers it to you because He loves you and cares for you. Do not hesitate to accept God's gift.

Lord Jesus, thank You for enabling me to be with You in paradise one day, although I deserve it as little as the criminal who was crucified with You. Amen.

"Father, Forgive Them ..."

When they came to the place called the Skull, they crucified Him there, along with the criminals. Jesus said, "Father, forgive them, for they do not know what they are doing."
Luke 23:33-34

Jesus loved us so much that He not only sacrificed heaven to come and live on earth as an ordinary man, but even died on the cross for us. Yet He was rejected by His own people, who had Him crucified, although He was completely innocent. But Jesus did not stop caring for them. He prayed that His Father would forgive those who sentenced Him to death, because they did not know what they were doing.

In contrast to Jesus' compassion and forgiving love for them, the behavior of those around Him was completely heartless. They divided up His clothes among them. The last sign of His human dignity was taken away from Him.

This is the kind of rejection that Jesus had to suffer in order to earn grace and salvation for those who believe in Him. This is how every believer can expect to be treated by a world that has rejected God's greatest gift.

Jesus demonstrated His love and compassion for you on the cross. Because He paid the price for your sins in full, God is now willing to forgive all of them.

Lord Jesus, thank You that You love me so much that You were willing to be crucified for me. Help me to demonstrate my love for You and my compassion toward others through my life. Amen.

A Widow Opens Her Heart

In Joppa there was a disciple named Tabitha (in Greek her name is Dorcas); she was always doing good and helping the poor. Acts 9:36

Luke described Tabitha as a woman who demonstrated her compassion in everything she did for others. She was always doing good and helping those less privileged than herself. Her good deeds were proof of her loving heart. She did not only give of her possessions, but also of her time and energy. We read that she made clothes for the poor.

When she suddenly fell ill and died, the widows to whom she had been so good were inconsolable. They called Peter to Joppa, took him to the room upstairs where her body was lying and told him how good she had been to them. They also showed him the clothing that she had made for them with her own hands.

Peter saw that the widows were truly sad about the death of their benefactor. He sent them out of the room and prayed fervently. Then he commanded, "Tabitha, get up," whereupon Tabitha opened her eyes and sat up. The widows were overcome with joy because God had given Tabitha back to them.

You can also serve God by doing good to others. Does your life bear testimony to the fact that you belong to God?

Heavenly Father, thank You that You take such good care of me. Grant me a heart that is open toward others, so that I, like Tabitha, may become aware of the needs of others and always be willing to do good. Amen.

One of the Least

"The King will reply, 'Truly I tell you, whatever you did for one of the least of these brothers and sisters of Mine, you did for Me.'" Matt. 25:40

Jesus concluded His last sermon before His crucifixion with a description of those things that will count the most with God during the last judgment. God sets a premium on the love and compassion that His children display toward others. When Jesus returns He is going to test the love and compassion that people demonstrated on earth. And this test will determine who will be allowed into His kingdom.

Jesus called the poor and the needy "brothers and sisters of Mine" and He clearly stated that if you care about such people, it is proof of your relationship with Him. What you do for others on this earth, you do for Jesus. But the opposite is also true: That which you have neglected to do, you have not done for Jesus either.

Your conduct toward others is an indication of how much you care about Jesus. That which you do to others, you indirectly do to Jesus. Therefore we need to go and truly think about what Jesus' words mean exactly before we again refuse a request of someone who needs our help. When a beggar knocks on your door, remember that he is "one of the least".

Lord Jesus, You were always ready to help others. Please make me willing to do the same. Let me never forget that what I do for others, I also do for You. Amen.

Forgive One Another

Bear with each other and forgive one another if any of you has a grievance against someone. Forgive as the Lord forgave you. And over all these virtues put on love. Col. 3:13-14

Christians should bear with each other and be willing to forgive one another, Paul wrote to the Christians in Colosse. The Greek word that has been translated as "bear with" implies giving someone a second chance. Jesus personally set us an example of forgiveness. He told Peter that we should be willing to forgive one another "seventy times seven" (see Matt. 18:22). (In the Bible the number seven represents perfection. But Jesus multiplied this ten times.) Therefore, according to Jesus, forgiveness should have no limits.

If you truly care for other people you should be willing to forgive them when they have transgressed against you. You should not record their mistakes, but rather overlook them. If you do not carry God's love in your heart, you will try in vain to forgive. To forgive as Jesus requires of us means that you will have to be willing to sacrifice many things and should forgive everybody.

This kind of forgiveness is not part of human nature. However, this is the kind of forgiveness you need to develop if you wish to be more like Jesus.

Lord Jesus, I pray that You would teach me to forgive like You, to be willing to offer my forgiveness freely – up to seventy times seven. I know that I will never be able to do this on my own – thank You that it is indeed possible through the working of Your Spirit. Amen.

Carry Each Other's Burdens

Carry each other's burdens, and in this way you will fulfill the law of Christ. Gal. 6:2

Many people today do not take notice of one another any more, because time has become a luxury. We simply no longer really care about each other, because of our hurried lifestyles. However, this is not how a Christian should live. You should really care about others and take notice when other believers suffer. Help them bear their problems. Do not let them wrestle with them all alone. This is what Jesus expects of us.

To really care about others implies that you should be willing to place yourself in their shoes so that you will really know what they think and how they feel. In Romans 12, Paul gives a practical description of this kind of caring: "Love must be sincere. Share with the Lord's people who are in need. Practice hospitality. Rejoice with those who rejoice; mourn with those who mourn" (vv. 9, 13, 15).

The way in which you treat other people reveals whether or not you belong to Christ. You should be a window of Jesus' caring love to others. When people observe the things that you do, they should notice Him. From now on, try to follow John's advice: "Whoever claims to live in Him must live as Jesus did" (1 John 2:6).

Lord Jesus, please enable me to care the way You cared, to live the way You lived, to notice other people's needs and help them. Amen.

Friends Sharpen One Another

Perfume and incense bring joy to the heart, and the pleasantness of one's friend springs from their heartfelt advice. As iron sharpens iron, so one person sharpens another.
Prov. 27:9, 17

Two friends who really care about each other have a lasting influence on one another. Through their mutual interactions, they sharpen one another. If your friend is honest, your crooked transactions are going to result in your having such a guilty conscience that you will begin doing the right thing. If you know that your friend does not like you to use bad language, you will do your utmost to get rid of this bad habit.

But the opposite is also true. Undesirable friends can have a negative influence on your life. If your friends drink too much or use drugs, you might feel pressured to follow their example. Ensure that your influence on your friends is always positive. True friends should reprimand one another if necessary, even though it is not always easy or pleasant to do so.

Jesus set us the perfect example with regard to friends: "Greater love has no one than this: to lay down one's life for one's friends. You are My friends if you do what I command" (John 15:13-14).

Do you care sufficiently about your friends to set a good example for them, and not to withhold your advice when you see that they are doing wrong?

Lord Jesus, thank You for friends who sharpen me. Make me a friend to them as You are a friend to me and help me to be totally obedient to You. Amen.

Submit to One Another

Submit to one another out of reverence for Christ. Wives, submit yourselves to your own husbands as you do to the Lord. Eph. 5:21-22

Ephesians 5:22 is a verse that many women do not like, because not all of us like to submit to our husbands! However, if we read verse 21 first, we really should have no problem with this command. In the first place, husband and wife must submit to one another out of reverence for Christ. When He comes first in our lives, we become less important. Our relationship with Christ should be the cornerstone of our marriages and our relationships. The submission of which Paul speaks means that we will demonstrate our caring love for one other in marriage by being willing to yield and put our marriage partner first.

A happy marriage requires two unselfish marriage partners who will demonstrate their caring love to each other in word and deed every day. Tell your husband that you love him, and admire him. Show him in a thousand and one little ways. Forget about your "rights" in marriage and do your utmost to make your husband happy. This kind of caring love is more infectious than measles and will cause him to assure you of his love. He will go out of his way to demonstrate that he really cares about you. And then it will be easy to submit to one another out of reverence for Christ.

Lord Jesus, thank You that You have given me a husband to love. Help me to demonstrate my caring love for him in our marriage by submitting to him. Amen.

Reach Out to People in Need

If you spend yourselves in behalf of the hungry and satisfy the needs of the oppressed, then your light will rise in the darkness, and your night will become like the noonday.
Isa. 58:10

T housands of people in the world die of hunger every day. Millions of people throughout the world live in extreme poverty. In the Indian city of Calcutta there are millions of people who live on the streets and have to survive on charity. They do not have access to even the most basic facilities. In many other countries hundreds of thousands of homeless people live in desperate conditions. Because most of us live in comfortable houses, with enough food every day, we can scarcely imagine how these people have to live.

God expects you to be willing to reach out to the poor, to share your food with the hungry, to provide the poor wanderer with shelter, to clothe the naked (see v. 7). Get involved with relief schemes in your area. If you are willing to give to people in need and to extend a helping hand to them, you will be rewarded. Then the Lord promises to bless you, to guide you always, to satisfy your needs and to strengthen you (see v. 11). You may gladly take Him at His Word – He always fulfills His promises!

Father, there are so many people around me who are in need that I sometimes feel it is not worth trying to help them. I pray that You would help me to meet their needs as You meet mine. Amen.

Comfort One Another

God, who comforts us in all our troubles, so that we can comfort those in any trouble with the comfort we ourselves have received from God. 2 Cor. 1:3-4

The people around you do not only have material needs, but also emotional needs. There are probably more people in your vicinity who need a hug or a sympathetic ear than there are people who suffer from a lack of food. If your heart is truly open to others, you will quickly realize when there is someone close to you who needs comfort.

Because you have been on the receiving end of God's comfort, you know full well how you, in turn, can comfort other people: "Strengthen the feeble hands, steady the knees that give way; say to those with fearful hearts, 'Be strong, do not fear; your God will come'" (Isa. 35:3-4).

If there are some of your friends or acquaintances who need to be comforted, be there for them. Visit them, pray for them, but above all, tell them that God loves them and that He is there with them. Find time for others in your busy program. Be willing to listen to them, without offering too much advice. Sometimes people are only looking for someone who will really listen. Offer your sympathy to people who need to be comforted.

And, when you are in need, pocket your pride and go and talk to your friends.

Lord Jesus, thank You that You are always there for me. Teach me to notice the pain of others and to comfort them as You comfort me. Amen.

October

Characteristics of God's Children

The Bible teaches us that there are various distinguishing features that God wants to see developed in the lives of His children.

Some of them can only be given to you by God, others depend to a large extent on your own attitude and outlook on life – the better you know God, the closer you live to Him, the more clearly these characteristics will be seen in your life. Each one of them is then also a distinguishing feature that was clearly evident in the life of Jesus.

Each day of the month that lies ahead, meditate on one of these distinguishing features. If there are some of these that are not yet visible in your life – do your best to acquire them. Perhaps you will need to work on some of these features – if you manage to incorporate them into your life with the help of God you will find that you will reap the positive fruit of them for the rest of your life.

Lord Jesus,
I really want to be more like You
by developing in my life the distinguishing
features that You lived out on earth.
Help me to trust You to
satisfy my desires and to care for me.
Help me to believe in You even though
Your promises have not yet come to pass in my life;
to be able to obey You completely and to follow
the guidelines in Your Word.
Make it possible for me to love God
with my whole heart, soul and mind
and to love my neighbor as myself.
I really want to serve You with the gifts that
I have received from You. I pray for Your wisdom
in my life and a thirst for knowledge of You.
I really do want to persevere in spite of my
circumstances; I want to be willing to serve
and be thankful in all things. I want to worship
You and radiate Your glory.
Make me hospitable to all people,
humble, honest, courageous and willing
to be of one mind, and dependent on You.
I praise You because You give me courage
when I am feeling discouraged and forgive my sins.
Thank You for Your joy that I can
pass on to others and for the hope
of the glory that lives in me.
Make me diligent and
patient with others as You are with me,
trustworthy and prepared to live a holy life.
I ask this in Your wonderful name,
Amen.

Trust in God

That is why I am suffering as I am. Yet this is no cause for shame, because I know whom I have believed, and am convinced that He is able to guard what I have entrusted to Him until that day. 2 Tim. 1:12

It seems as if Timothy's zeal was cooling down. He was no longer as enthusiastic about proclaiming the gospel as he had been in the beginning. In his letter, Paul encourages him to once again stir up the gifts that he has received from God and to work through the difficulties with the strength that God provides. Paul wrote this letter while he was in prison, but in spite of the troubles that he had to endure he knew the One in whom he trusted and was convinced that God was mighty enough to care for him until Jesus returned.

God wants you to trust Him at all times; to yield your whole life to Him with the certain knowledge that He will undertake on your behalf. Trusting in God is a way of life. And no one who has completely trusted in God has ever been disappointed.

If you are prepared to put your trust in God, you will be able to make the beautiful promise in Psalm 37:3-5 your own: "Trust in the LORD and do good; dwell in the land and enjoy safe pasture. Take delight in the LORD, and He will give you the desires of your heart. Commit your way to the LORD; trust in Him and He will do this."

Heavenly Father, I praise You that You are the One in whom I can trust. I now want to take Your promise for myself: Thank You that You will make my heart's desires a reality and will care for me always. Amen.

Have Faith

Now faith is confidence in what we hope for and assurance about what we do not see. This is what the ancients were commended for. Heb. 11:1-2

Faith and trust lie very close to each other. Faith is, after all, a steadfast trusting in the things we hope for; the evidence of the things that we cannot yet see, according to the writer of Hebrews. And if we do not have this faith in our hearts, it is impossible for us to please God.

If you sometimes struggle to believe, look at the faith of a child. Children believe without insisting on proof, simply because they love their heavenly Father and trust Him. Faith is not knowing what the future holds, but knowing Who holds the future. Faith asks you to make the promises of God your own, even if they have not yet come to pass in your life. It is impossible to believe from within yourself, because it is only God who can establish faith in your heart.

The Scripture verse that sums up faith so well comes from Mark 9:23-24: "Everything is possible for one who believes," Jesus said to the father of the son who was possessed by evil spirits. The father of the boy cried out immediately, "Help me overcome my unbelief!"

If you believe, all things will be possible for you, and God Himself will help you in the areas where you still doubt.

Heavenly Father, sometimes I struggle to believe – thank You that everything is possible for the one who believes. Please strengthen my faith. Amen.

Obedience

In the way of righteousness there is life; along that path is immortality. Prov. 12:28

Faith and obedience are closely linked. The person who obeys God also trusts in Him. Dietrich Bonhoeffer declares frankly, "He who is not obedient cannot believe."

How obedient are you? God asks for and expects obedience from His children. Unfortunately we are not always prepared to give Him this absolute obedience – we are far too fond of getting our own way and following our own direction. Do you see your way clear to obeying the commands of God without questioning and without counting the cost if you obey?

Jesus is the perfect example of someone who was absolutely obedient. He was even willing to leave heaven and come to earth as an ordinary person, to die on a cross because His Father asked Him to. In Philippians 2:8 Paul writes, "Being found in appearance as a man, He humbled Himself and became obedient to death – even death on a cross!"

If you are prepared to obey the commandments and guidelines God gives you in His Word, the promise in Exodus 19:5 is addressed to you: "If you obey Me fully and keep My covenant, then out of all nations you will be My treasured possession."

Heavenly Father, please forgive me for my stubborn disobedience and help me from now on to be absolutely obedient to You. Amen.

Love for God

Jesus replied: "'Love the Lord your God with all your heart and with all your soul and with all your mind.' This is the first and greatest commandment." Matt. 22:37-38

When one of the teachers of the law wanted to know from Jesus what the greatest commandment in the law was, Jesus immediately had an answer ready: To love the Lord your God with all your heart and with all your soul and with all your mind – the first and greatest commandment, He told him. Jesus clearly indicated that no exceptions can be made here: It is imperative that love for God must be the most important thing in your life.

"To love God with the strength of the understanding, the strength of the emotions and the strength of the will – this forms the foundation for a true Christian and a truly balanced and strong character," writes Stanley Jones.

This love for God is again linked to obedience: "This is how we know that we love the children of God: by loving God and carrying out His commands. This is love for God: to keep His commands" (1 John 5:2-3).

How much do you love God? Can you honestly say that you love God with all that you are? That there is absolutely nothing in your life that is as important as He is? If so, you will be obedient to Him and your love for Him will be seen in the things that you do.

Heavenly Father, I truly want to love You with my whole heart, my whole soul and my whole mind. Help me to show my love through the things that I do for You. Amen.

Love for One Another

"A new command I give you: Love one another. As I have loved you, so you must love one another. By this everyone will know that you are My disciples, if you love one another."
John 13:34-35

When Jesus answered a trick question from an "expert of the law" about the most important commandment, He added something else after saying we should love God with all that we are: "And the second is like it: 'Love your neighbor as yourself.'" (Matt. 22:39).

"The love of God is meaningless if it is not crowned with love for your fellow human beings," writes Martin Buber. Jesus issued a command to His disciples: They were to love one another in the same way He loved them. And He was prepared to give His life for them.

Jesus' command is still valid today. The only way in which other people can see that you belong to God is when you love all people unconditionally, just as Jesus did. Love has always been the distinguishing mark of Christians. John puts it very clearly: "If anyone has material possessions and sees a brother or sister in need but has no pity on them, how can the love of God be in that person?" (1 John 3:17).

Whether you love other people as much as God asks you to can be seen from the things that you are prepared to do for others. Love is never a feeling but a sacrificial attitude; of being prepared to wash the feet of others, just as Jesus did.

Lord Jesus, teach me to love others with the same unconditional, sacrificial love with which You love me. Amen.

Creativity

A wife of noble character who can find? She is worth far more than rubies. In her hand she holds the distaff and grasps the spindle with her fingers. She makes coverings for her bed; she is clothed in fine linen and purple. She makes linen garments and sells them, and supplies the merchants with sashes.
Prov. 31:10, 19, 22, 24

Creativity comes from God because He is the Creator God. In the beginning God created the universe, the world and all that is in it out of nothing. He also gives His children talents and abilities so that they can be creative.

In 2 Chronicles 2:14 the master craftsman Hiram's exceptional creativity is described: "He is trained to work in gold and silver, bronze and iron, stone and wood, and with purple and blue and crimson yarn and fine linen. He is experienced in all kinds of engraving." When the writer of Proverbs gives us one of the most complete prototypes of a wife in today's Scripture reading, her creativity is an important aspect of her character.

God gave you creative talents with which you can serve Him. How creative are you? Consider carefully whether or not you have done everything in your ability to develop your creativity; to be able to look at things with different eyes. It is only when you are prepared to work on your creativity that God will bless it. Do not delay any longer!

Lord, thank You that You have made me a creative person. Help me to develop my talents and to build them up so that I can use them in Your service. Amen.

Knowledge

His God instructs him and teaches him the right way. All this also comes from the LORD Almighty, whose plan is wonderful, whose wisdom is magnificent. Isa. 28:26, 29

K nowledge and wisdom to be able to do the right thing at the right time comes from the Lord, says the prophet Isaiah to the leaders of Jerusalem. Only God can help us to live right and to do the right things. People who refuse to listen to Him are heading for disaster.

In the book of Proverbs knowledge is very highly esteemed: "My son, pay attention to my wisdom, turn your ear to my words of insight, that you may maintain discretion and your lips may preserve knowledge" (Prov. 5:1-2). "Whoever loves discipline loves knowledge, but whoever hates correction is stupid" (Prov. 12:1).

Although knowledge comes from God, you can do much to sharpen your own knowledge of God and His Word. There are many ways to broaden your spiritual knowledge. One such way is to invest in a library of spiritual books about various topics that interest you.

The more you read, the more you will learn and the more knowledge you will gather. And the more knowledge of God you have, the more you will realize exactly how wonderful He is.

Heavenly Father, thank You that there are so many resources available to me to broaden my knowledge of You. Help me to use my knowledge to structure my life according to Your will. Amen.

Wisdom

The fear of the LORD is the beginning of wisdom, and knowledge of the Holy One is understanding. For through wisdom your days will be many, and years will be added to your life. Prov. 9:10-11

There is a very fine distinction between knowledge and wisdom. Wisdom means to know how to correctly use the knowledge you have at your disposal. Knowledge is to know why the sea is dangerous in certain places; wisdom is the insight not to go and swim in that particular place.

Like knowledge, wisdom also comes from God. Unlike knowledge, wisdom usually only comes with the passing of time. An intelligent child can have more knowledge than an old person, but the latter will reveal more wisdom.

The wisdom that the Bible speaks of can be found through studying the Word of God and through living close to the Lord. You will need to work to gain knowledge about various subjects, while you can pray to God for wisdom: "If any of you lacks wisdom, you should ask God, who gives generously to all without finding fault" (James 1:5). If you need more wisdom in your own life so that you can better discern between right and wrong, you can ask God to give you that wisdom. He will do so willingly.

Heavenly Father, I know that wisdom begins with serving You. Please give me wisdom in my life so that I can discern between right and wrong. Amen.

Humor

I know that there is nothing better for people than to be happy and do good while they live. Eccles. 3:12

Of all the things that God created, it is only human beings to whom He has given a sense of humor. And without this sense of humor we would have been insipid, joyless beings! It has often been said that humor makes the dark side of life a little lighter. It helps you to put things in perspective and it brings people closer together. It not only feels good to laugh – it has been scientifically proven that it is good for you.

A sense of humor makes it possible for you to tackle most of your problems with a smile; it helps you to handle the crises in your life with greater ease and it allows you to be aware of the brighter side of life at all times. Furthermore, it relieves stress and tension. When you are sick or feel bad, laughing from your belly will help you feel much better. People who have a well-developed sense of humor are always popular, because we like people who make us laugh.

A humorous person is also able to laugh at himself. No wonder the writer of Proverbs came to the conclusion that things always go badly for a despondent person, but that a cheerful person's whole life is a feast (see Prov. 15:15).

Heavenly Father, thank You very much for the gift of humor and the enjoyment of a good laugh. Teach me not to take life so seriously – to be aware of the comic side of life and to share it with others. Amen.

Perseverance

You need to persevere so that when you have done the will of God, you will receive what He has promised. Heb. 10:36

There is a wonderful story of a snail that started climbing up an apple tree one cold winter's day. While he was creeping up the bottom of the trunk, a worm stuck its head out of a hole in the bark, "You're wasting your time, there is not one single apple up there," he said. "By the time I get there, there will be," answered the snail. Perseverance means that you are prepared to endure right to the end, in spite of your circumstances.

There are quite a few places in the Bible where believers are encouraged to persevere. In Matthew 10:22, Jesus warns His followers about the persecution that lay ahead, but at the same time He promised, "The one who stands firm to the end will be saved." James writes, "The testing of your faith produces perseverance. Let perseverance finish its work so that you may be mature and complete, not lacking anything" (James 1:3-4).

Is perseverance a value that is evident in your life? Usually it is difficulties that nurture perseverance. With God's strength He will truly make it possible for you to be able to continue and persevere – to be able to endure to the end, so that you will be able to do the will of God and receive the things that He has promised.

Heavenly Father, I pray that You would help me to endure to the end, to persevere until each one of Your promises comes to pass in my life, and that I can receive the heavenly prize that You have promised. Amen.

Thankfulness

Give thanks in all circumstances; for this is God's will for you in Christ Jesus. 1 Thess. 5:18

T hankfulness ought to be a distinguishing characteristic of every Christian. We know that everything we have is because of God; everything we are and own comes from Him. And that is why we should never stop thanking Him. "Be thankful," writes Paul to the church in Colosse: "Let the message about Christ, in all its richness, fill your lives. Teach and counsel each other with all the wisdom He gives. Sing psalms and hymns and spiritual songs to God with thankful hearts" (Col. 3:16).

Most of us manage to be thankful without great struggle when things are going well for us. But when we are sick or confronted with problems or if a disaster occurs in our lives, it is much more difficult. "One act of thanksgiving when things go wrong is worth a thousand thanks when things go right," says John of Avila.

And yet God can make it possible for you to remain thankful in all situations. No matter how badly things are going for you, you still know that God is with you, that He will carry you through adversity and will protect you in dangerous situations. Therefore, when you are tempted to doubt God's love in times of hardship, remember that He is in control; He will ultimately work all things out for your good!

Heavenly Father, I am sorry that my gratitude is sometimes shipwrecked when things do not go well for me. Make me thankful in all things because that is what You expect from me. Amen.

Willingness to Serve

Brothers and sisters, each person, as responsible to God, should remain in the situation they were in when God called them. 1 Cor. 7:24

Trrue ministry implies being willing to be of service to God and others without receiving any acknowledgement for it. Jesus came to teach us exactly what is meant by being willing to serve. Matthew 20:26-28: "Whoever wants to become great among you must be your servant, and whoever wants to be first must be your slave – just as the Son of Man did not come to be served, but to serve, and to give His life as a ransom for many," He said to James and John when they came to ask Him if they could sit one on either side of Him in His kingdom.

Paul impresses upon us that God has already placed each one of us in the exact place where He wants us to serve. You need never look for a different place to serve God. Rather be prepared to serve in your own town and in your own community: Be available for other people, take note of their needs and do something about them.

God is Almighty, but He works on earth through His children. It is with your hands that He does His work here and with the money in your purse His kingdom is extended. Therefore, report for service in His kingdom and see how He will use you for His honor.

Lord Jesus, please prepare me to serve You and other people in the place where You have placed me. Thank You that I can be Your hands and feet in this world. Amen.

Hospitality

Don't forget to show hospitality to strangers, for some who have done this have entertained angels without realizing it! Heb. 13:2

I t is rather pertinent that Bible characters were extremely hospitable. Abraham actually did entertain angels through his hospitality (see Gen. 18:1-8) and in the New Testament Christians are frequently urged to be hospitable. Peter writes that we should be hospitable without complaining about it (see 1 Pet. 4:9) and Paul singles out hospitality as one of the guidelines for Christian behavior (see Rom. 12:13).

It is rather dangerous to offer your hospitality to just anyone who knocks on your front door these days. But God still expects His children to reach out to others, and to be hospitable to other Christians.

Hospitality is a deeply rooted, inward attitude of openness and sharing. Perhaps our hospitality in the busy world in which we live has suffered because we put too much effort into it. It is not necessary to go to all sorts of trouble when you invite people for a meal. Soup and bread is enough because hospitality is not about how smart the host is or about how wonderful the food tastes – it is about the art of letting people feel welcome and at home and opening your house to them.

Do not hold back from being hospitable to others. Open your heart and your home.

Lord, forgive me for so often being reluctant to receive other people into my home. Please give me an attitude of true hospitality. Amen.

Worship

Yet a time is coming and has now come when the true worshipers will worship the Father in the Spirit and truth, for they are the kind of worshipers the Father seeks. God is spirit, and His worshipers must worship in the Spirit and in truth." John 4:23-24

God takes pleasure in His children coming to kneel before Him in worship. Worship is more than simple prayer. Rick Warren explains it very well: "Worship is far more than praise, singing and praying to God. Worship is a lifestyle of finding delight in God, loving Him and giving ourselves to Him so that we can be used for His purposes. When you yield your life to seeing God glorified, everything that you do becomes an act of worship."

It is wonderful to communicate with God through prayer in your quiet time. But your worship should not end when you get up from your knees – it should continue through your busy day so that you are connected to God: when you are driving to work, when you are at work, in your interaction with other people, when you admire the beauties of nature … In everything that you do, say and think, you should be worshiping God.

The more you learn to know God and the more time you set aside for Him, the easier it will be for you to worship Him. Ask the Holy Spirit to teach you to learn to worship God in Spirit and in truth.

Holy Spirit, teach me the secret of worship: to acknowledge the greatness of God every moment of my life and to praise Him for that. Amen.

Unity

I appeal to you, brothers and sisters, in the name of our Lord Jesus Christ, that all of you agree with one another in what you say and that there be no divisions among you, but that you be perfectly united in mind and thought. 1 Cor. 1:10

One of the distinguishing features that God expects to see in us and with which Christians struggle the most is unity. We just can't get it right to be truly one, and the reason for this is due to our inherent stubbornness and selfishness.

We all want to follow our own lead and expect that the rest of the community should fall in with us. When Jesus prayed for His disciples, He asked, "I pray that they will all be one, just as You and I are one – as You are in Me, Father, and I am in You. And may they be in Us so that the world will believe You sent Me" (John 17:21).

Our faith in Jesus requires that we, as His children, should be one; that we would, as described in the book of Acts (2:44), be of one mind. Oneness in Christ does not require of us to all think the same and be exactly the same, but for unity to appear in our actions because we do what He asks of us and are obedient to Him.

Like God's team in this world we need to follow God's pattern and have the same goal. This is, after all, what Jesus did. Are you willing to be one with your brothers and sisters in the faith?

Lord Jesus, I pray that You would make me prepared to let go of my inflexibility and become one with the rest of my church community, just as You and the Father are one. Amen.

Simplicity

Better to be lowly in spirit along with the oppressed than to share plunder with the proud. Prov. 16:19

Any experienced traveler will know that the less baggage you take with you the easier and more satisfying the journey is. This is also true of your journey through life.

Unfortunately, most people in the world today have become so attached to their earthly possessions that very few are satisfied with simplicity. We want everything that our neighbors have and we buy everything that our eyes see, whether we can afford it or not. Our possessions demand all our time, energy and money, to such an extent that we forget to be happy because we are so absorbed in gathering things. Rather follow the example of Jesus; He had very few possessions and He did not even have a place to lay down His head.

Perhaps the time has come for us to focus on simplicity and get rid of the things that we do not really need: the clothes from years ago, the "time saving" gadgets that never get used … The older people get the more they realize that one can live quite happily with half the number of possessions.

Make a point of simplifying your life by channeling the excess things that complicate your life to the people who really need them. Then you will once again discover how simplicity can set you free and make you happy.

Lord, please forgive me for being like a magpie who hoards attractive things. Teach me how to live a simple life. Amen.

Humility

For this is what the high and exalted One says – He who lives forever, whose name is holy: "I live in a high and holy place, but also with the one who is contrite and lowly in spirit, to revive the spirit of the lowly and to revive the heart of the contrite." Isa. 57:15

God is always on the side of people who have learned to be humble. In different places in the Bible we hear about how the arrogant and proud will fall, while the humble will receive mercy.

Humility is thus also one of the characteristics that is specific to Christians. "Submit yourselves to your elders. All of you, clothe yourselves with humility toward one another, because, 'God opposes the proud but shows favor to the humble.' Humble yourselves, therefore, under God's mighty hand, that He may lift you up in due time" (1 Pet. 5:5-6).

Jesus Himself was absolutely humble. "Learn from Me, for I am gentle and humble in heart," He testifies in Matthew 11:29. "God made the world out of nothing and as long as we are nothing He can make something out of us," writes Martin Luther.

As soon as you realize your limitations and acknowledge your dependence on God; and discover that you can succeed at nothing on your own because everything comes from God, it is not that hard to be humble.

Lord Jesus, I am sorry that I struggle to be humble sometimes; that my pride and selfishness raise their heads time and time again. Make me humble so that others will be more important than me. Amen.

Honesty

The righteous lead blameless lives; blessed are their children after them. Even small children are known by their actions, so is their conduct really pure and upright? Prov. 20:7, 11

Honesty has been a very rare value throughout the centuries – but was ever as scarce as it is now in the twenty-first century? These days it is indeed a rarity to leave your handbag somewhere and to have it returned – with everything still in it.

Even in business transactions and the paying of income taxes – and this includes Christians! – it is too easy to find excuses about why it is impossible to be completely honest. In the late twentieth century the Institute of Motivational Behavior found that ninety-seven percent of all people tell lies – and that each one does so about a thousand times a year.

It seems like this dishonesty comes a long way. Just listen to what the prophet Isaiah said thousands of years ago: "No one calls for justice; no one pleads a case with integrity. They rely on empty arguments, they utter lies; they conceive trouble" (Isa. 59:4).

If you are serious about your Christianity you will need to learn to be honest and to live with integrity. Christians are supposed to be different: honest in their business transactions and money matters as well as in the things they say. If you have not yet been able to get this right, ask God to help you with it.

Lord, I realize now that I do not always act honestly. Please show me the areas where I need more integrity. Make it possible for me to be honest and upright at all times. Amen.

Courage

"The LORD Himself goes before you and will be with you; He will never leave you nor forsake you. Do not be afraid; do not be discouraged." Deut. 31:8

When Joshua was appointed as Moses' successor, Moses made him a beautiful promise: There was no reason to ever be discouraged or afraid. God Himself would go before Joshua and would be with Him. He would never let him down or leave him alone. "I will refresh the weary and satisfy the faint" (Jer. 31:25).

You and I can still depend on that same promise today, even though there are currently a whole lot of reasons to feel discouraged. If we consult the media, watch the news on TV or take our own situations into consideration, it looks like there will never be an end to the raging spiral of violence and crime. And yet the children of God ought not to get discouraged for the simple reason that God is with us; He Himself undertakes to make us courageous.

"Courage is not a permanent condition of the human spirit but a gift that people need and will receive – if they have learned to look up at heaven," writes Johan Heyns. If you ever find yourself in the Slough of Despondency you simply need to remember the promise that is written in Isaiah 35:4: "To those with fearful hearts, 'Be strong, do not fear; your God will come.'"

Heavenly Father, thank You for the promise that You will give courage to those who have become discouraged. Please do this for me today. Amen.

Forgiveness

In Him we have redemption through His blood, the forgive-
ness of sins, in accordance with the riches of God's grace that
He lavished on us. Eph. 1:7-8

When the blood of Jesus flowed on the cross, He made it possible for God to forgive your sins and mine. This is not only the sins that we have committed in the past, but also sin that we are still going to commit in the future. God is always prepared to forgive us on the grounds of the work of reconciliation of His Son. And God forgives us because He is merciful. We have to do nothing ourselves other than confess our sins in order to receive God's forgiveness.

And yet the forgiveness of God lays a great responsibility on us. When Paul gave the Ephesians a number of guidelines for new believers in Christ, he writes, "Be kind and compassionate to one another, forgiving each other, just as in Christ God forgave you" (Eph. 4:32). If you have found it difficult to forgive other people in the past, read what Jesus said in the Sermon on the Mount about forgiveness: "If you forgive other people when they sin against you, your heavenly Father will also forgive you. But if you do not forgive others their sins, your Father will not forgive your sins" (Matt. 6:14-15).

Ask God to help you to forgive other people with your whole heart, just as He is prepared to do for you.

Lord Jesus, I praise You because You died on the cross so that
my sins could be forgiven. Help me to wholeheartedly forgive
other people who have offended me. Amen.

Joy

Sing to God, sing in praise of His name, extol Him who rides on the clouds; rejoice before Him – His name is the LORD.
Ps. 68:4

God is the source of all true joy. If we do not know Him we do not yet know what it means to be happy. "God cannot give us a happiness and peace apart from Himself, because it is not there. There is no such thing," writes C. S. Lewis.

Joy, then, ought to be a distinguishing feature of the children of God. After all, you know that you have been saved, that He will always cause things to work out for your best, and that heaven awaits you.

Christians can even manage to testify as Habakkuk did, "Though the fig tree does not bud and there are no grapes on the vines, though the olive crop fails and the fields produce no food, though there are no sheep in the pen and no cattle in the stalls, yet I will rejoice in the LORD, I will be joyful in God my Savior" (Hab. 3:17-18).

If your flame of joy is burning low at the moment, you can do something about it. True joy is contagious – if you make someone happy, you will also share in their joy. God really wants to share His joy with you – stay close to Him and make other people happy; then you will be able to live each day in the sunshine of His joy.

Heavenly Father, I praise You for the joy that I experience because You are with me, and because I know You. Help me to convey this joy to every person who crosses my path. Amen.

Truth

"These are the things you are to do: Speak the truth to each other, and render true and sound judgment in your courts; do not love to swear falsely. I hate all this," declares the LORD. *Zech. 8:16-17*

T he prophet Zechariah spoke to the people about the way they were acting towards others and asked them to always speak the truth to one another and to behave righteously. In this way, service to others becomes service to God. Your social life becomes the place where you practice your faith.

Through the way you speak and behave it is easy for other people to know if you are twisting the truth or if you are honest at all times. When you are always truthful, you are trustworthy. Then other people can rely on what you say; they will know that you are dependable.

Unfortunately, there are far too many people who twist the truth rather than sticking to it. If you also assume that a little white lie is really not wrong, think again! God expects His children to speak the truth. The Bible calls the Devil the "father of lies" (John 8:44) and it is he who incites you to tell lies.

To be able to speak the truth, you need the Spirit of Truth in your life. "When He, the Spirit of truth, comes, He will guide you into all truth," Jesus promises His disciples (John 16:13). Decide to speak the truth from now on and ask the Lord to help you do so.

Father, please forgive me for the times when I have spoken untruthfully. Make it possible for me to always speak the truth so that I will be a reliable person. Amen.

Hope in the Lord

Yet this I call to mind and therefore I have hope. The LORD is my portion; therefore I will wait for Him. Lam. 3:21, 24

Things went so badly for the prophet Jeremiah that he lost all hope. "My splendor is gone and all that I had hoped from the LORD," he confesses in Lamentations 3:18. But then his hope is reignited. The reason for this is that there is no end to the mercies of God; His faithfulness is new every morning; He is good to those who continue to hope in Him.

The reasons Jeremiah had for hoping in spite of his unbearable circumstances is still applicable to you. If you believe in Jesus, you know that your hope will never be put to shame. Hope is not a feeling, but a Person: "Christ in you, the hope of glory," Paul wrote to the people in Colosse (Col. 1:27).

Thus you can fix your hope on God, because Christian hope is the certain knowledge that the promises of God will come true for you in the future; that heavenly glory awaits you. This hope can never be taken away from you, because it is fixed in God Himself.

May your hope become ever stronger until the day Jesus returns.

Lord Jesus, thank You that You are my hope for glory; that I can know for certain that You are busy preparing a place for me in heaven where I will one day be with You forever. Amen.

Diligence

Our people must learn to devote themselves to doing what is good, in order to provide for urgent needs and not live unproductive lives. Titus 3:14

P aul writes to the believers in Crete that it is necessary for them to work so that they can help other believers and make sure that they do not lack anything. The emphasis here is not on enjoyable work or well-paying work, but rather on honest work. Diligence is the answer for many whose lives are unfruitful.

In many countries there are people who really want to work, but cannot find any; there are others who do have work, but are constantly looking for ways to get out of it. It is a privilege and an opportunity to be able to work; never a right or something to try and avoid. If you are fortunate to have a job that is at the same time a calling for you, you should thank God for that every day. "I saw that there is nothing better for a person than to enjoy their work, because that is their lot. When God gives someone wealth and possessions, and the ability to enjoy them – this is a gift from God," says the writer of Ecclesiastes (see Eccles. 3:22; 5:19).

Always do your work to the very best of your ability; be thankful that you have a job and reach out to others who are not so fortunate by providing them with the basic necessities of life.

Heavenly Father, thank You so much that I have a job in which I can use my gifts. I pray for all those who cannot find a job. Please show me where I can help them. Amen.

Friendliness

The Lord's servant must not be quarrelsome but must be kind to everyone, able to teach, not resentful. 2 Tim. 2:24

Mother Teresa is surely one of the people in whom the characteristics of Jesus could clearly be seen. She committed her whole life to helping. "We shall never know all the good that a simple smile can do. Be a living embodiment of God's love – with compassion in your smile, in your eyes, in your words, in the touch of your hands," she wrote.

People ought to be able to see from the friendliness you radiate that you are a Christian. Some people are by nature friendlier than others, but each one of us can learn to be more friendly; to smile more and to do more for others in an attitude of love and friendliness.

It is not always easy to be friendly; we do not always feel equally friendly. One way of looking at it is to say that a person should put on a smile on the outside and then it will move to the inside.

How friendly are you? A smile is one of the most attractive things that there is. If someone gives one to you, you spontaneously give one back. Make a decision right now that from now on you will deliberately be friendlier to others.

Father, please forgive me for not always being as friendly as I could be. Help me to give a smile to every person I meet. Amen.

Patience

Be completely humble and gentle; be patient, bearing with one another in love. Eph. 4:2

God is unbelievably patient with us. When we read the history of the people of God in the Old Testament, we can hardly believe the extent of patience that God reveals. Over and over again He is prepared to forgive His disobedient people. Thankfully, God treats us with exactly the same patience – He is always prepared to give us another chance.

Patience is also one of the characteristics of the fruit of the Holy Spirit that Paul writes about in Galatians 5:22-23. It is therefore a quality that God seeks in each one of His children. Paul tells the Christians in Ephesus that they should always be polite, friendly and patient, and should bear with one another in love. Unfortunately, that kind of patience is not often seen among Christians. Christian patience doesn't mean to bear with one another but be bursting with irritation and frustration on the inside. Patience needs to be demonstrated through purposeful, never-ending friendliness.

If you are by nature an impatient person, ask the Lord to grant you more patience.

Heavenly Father, thank You so much for Your great patience with me. I am sorry that I am so impatient with myself and other people. Please make it possible for me to be polite, friendly and patient. Amen.

Dependence

"Blessed are the poor in spirit, for theirs is the kingdom of heaven." Matt. 5:3

In the time in which we live it is not really much of an advantage to be dependent. We would all much rather be independent; we want to be able to take care of ourselves without having to rely on someone else.

But in the Sermon on the Mount, Jesus said that it is the person who is aware of their dependence on God who is happy and blessed. It is so important to God that His children should be absolutely and completely dependent on Him, that it is the very first sentence of the Sermon on the Mount.

It is usually only when disaster strikes or when you come to the end of your own strength that you are willing to acknowledge your dependence on God. In 2 Corinthians 1:8-10 Paul talks of the problems that they experienced in Asia, and then he testifies, "Indeed, we felt we had received the sentence of death. But this happened that we might not rely on ourselves but on God" (v. 9).

Are you ready to be dependent on God in all things? To give up your independence and your will so that your life is lived in dependence on God and in line with His will? Do not put off becoming dependent and acknowledging that you are dependent on the Lord.

Lord, I am still reluctant to be dependent on You. Help me to understand that if I am willing and acknowledge my dependence, I will be part of Your kingdom. Amen.

Holiness

Let the Spirit renew your thoughts and attitudes. Put on your new nature, created to be like God – truly righteous and holy. Eph. 4:23-24

Jesus was a person just like us, with one difference: He was holy and without sin. In fact He came to earth to make it possible for us to also be holy. "Now He has reconciled you by Christ's physical body through death to present you holy in His sight, without blemish and free from accusation," writes Paul to the church in Colosse (Col. 1:22).

God wants each one of His children to be holy, just like Jesus was. For this to be possible, we need to undergo a makeover, because each one of us is born in sin. Because God is holy, you need to do everything possible to also be holy by getting rid of all the things in your life with which God is not happy. Ask Him to show you what sins are still in your life; confess these sins and let go of them. But be warned, it is not going to be easy.

How to succeed in becoming holy is clearly explained in today's Scripture verse: Your soul and mind must be made new; from now on you should live like a new person who has been created in the image of God.

Your lifestyle must be completely in line with God's will so that you can be holy, as Jesus was.

Heavenly Father, I really want to be holy like You are. Please show me what things in my life I need to get rid of so that I can live and think in a new way. From now on I want to be completely surrendered to You. Amen.

Trustworthiness

Since we have these promises, dear friends, let us purify ourselves from everything that contaminates body and spirit, perfecting holiness out of reverence for God. 2 Cor. 7:1

God is completely trustworthy. When He promised something to His people He fulfilled those promises to the letter every time. They knew that they could trust in these promises. Unfortunately, the same cannot be said of the unfaithful Israelites. They repeatedly promised to be faithful to God and His covenant, and over and over again they broke their promises.

We, like the Israelites, are also unfaithful. When we are in trouble we promise the Lord that we will turn over a new leaf if He will help us, and then we conveniently forget our promise when things go well again. Thankfully, God is still the same as He was in biblical times: Not only does every promise in the Bible apply to you, but God is still as trustworthy as He was then. "Not one of all the LORD's good promises to the house of Israel failed; every one was fulfilled" we read in Joshua 21:45.

You can depend on every promise that has been recorded in the Bible. Don't you want to undertake from now on to be more reliable and to fulfill the promises you have made to God? If you ask Him to make you more trustworthy, He will gladly do so.

Heavenly Father, please forgive me for having such a history of untrustworthiness. Make it possible for me to be trustworthy from now on and to fulfill all my promises to You to the letter. Amen.

Merciful

"Blessed are the merciful, for they will be shown mercy."
Matt. 5:7

I n the Sermon on the Mount, Jesus promises that the people who are merciful to others will themselves receive mercy. "You're blessed when you care. At the moment of being 'care-full', you will find yourselves cared for," says *The Message*. In Luke's account of the Sermon on the Mount, Jesus requests, "Be merciful, just as your Father is merciful" (Luke 6:36).

To be merciful means to have an open heart. God asks us to be merciful just as He is merciful. He asks that we be willing to help other people just as He is always prepared to help us. The compassion of God for the world does not stand apart from the compassionate actions of His children. The love of God is given visible hands when His children protect orphans, welcome strangers and help the poor.

If you are prepared to pass the compassion that God has shown to you on to other people, there is a beautiful promise for you: "If you spend yourselves in behalf of the hungry and satisfy the needs of the oppressed, then your light will rise in the darkness ... The LORD will guide you always; He will satisfy your needs in a sun-scorched land and will strengthen your frame. You will be like a well-watered garden, like a spring whose waters never fail" (Isa. 58:10-11).

Father, I pray that You would give me a heart for those in need and hands that would offer them help so that I may be merciful as You are merciful. Amen.

Peace

"Peace I leave with you; My peace I give you. I do not give to you as the world gives. Do not let your hearts be troubled and do not be afraid." John 14:27

The coming of Jesus into the world brought us peace. When He came into the world He came to make peace between God and people and He made it possible for us to live in peace with one another.

When Jesus went away He promised to leave His peace behind for His children. And this peace differs in every way from worldly peace, which in most cases means nothing more than a truce. The peace of Jesus includes an inner serenity, an absolute trust that wipes out fear and equips us to be peacemakers and to promote peace in the lives of others.

Without God in your life this kind of peace is impossible. When all is said and done, it is only God who can guarantee true peace. "Jesus Himself is our peace," writes Paul to the church in Ephesus (Eph. 2:14).

At this moment we are desperately in need of the peace of God in our country and in the world. He is still prepared to give it to us. Pray that the peace of God will come and settle in your heart; that He will make it possible for you to exchange your many fears for His peace; and that nothing will ever be able to take this peace away again.

Lord Jesus, I pray that You will give me Your peace in my life; that I will experience tranquility and be able to shake off my fears. Help me to be a peacemaker. Amen.

November

What Makes a Christian Different

While Jesus was on earth, He often talked ab[...]
love and emphasized to His followers that to [...]
God, ourselves and even our enemies is the fulfi[...]
of God's law. This love makes it possible for us[...]
off our masks that we hide behind and to be [...]
because we believe that our lives are worth[...]
eyes.

Romans 12 is the chapter in the Bible t[...]
trates the essence of Christian love. It i[...]
sacrificial love that sets a Christian apa[...]
else. In the month ahead, you will lea[...]
you to live, so that those inseparab[...]
may become evident in your life. [...]
of the month you will realize h[...]
kind of love in a practical and [...]

Use Your Gifts

We have different gifts, according to the grace given to each of us. If your gift is prophesying, then prophesy in accordance with your. Rom. 12:6

God gives a gift to each of us. You, too, have received a particular gift with which to honor Him. If you still don't know what your gift is, don't hesitate to ask a member of your family or your best friend what it is that you are really good at. Once you've done this, explore your gift and use it in your church.

Everyone's gifts are different and not everyone's gifts re equally evident. Some talents are more spectacular an others. A big fuss is often made over such people. t everyone's particular gift is equally important in d's eyes.

he significance of your gift is not as important as t you do with it. Use your gift to the honor of God ing it in His kingdom in the best possible way and ving others.

't compare your gifts to those of others. People mpare themselves with others become bitter and ied, because, in their own eyes, they always get g end of the stick.

can achieve great things with your gift, you ze that this is because of God's blessings. Give nor for it and serve Him with it.

ather, help me always to realize that my gifts ou and that I should serve You with them and he honor. Amen.

November

What Makes a Christian Different

While Jesus was on earth, He often talked about love and emphasized to His followers that to love God, ourselves and even our enemies is the fulfillment of God's law. This love makes it possible for us to take off our masks that we hide behind and to be ourselves, because we believe that our lives are worthy in God's eyes.

Romans 12 is the chapter in the Bible that most illustrates the essence of Christian love. It is precisely this sacrificial love that sets a Christian apart from everyone else. In the month ahead, you will learn how God wants you to live, so that those inseparable qualities of Jesus may become evident in your life. Hopefully, by the end of the month you will realize how to demonstrate this kind of love in a practical and real way.

Heavenly Father,
on that day that I chose You for the first time,
love entered with You into my life. I could no longer remain
the same, because Your love changes people, so that Jesus'
characteristics can be seen increasingly in their lives.
Make this change in me one that will continue:
Teach me anew how to think;
to be humble, because I know my gifts come from You.
Make it possible for me to love other people with
a love like Yours, and to hold on to the good in life.
Give me the vibrant enthusiasm I had
when I first came to Christ – and make me
completely dedicated to You again.
Help me to serve You and others unselfishly.
I praise You that every day I may rejoice in hope,
because you fulfill all of Your promises.
Help me to stand firm in tough times, to be hospitable,
to bless those who persecute me, to rejoice with those
who are happy and to mourn with those who are sad.
Make me of one mind with other Christians
and help me to be kind to them, willing to put others first,
and to live in peace with everyone. Keep me from relying on
my own wisdom, and repaying evil with evil. Show me how
to overcome evil in Your power. You first loved me, Lord,
therefore I owe all other people my love – make me willing
every day to pay off this debt of love.
Amen.

Offer Yourself to God

Offer your bodies as a living sacrifice, holy and pleasing to God – this is your true and proper worship. Rom. 12:1

Being a Christian is not always easy. That's why all of us are tempted to do things we know we shouldn't do. Today's verse challenges you to prove in all circumstances that you belong to God, even if it requires giving up something. But even more than that – you must also offer yourself as a sacrifice to God.

According to *The Message*, you should give your whole life to Him: "Take your everyday, ordinary life – your sleeping, eating, going-to-work, and walking-around life – and place it before God as an offering" (v. 1).

Fortunately, God does not only give you this instruction; He also teaches you how to achieve it. Romans 12 provides a step-by-step explanation of the general principles that should characterize a Christian's life. Paul writes that we should prove to God with all of our lives how thankful we are for the salvation He gives us.

If you really begin to live like a Christian, you can expect resistance and persecution. In the Old Testament the sacrifice of an animal was the symbol of someone's surrender to God. If you are willing to offer yourself as a sacrifice to God, you will have to allow your entire life to be controlled by His Spirit.

Are you prepared to become such a living sacrifice?

Lord Jesus, I want to give myself to You so that my entire life can be in Your service. Please make this possible for me. Amen.

Renew Your Mind

Be transformed by the renewing of your mind. Then you will be able to test and approve what God's will is – His good, pleasing and perfect will. Rom. 12:2

As God's children we must be different from the world. We must not only act and speak differently, but also think differently. We must allow God to change our thought processes and renew our minds so that we know which things are in accordance with His will.

The renewal God wants to achieve in your life begins on the inside and eventually spreads to every part of your life. God will also teach you to distinguish between your own way and God's perfect will for your life; He will help you to surrender your will and to be obedient to Him.

When God renews your mind, you will discover that you will start thinking differently about many things. You will think differently about your religion, about your relationship with God and with other people, about your calling in life. You will exchange your old, selfish way of life for a life in which other people are more important.

Slowly, in the cocoon of God's love, the caterpillar of selfishness changes into a butterfly gracefully displaying the glory of God's salvation in acts of sacrifice. Only then will you become the person God intended you to be.

Heavenly Father, please teach me to think differently. Renew my mind and give me the wisdom to know and obey Your perfect will for my life. Amen.

Don't Become Arrogant

By the grace given me I say to every one of you: Do not think of yourself more highly than you ought, but rather think of yourself with sober judgment. Rom. 12:3

Your church is where you practice self-sacrificing love and your attitude toward others should be right. Don't think more – or less – of yourself than you should. God gives gifts to each of us, and if you happen to have received more gifts than some of your friends, it is easy to forget that everything you have comes from God. It is even easier to become arrogant when people constantly praise and compliment you.

Christians should be humble and modest. After all, they are people who have discovered that their gifts and talents come from God, and should therefore use these gifts and talents in the church in His service and to His honor.

Consider your own position in your church. What are your gifts and how can they be used fruitfully in your church? Perhaps you are musical and you can join the church choir; perhaps you have leadership qualities and can offer to be on the church committee. Perhaps your gift is less evident, but you can still help by making yourself available to assist in the kitchen or to look after the children.

Everyone has a gift. Find out what yours is and use it fully – without becoming arrogant in the process.

Heavenly Father, thank You for the gifts and talents You entrusted to me. Help me to apply my particular gifts and talents to serve You and my church. Amen.

Use Your Gifts

We have different gifts, according to the grace given to each of us. If your gift is prophesying, then prophesy in accordance with your. Rom. 12:6

God gives a gift to each of us. You, too, have received a particular gift with which to honor Him. If you still don't know what your gift is, don't hesitate to ask a member of your family or your best friend what it is that you are really good at. Once you've done this, explore your gift and use it in your church.

Everyone's gifts are different and not everyone's gifts are equally evident. Some talents are more spectacular than others. A big fuss is often made over such people. But everyone's particular gift is equally important in God's eyes.

The significance of your gift is not as important as what you do with it. Use your gift to the honor of God by using it in His kingdom in the best possible way and by serving others.

Don't compare your gifts to those of others. People who compare themselves with others become bitter and dissatisfied, because, in their own eyes, they always get the wrong end of the stick.

If you can achieve great things with your gift, you must realize that this is because of God's blessings. Give Him the honor for it and serve Him with it.

Heavenly Father, help me always to realize that my gifts come from You and that I should serve You with them and give You all the honor. Amen.

Love Must Be Sincere

Love must be sincere. Rom. 12:9

Children of God are recognized by their love for God and for each other. Paul tells the Christians in Rome that their love must firstly be sincere. All of us are usually so busy with our own things that we have precious little time and attention left for other people. This is one of the reasons why our love is not always sincere. We pretend to be interested in other people's issues, while we actually only care about our own problems.

The original Greek text refers to an actor wearing a mask. Sincere love is therefore love without a mask. It is a love that is genuine and sincere, a love that puts others first, so that our own interests are less important.

In ourselves we are not capable of such a love, because it is the type of love with which God loves us. God is love, and only He can teach us to love like that; to see other people as He sees them; to look past the faults and shortcomings and love the people behind them.

Ask Him to give you this sincere love through His Holy Spirit who lives in you.

Heavenly Father, I pray that You would make it possible for me through Your Holy Spirit to love other people sincerely, with the same love with which You love me. Amen.

Cling to What Is Good

Hate what is evil; cling to what is good. Rom. 12:9

The many instructions that Paul provides in Romans 12:9-16 help us to make visible the self-sacrificing love of Jesus through our actions in our lives and in our church. All these qualities were characteristic of Jesus' own life on earth. He always chose the best option.

If we see things through the eyes of Jesus, we will automatically hate what is wrong and cling to what is good. To hate what is evil means that you will choose to walk in the light of Jesus; that you will trust in Him and live every day in dependence on Him.

The prophet Micah wrote, "He has shown you, O mortal, what is good. And what does the LORD require of you? To act justly and to love mercy and to walk humbly with your God" (Mic. 6:8).

God requires you to fulfill your responsibility toward your brothers and sisters in Jesus; to look after them and to show them love and mercy. You must constantly test yourself to make sure that you are living according to God's will.

Christianity is a way of life. If you are truly willing to hate what is evil and cling to what is good, your entire way of life will reflect your relationship with God.

Can this be said of you?

Heavenly Father, I so much want to do what is good, but before I know it I have already done something wrong. Please forgive me and help me to live according to Your will. Amen.

Brotherly Love and Devotion

Be devoted to one another in love. Honor one another above yourselves. Rom. 12:10

B e good friends who love deeply; practice playing second fiddle" reads *The Message*. This is no easy task.

By nature we much rather tend to distrust one another, to be jealous of each other and to look after our own interests. This selfishness constantly impedes us when we want to obey the law of God.

After all, in His summary of the law Jesus says that we must love God above all things and our neighbor like ourselves. These two commandments are a summary of the entire law.

Only when your love for God is stronger than your love for yourself will you learn to be free to love and respect other people in the way God requires of you.

Only then can you (still with the help of God) love and respect other people unconditionally, even when they have fewer accomplishments and gifts than you do. Only then will the superior talents of others cease to be a threat to you – you will not begrudge them their talents and achievements.

After all, this is what Jesus did. Your attitude should be the same as that of Christ Jesus. Do nothing out of ambition or conceit, but in humility consider others better than yourselves (see Phil. 2:5, 3).

Lord Jesus, I pray for the same spirit of humility and unselfish service that You had. Teach me to consider others better than myself. Amen.

Never Be Lacking in Zeal

Never be lacking in zeal, but keep your spiritual fervor, serving the Lord. Rom. 12:11

C hristians often discover that the zeal and devotion they had when they started to serve the Lord gradually grows weaker until it dwindles away almost entirely.

"Yet I hold this against you: You have forsaken the love you had at first. Repent and do the things you did" (Rev. 2:4-5) is the message to the church in Ephesus.

This also applies to many marriages. When the honeymoon is over the spouses discover that they don't love each other as much as they initially thought. They are not prepared to work on their marriage, with the result that two out of three marriages end up in the divorce court.

Do you love the Lord as much now as you did when you were converted, or has your love for Him grown weaker with time? Do you find it a joy to talk to Him in prayer, to study your Bible and listen to His voice, or do you often fall asleep on your knees or constantly find excuses not to spend time in devotions?

This must never happen. If you have recently inadvertently started to stray from the Lord, make a U-turn and return to Him. Be prepared to work on your relationship. He loves you and waits impatiently to be merciful to you again.

Heavenly Father, please forgive me for not serving and loving You with the same zeal as I did at first. I pray that You would return that enthusiastic first love to me. Amen.

Keep Your Spiritual Fervor

Keep your spiritual fervor. Rom. 12:11

Never become lukewarm in your spiritual life. Rather, serve and love God fervently and eagerly. God does not tolerate lukewarm Christians. Because the church in Laodicea was spiritually lukewarm, they were unacceptable to Him. "I know your deeds ... I wish you were either one or the other! So, because you are lukewarm ... I am about to spit you out of My mouth" (Rev. 3:15-16).

Fire played an important role in the spiritual sacraments of the Israelites. In the Old Testament sacrifices had to be burned with fire. God appeared to Moses in a burning bush and at night accompanied His people through the desert as a column of fire.

Fire therefore represented the holiness of God. Fire could purge and cleanse. The prophet Jeremiah writes that God's Word is like fire (see Jer. 23:29). It is God's Spirit that wants to bring this word to life for us and that sees to it that this fire will touch and change us.

In order to remain fervent and enthusiastic about the things of the Lord, you will have to serve God with absolute devotion and read and obey His Word with the same devotion. You also need to make time for Him in your busy schedule. Only if you remain close to Jesus will He give you this fervent devotion to Him.

Lord Jesus, I come to You to confess that I have become lukewarm in my relationship with You. Please forgive me and once again give me a fervent faith and devotion so that I will serve You with fervor. Amen.

Serve the Lord

Work hard and serve the Lord enthusiastically. Rom. 12:11

If we truly love God with devotion and fervor, it goes without saying that we will be willing to serve Him. Serving others was one of Jesus' most important qualities. "For even the Son of Man did not come to be served, but to serve, and to give His life as a ransom for many," Jesus tells His disciples in Mark 10:45.

Jesus' entire life was a life of service to others. His instruction that His children must be each other's servants still applies to all Christians today. And this willingness to serve should change the lives of His children irrevocably.

Jesus' example should inspire you to be willing to serve others as He did. "Don't burn out; keep yourselves fueled and aflame," warns *The Message*. "Be alert servants of the Master, cheerfully expectant" (Rom. 12:11).

Service without love is impossible: "Serve one another humbly in love," Paul writes to the church in Galatia (Gal. 5:13). If you are willing to follow Jesus' example of service – not only serving God but also your neighbor – you must begin by truly loving your neighbor, in spite of the fact that they may differ from you or may wish you harm.

God will make it possible for you to do this if you make the decision to be willing to serve.

Lord Jesus, I want to report for service. Make me willing to serve others as You did when You were on earth. Amen.

Be Joyful in Hope

Be joyful in hope. Rom. 12:12

Although Jesus experienced the uncertainty of the world, He never lost hope because He knew that His Father was in control. "In this world you will have trouble. But take heart! I have overcome the world," He tells His disciples (John 16:33). In other words, Christians can succeed in living in hope in this world, even if things are not going well.

When Paul talks about hope here, he is referring to a fixed certainty that each Christian already has. This hope is not accompanied by a measure of uncertainty as we sometimes use it when we say, "I hope it will rain soon."

Christian hope is always entwined with God's promises, which He gives us in His Word. And we can trust in these promises because they are fixed and sure.

This is why God's children can be joyful in hope. They know that the things they hope for will come true.

The Christian hopes with an eye on Jesus Christ, with the desire to live more and more like Him. We place our hope in the clouds, the clouds of Jesus' Second Coming. The Christian's hope does not end in death; we have the certainty of eternal life.

Do you succeed in remaining joyful because of this hope that lives in your heart?

Lord Jesus, thank You that I may live every day with hope in my heart because I know that You will keep every one of Your promises to me. Amen.

Be Patient in Affliction

Be patient in affliction. Rom. 12:12

In our own country we hardly know what the oppression the early Christians were subjected to must have been like. They were tortured and persecuted on account of their faith, and still they remained true to God. However, there are still many countries in which Christians suffer and are persecuted because they believe in Jesus. Paul tells these people to remain patient in affliction.

Although we are not physically oppressed, nobody can escape suffering. In everybody's life there are times when we fail to understand God; when, like Job, we want to know why we have to suffer.

At times we also have to endure ridicule because we air our opinions on topics such as abortion, pornography and extramarital sex – things that are accepted without question in our modern society.

If you are currently experiencing such a moment of "oppression" because you profess your Christian faith; if people avoid you because you stand up for your faith, don't be disheartened. Wait patiently for God to deliver you. Paul's message also applies to you: remain patient. After all, you know that this oppression will only last a short time. God loves you and although He allows crises to arise in your life at times, He will provide deliverance in His good time and in His way.

Lord Jesus, I am sorry for protesting when I sometimes have to sacrifice things for my faith. Help me to remain patient in affliction and to trust in You always. Amen.

Be Faithful in Prayer

Be faithful in prayer. Rom. 12:12

When we pray and don't receive an answer, we easily grow despondent. But God wants us to continue praying, then more than ever. Jesus said, "Ask and it will be given to you; seek and you will find; knock and the door will be opened to you. For everyone who asks receives; the one who seeks finds; and to the one who knocks, the door will be opened" (Matt. 7:7-8). With these words Jesus tells us that we need to continue to seek God in prayer even when we don't immediately receive an answer.

God is always there to listen to your prayers. But you must not lose hope if He takes time to answer your prayers.

Abraham had to wait years for his heir, but he continued praying and believing even when it became physically impossible for him and his wife to have a child. Because Abraham persevered in faith and prayer, God gave him his promised heir.

God wants to answer your requests, but only if you are willing to persevere in asking. He will answer your prayers when He deems fit. Sometimes God's answer is different from what you would have liked. But even then you can know that God loves you so much that He wants to give you only what is best for you.

Lord Jesus, please forgive me for growing despondent at times and for sometimes giving up when my prayers are not answered when I think they should be. Help me to persevere in prayer. Amen.

Share with Those in Need

Share with the Lord's people who are in need. Rom. 12:13

W hen Jesus tells His followers to help each other, He means that we must help all people, starting with our fellow believers. Love for God cannot be separated from service to others. "Share with the Lord's people who are in need," Paul asks. My husband likes saying that this text requires love with rolled-up sleeves. In Paul's time Christians often suffered and were dependent on fellow Christians for help.

This need that Paul mentions is more than a financial need. Need means that you are no longer in a position to handle circumstances on your own. Fellow believers may live in a beautiful house with plenty to eat, but they may still have a need you can meet.

And precisely because we are so wrapped up in our own problems and crises, we are often oblivious to the needs of other Christians. Perhaps the time has come to tear your attention away from your own problems and focus on other people's needs. Get involved with other people. There are many people around you who need you. Support them, pray for them and encourage them.

Ask the Lord to open your eyes and ears to their need, to enable you to be at the disposal of people in need and to play an active part in helping them.

Heavenly Father, I come to You to confess that I am so busy with my own things that I am often oblivious to the needs of others. Please forgive me and help me to see their need in future and to do something to help them. Amen.

Practice Hospitality

Practice hospitality. Rom. 12:13

While I was studying this Scripture passage, it struck me how often our own activities prevent us from treating others as God wants us to. Hospitality is an instruction from God. "Offer hospitality to one another without grumbling," Peter writes in 1 Peter 4:9.

The Jews were very proud of their tradition of hospitality and this custom was built into several of their laws. Read with what hospitable abandon Abraham received the three foreign visitors in Genesis 18. This custom is sadly disappearing from our Western civilization. When we hear that somebody wants to visit us, we often think first about the time, effort and expense it will require from us. Some of us would much rather give money than open our homes to others.

True hospitality involves much more than this. It means that you are also prepared to open your heart to visitors and make them feel truly welcome.

Unfortunately, the kind of society we live in today makes it almost impossible to open our doors to strangers as people could do in the past. But this does not mean that we cannot at least try to be more hospitable to our acquaintances. We need to be more genuinely compassionate toward each other; to receive our friends and acquaintances in our homes with more hospitality.

Are you willing to try?

Lord, I am sorry for often being so inhospitable toward others. Please make me willing to open my heart and my home to others. Amen.

Bless Your Persecutors

Bless those who persecute you; bless and do not curse.
Rom. 12:14

We so easily fail when it comes to Jesus' most important instruction to love our neighbor. Loving the people who love you isn't always all that easy, but to love those people whom you hate just seems like too much to ask. No one likes to come off second best, and usually we are quite indignant when we do. Because we are only human, we find it virtually impossible to bless those who have persecuted us.

And yet the Lord asks it of us. Jesus was willing to pray for and bless the people who persecuted Him time and again. Even on the cross He prayed to God to forgive His persecutors because they did not know what they were doing.

In His Sermon on the Mount He similarly states that His children should love their enemies: "But I tell you, love your enemies and pray for those who persecute you" (Matt. 5:44).

To obey this command is impossible if you are not yet a child of God. It is only He who can enable you to conquer your innate selfish nature and to love and bless those people for whom you feel no love. Are you able to wish your persecutors well? If not, God would like to make it possible for you to do so.

Heavenly Father, You know that I cannot bless those people who persecute me. Please enable me to love them because You loved me first. Amen.

Rejoice with Those Who Rejoice

Rejoice with those who rejoice. Rom. 12:15

It is easy to be happy when joyful events take place in our lives. We celebrate the marriages of our children with great gladness and we radiate joy when our grandchildren are born. We love hearing that our husbands got a promotion at work; that our children passed their exams with flying colors.

It is more difficult to be joyful for other people when one of your colleagues receives the promotion that you expected to get, or when one of your friends' children gets better results at school than your child.

Paul's instruction to rejoice with those who rejoice goes against the grain of our innate selfish nature. The only way in which we will really be willing to share spontaneously in other people's joy is when we become truly emotionally involved with these people; when we start caring for them from the heart and start loving them with the same unselfish love that Jesus shows toward us.

And this, unfortunately, is impossible. But by this time you should know the solution to the problem. The Holy Spirit who lives within you can help you to accomplish this goal. Ask Him right now to do this and immediately start to assure other people that you rejoice with them when something exciting happens in their lives.

Lord, make it possible for me to love other people so much that I will truly rejoice with those who rejoice. Amen.

Mourn with Those Who Mourn

Mourn with those who mourn. Rom. 12:15

Selfish people find it much easier to mourn with others than to rejoice with them. And yet it requires sincere compassion to really cry with someone who is sad, because this sympathy should go much deeper than a little card or a few words of condolence.

What do you do when someone close to you loses a loved one? When your neighbor's wife succumbs to a serious illness, or when an acquaintance's new grandchild turns out to be disabled? It is all too easy just to mumble a quick "I'm sorry" in passing, rather than to become truly involved or sincerely mourn with people who are sad.

Jesus truly cared for the people around Him. It did not matter to Him whether they were cast out by society. He loved everyone unconditionally. He always helped people, healing the sick, reaching out to those who were downcast.

If you have suffered in your own life, you are better equipped to mourn with those who mourn, because then you are able to console them from your experience. Ask the Holy Spirit to teach you and lead you to reach out to those people who need your compassion most. Show a sincere interest in the people around you. Make yourself available to them and offer your sympathy and help.

Lord Jesus, make it possible for me to have real sympathy with people who are sad and make me willing to help them in a practical way. Amen.

Live in Harmony

Live in harmony with one another. Rom. 12:16

When Paul writes that Christians should live in harmony with one another, he doesn't mean that we should all be the same. Rather, he means that we should think and act from our mutual love for God.

In Philippians 2:2-4 this spiritual harmony is explained beautifully: "Make my joy complete by being like-minded, having the same love, being one in spirit and of one mind. Do nothing out of selfish ambition or vain conceit. Rather, in humility consider others above yourselves, not looking to your own interests but each of you to the interests of others."

Unfortunately we hear much more about division among Christians than about harmony. In just about every church disputes among God's children regularly occur. And the reason for these disputes are, once again, selfishness and self-interest. When you are so involved in your own life and interests that there is no room for other believers in your life, you are disobedient to God's command.

The same is true when you are unable to live in peace with other Christians. But if you are willing to live in harmony with your fellow Christians, as God commands you, you will gladden God's heart because you will be glorifying His name.

Heavenly Father, forgive me for not living in harmony with my fellow believers. Help me to be one in spirit and purpose with other Christians. Amen.

Do Not Be Proud

Do not be proud. Rom. 12:16

"Get along with each other; don't be stuck-up," is how *The Message* interprets this command. People who are proud believe they are just that little bit better than everyone else. They believe that they are always right and they tend to look down on other people.

They are usually people who are successful in their career, people others look up to – at least in worldly terms. But God does not tolerate pride in His children. At the beginning of Romans 12, Paul writes without mincing words, "Do not think of yourself more highly than you ought, but rather think of yourself with sober judgment, in accordance with the measure of faith God has distributed to each of you" (Rom. 12:3).

What is your position? Are you successful and popular? If you have accomplished much in life; if the things that you have achieved tend to make you conceited, just remember that you have nothing that you didn't receive from God. All your abilities and talents come from Him; your success and achievements are all His work. It is He who helped you to become what you are today. And for this reason you have no right to think too much of yourself. Rather, you should always give the honor for the things that you have accomplished to God.

Do you?

Heavenly Father, forgive me for being conceited about my successes and achievements. Teach me that all these things are undeserved grace from Your hand. Amen.

Associate with the Humble

Be willing to associate with people of low position.
Rom. 12:16

One of Jesus' most outstanding characteristics was His absolute humility: "Christ Jesus ... being in very nature God ... made Himself nothing by taking the very nature of a servant, being made in human likeness," Paul writes (Phil. 2:5-7). Despite the fact that He was God Himself, He was willing to come to the world as an ordinary human being. He was prepared to be born here in a dirty stable, to wash His disciples' feet and to die the cruelest death conceivable.

And this attitude of Jesus, Paul writes, should also be in every one of His children. We sometimes think that humble people are rather cowardly, that they are people who are too afraid to assert themselves. But this is far from the truth. People who are truly humble are willing to put other people's interests before their own, and this takes a tremendous amount of courage.

God wants you to be willing to be associated with humble people. "All of you, clothe yourselves with humility" (1 Pet. 5:5).

It is not that difficult to be humble if you see yourself as God sees you. In your own strength you can accomplish nothing that is good and right. Ask God to help you to live humbly from now on.

Heavenly Father, forgive me for struggling so much to be truly humble and to hold others in higher regard than I do myself. Please make it possible for me to accomplish these goals. Amen.

Do Not Be Conceited

Do not be conceited. Rom. 12:16

W hat exactly does it mean to be conceited? To be conceited is to:
- Always know better than anyone else.
- Be convinced that you are always right.
- Have a tendency to always correct others.

People who are conceited find it very hard to put themselves in other people's shoes because in their own reckoning they always know best.

The wisdom of which the Bible speaks stands in direct opposition to conceit. This wisdom means to rely on God to distinguish between right and wrong. James asks, "Who is wise and understanding among you? Let them show it by their good life, by deeds done in the humility that comes from wisdom" (James 3:13). He continues to explain what this wisdom involves: "But the wisdom that comes from heaven is first of all pure; then peace-loving, considerate, submissive, full of mercy and good fruit, impartial and sincere" (James 3:17).

Do you think that you always know best; that you possess all the wisdom in the world? All people are fallible and make mistakes. Be prepared to listen to others and to admit that you might be wrong. Pray for God's wisdom in your life and ask Him to exchange your conceit for His wisdom.

Lord Jesus, forgive me for sometimes thinking that I am always right. Grant me the wisdom that comes from You and help me to give others a chance. Amen.

Do Not Repay Evil with Evil

Do not repay anyone evil for evil. Rom. 12:17

I f someone has wronged you or someone close to you, you naturally want to take revenge on that person. But Paul insists that Christians should not repay evil with evil.

To be able to forgive and not harbor bitterness you will have to start with your thoughts, because if you harbor vengeful thoughts toward someone, you will find that before long those thoughts are transformed into deeds.

You should be willing to wholeheartedly forgive people who have wronged you. People who cannot forgive and forget the wrongs that others have done to them cannot truly love other people.

It is natural to wish suffering on people who have treated you unjustly. It is also natural to want to have a hand in their suffering; to get back at them. But if you are sincere in your commitment to God, you will undertake not to repay evil with evil.

Are you prepared to offer your love and forgiveness to people who have wronged you? You will not be able to do it in your own strength, but God will enable you to do it.

Heavenly Father, You know that it sounds very unfair to me that those who have wronged me will get off scot-free. Please help me to relinquish all my vengeful thoughts and to forgive them. Amen.

Do What Is Right

Be careful to do what is right in the eyes of everyone.
Rom. 12:17

This instruction would have been much easier if only Paul had left out the word "everyone." In this context, to do what is right means to have a benevolent attitude and demeanor toward all people, to wish only the best for others and to do everything in your power to give it to them.

In God's eyes a benevolent attitude should always be accompanied by good deeds. It serves no purpose to have a friendly word for everyone, but no good deeds to confirm their authenticity.

As far as this instruction is concerned, you can once again turn to Jesus' example. He did right to all people, including His persecutors, the people who betrayed and killed Him, and His disciples who betrayed and deserted Him.

With what attitude do you view other people? Do you distrust everyone without exception, or do you trust people? Do you live a selfish life that is focused only on your personal gain, or do you have a benevolent attitude towards other people?

Make benevolence toward all people a part of your life. See the good in others and develop it. Give other people a fair chance – just as God is willing to do for you every day.

Heavenly Father, thank You for always seeing the good in me and for forgiving my sins time and time again. Help me to be prepared to do the same for others. Amen.

Live at Peace with Everyone

If it is possible, as far as it depends on you, live at peace with everyone. Rom. 12:18

To live at peace with other people implies that you should do your best, as far as possible, to maintain good relationships with other people. And yet again Paul includes that pesky little word "everyone"! You need to do your best to live in harmony with all other people and undertake to act as a peacemaker in the lives of others.

In His Sermon on the Mount, Jesus says, "Blessed are the peacemakers, for they will be called children of God" (Matt. 5:9). It is therefore not enough merely to live at peace with others. You should also be willing to be a peacemaker, to resolve and put to rest disputes among others.

The peace the Bible speaks refers to is something that transcends worldly peace, which actually requires nothing more than a truce. The peace of the world means simply concluding an agreement with someone, but biblical peace means reconciliation, reaching out in love, putting an end to conflict, being prepared to forgive the other person wholeheartedly.

However, making peace does not mean that you should be willing to relinquish your Christian principles. Live in peace as far as it depends on you, Paul writes.

Lord, I pray that You would grant me Your peace in my life and that I will be willing to pass this peace on to others, so that I may be a peacemaker for You in this world. Amen.

Do Not Take Revenge

Do not take revenge, my dear friends, but leave room for God's wrath, for it is written: "It is Mine to avenge; I will repay," says the Lord. Rom. 12:19

Paul filled Romans 12 with extremely difficult instructions! No one wants to wait until the Lord one day sets things right for us. We want to do it right now. But God asks His children to leave all reprisal to Him.

In all of our lives there is at least one thing that we struggle to deal with and forgive. In my own life it was something that someone did to my husband years ago. I simply couldn't manage to forgive that person. What's more, I kept thinking that the Lord would see to it that that person would get what he deserved.

It took long years for me to realize that this is not at all what Paul means in this passage. You should not dredge up the pain from the past time and again, and make elaborate plans to get back at the person who wronged you. You should also not delight in the thought that God will take revenge for you. If you are obedient to God's commands, you will be willing to surrender this thing that torments you completely to God. He will deal with the matter in His own way and in His own time.

Make a conscious decision to forgive the person. God will enable you not only to forgive the injustice, but also to forget it.

Lord, You know that there are things in my past that still hurt me. Grant me the mercy to forgive the people responsible for my pain, and to forget it altogether. Amen.

Feed Your Enemy

"If your enemy is hungry, feed him; if he is thirsty, give him something to drink. In doing this, you will heap burning coals on his head." Rom. 12:20

When you have an enemy, that person actively campaigns for your destruction; he will do everything in his power to harm you. And the Bible expects you to do good to your enemy in return!

This verse compares the effect of being kind to your enemy to heaping burning coals on his head. In Paul's time people used little stoves that generated heat from hot coals to cook their food. When someone ran out of coals, he had to go out and find more coals.

These burning coals were carried in a container on the head, and generous people who had enough coals for their own use often supplemented another person's supply of coals by placing hot coals in this container.

It was this same benevolence toward his enemies that Jesus manifested when He healed Malchus's ear that had been severed by Peter's sword. If the love that lived in Jesus is also present in your own heart, you will be willing to do good to those people who are actually your enemies.

Are you doing this yet?

Lord Jesus, I don't always like helping those who are my enemies. Please enable me not only to help them, but also to love them. Amen.

Do Not Be Overcome by Evil

Do not be overcome by evil. Rom. 12:21

We have already seen that that the concepts of "evil" and "good" actually refer to the attitude of your heart.

This is the place where the good and the evil things in your life reside. In itself your heart is filled with darkness. Paul writes in Romans 3:12 that "there is no one who does good, not even one." And yet God makes our hearts new, and His love enables His children to pass on this love to others, to live lives filled with goodness.

When we look at the world around us, it is all too obvious that evil reigns supreme in contemporary society. When we open the newspaper, we read of crime and violence. It would appear as if evil has already claimed the victory.

Fortunately this is not the case. But there is good as well as bad news. Even if you think that your life isn't going altogether badly, you can never pass the test in God's eyes. All people are sinners, and because God hates sin, He punishes it with death. Fortunately for you Jesus has already taken your punishment on Himself through His crucifixion.

Because He died for you, God is willing to forgive your sin. Do you think you will be able to deal evil a death-blow by living a life dedicated to God from now on?

Lord Jesus, thank You for enabling me to get the upper hand over the evil in my life through Your crucifixion. Help me to live only for You every day. Amen.

Overcome Evil with Good

Overcome evil with good. Rom. 12:21

You have already discovered that you can conquer evil because Jesus has enabled you to do so through His death on the cross.

In this verse Paul provides another weapon that you can use with good effect against evil: overcome evil by doing good; by fighting your evil nature; by saying no every time you are tempted to commit a sin.

You can fight the evil in you and around you with the love that God Himself has put in your heart. You can take a stand against things that you know run counter to biblical standards. You can obey God's law. You can choose your friends, your television programs and your reading material carefully. You can tell people that you do not agree with things like abortion, pornography and fraud.

You can also do what is good by filling your life with positive things, by blocking all negative things from your thoughts. You can live as a child of God by helping and supporting others and by making a positive contribution to society.

If you succeed in doing this – with God's help and in His strength – then you will overcome evil with good. And then you will fulfill Peter's instruction: "They must turn from evil and do good; they must seek peace and pursue it" (1 Pet. 3:11).

Lord Jesus, I pray that You would enable me to conquer the evil in my own life as well as the evil that reigns supreme in the world through Your strength. Amen.

People Owe One Another Love

Let no debt remain outstanding, except the continuing debt to love one another, for whoever loves others has fulfilled the law. Rom. 13:8

*T*he Message paraphrases this verse as follows: "Don't run up debts, except for the huge debt of love you owe each other. When you love others, you complete what the law has been after all along." If you love other people, you have fulfilled the entire law of God. If you are a child of God, you will never be able to settle this debt completely.

And this is a formidable debt. You know exactly what your love for other people should be like. This love must be sincere; it must not be put-on or the kind of love that wears masks. You cannot simply pretend that you care for other people. You should love them unconditionally, even those who anger you or do you wrong.

Furthermore, you should also be willing to transform your love into deeds, to roll up your sleeves and to help people in distress. "Let us not love with words or tongue but with actions and in truth" (1 John 3:18).

Sincere love can never remain a mere theory; it must always be transformed into deeds. It is precisely in this active kind of love that people will be able to see that you belong to Jesus. Love is the hallmark of the Christian. How much of your debt of love have you paid off?

Lord Jesus, thank You for loving me unconditionally. Grant me more and more of Your love so that it will run over to others, thus enabling me to start paying off my debt of love. Amen.

December

Through God's Eyes

God is not only almighty, He is also omniscient – His eyes see everything on earth, even from heaven.

We can hide nothing from Him. He made us, and He knows all about us. It can be comforting to know that there is Someone who knows us through and through – that He knows what we are thinking even before we have put our thoughts into words. It is wonderful to know that we worship a God whose eyes are always on His children, that He knows exactly where we are at any given moment and takes careful note to see if one of us might need something so that He can help us. It would also be good if you could learn to look at other people with God's eyes and treat them with the same love and empathy that He shows you.

Heavenly Father, You are a God who sees.
You see me; You also see straight through me.
You know me through and through
and know exactly what I do and think.
You see every step that I take,
my whole life lies open before You.
I praise You for the promise that I will also
one day be able to see You like You really are.
Thank You for sending Jesus to bring about reconciliation.
Help me to play a positive role of
reconciliation in our country.
Lord Jesus, You came to light
up a world dark with sin.
Make me a light for You,
so that I can reflect Your light to others.
You show me how much God loves me,
You inspire me to pass on Your love to others
and to help the people who need help.
Make me obedient to You
and give me lasting joy and peace.
I want to love like You do,
and pass on Your message of love
to every person that I come across.
I pray that my love for You and others will grow,
and become more and more –
so that I will be prepared to reach
out to others and become holier every day.
Help me to live so that my life will honor You,
to successfully carry out Your tasks in Your power.
Take care of me and bless me, Lord.
This I ask in Your precious name.
Amen.

The Lord's Eyes Search the Earth

The eyes of the LORD search the whole earth in order to strengthen those whose hearts are fully committed to Him. 2 Chron. 16:9

Hanani, the seer, brought God's message to King Asa: Because Asa put his trust in the king of Aram instead of in the God of Israel, he missed his chance of defeating Aram's army with God's help. Hanani said that God's eyes search the whole earth so that He can help those who trust in Him with all their heart.

King Asa was so angry about this message that he had Hanani thrown into prison. After Asa had reigned for 39 years, he developed a serious foot disease. Even when his life was threatened by this disease, he preferred putting his trust in his physicians instead of in the Lord.

Those who trust other people instead of God always lose out. Hanani's message concerns you too, even today. God watches His children here on earth from heaven, so that He can see who needs His help at a specific moment. He is always ready to take action and help those who put their trust in Him. If you undertake to firmly trust in God, you can rest assured that He will keep an eye on you, that He will help you right away when you need His help.

Lord, I find it comforting to know that You look upon the earth and can see just when I need help. Thank You so much for keeping an eye on me! Amen.

God Notices You

This is what the LORD says: "Heaven is My throne, and the earth is My footstool. Could you build Me a temple as good as that? Could you build Me such a resting place? My hands have made both heaven and earth; they and everything in them are Mine. I, the LORD, have spoken! I will bless those who have humble and contrite hearts, who tremble at My word." Isa. 66:1-2

When you think about God's greatness, it boggles the mind. Although the mighty Creator God made the world and everything in it, the sea and everything in it, the millions of galaxies and the entire universe, and maintains everything daily, He knows each one of us personally. He takes notice of every one of His children on earth, and loves each one of us personally. He was prepared to give His only Son so that our sins could be forgiven. He knows exactly when we need Him.

Isaiah gives a description of the person God notices: It is a humble person who is remorseful about their sins, someone who has respect for God's Word.

Although God is so great and almighty, He knows everything about you; He also sees everything you do. If you want God to keep on taking notice of you, start being humble, show remorse for your sins and confess them before God. You must also respect God's Word.

Lord, it is unbelievable that You concern Yourself with me. Make me humble and willing to confess my sins before You. Help me to respect Your Word, so that You will take notice of me. Amen.

God Is Watching

"They practice deceit, thieves break into houses, bandits rob in the streets; but they do not realize that I remember all their evil deeds. Their sins engulf them; they are always before Me." Hosea 7:1-2

The prophet Hosea drew a picture of God's people in his time: they were liars, they broke in and stole, they didn't ask what God's will was and didn't even care that God knew about all their sins. (This scenario seems all too familiar!) The Lord gave them one chance after the other, but when they still refused to listen, He promised to scatter them among the pagan nations.

When Jonah managed to convince the people of Nineveh of their sin, they were filled with remorse and decided to stop sinning. We read in Jonah 3:10, "When God saw what they did and how they turned from their evil ways, He relented and did not bring on them the destruction He had threatened." The writer of Proverbs says, "The Lord is watching everywhere, keeping His eye on both the evil and the good" (Prov. 15:3).

God is also watching you today. You must always keep in mind that He knows your sin, that it lies before Him like an open book. If you carry on with your sinful ways too long, and refuse to listen, God will punish you, but if you confess and give up your sins, like the people of Nineveh, God will be merciful and forgive you.

Lord, forgive me that I don't listen to Your warnings and keep on sinning. I am sorry about the wrong things I did in the past. Please forgive my sins. Amen.

God Sees Every Step You Take

Doesn't He see everything I do and every step I take? Have I lied to anyone or deceived anyone? Let God weigh me on the scales of justice, for He knows my integrity. Job 31:4-6

Job made excuses for himself all the way. He realized that God saw every step that he took, and that is why he couldn't really understand why he – who lived such an innocent life in his own eyes – was now being punished so severely by God. He even insisted that God should weigh him on a reliable scale so that He could see for Himself that Job was innocent.

But Job was way off the mark. He didn't reckon on the fact that all of us – even the most God-fearing – are sinners in God's eyes. The prophet Isaiah understood better what a sinner looks like from God's point of view: "We are all infected and impure with sin. When we proudly display our righteous deeds, they are nothing but filthy rags. Like autumn leaves, we wither and fall, and our sins sweep us away like the wind" (Isa. 64:6).

You are also guilty before God. He sees every step that you take and He knows about every one of your sins. So never think that you are innocent before Him. It would be better for you to make yourself aware of your sins and confess them.

Lord, when I think that You see every step I take, I realize again how guilty I am before You. Please forgive my sins and help me to live the way You want me to. Amen.

God Sees Your Hidden Sins

You spread out our sins before You – our secret sins – and
You see them all. Ps. 90:8

When Jesus met people, He saw deep inside them and He knew about all the things they tried to hide from others.

At the well in Samaria He started talking to a Samaritan woman who had come to fetch water. He asked her to go and call her husband. "I don't have a husband," she replied. "You're right! You don't have a husband," Jesus said. "You have had five husbands, and you aren't even married to the man you're living with now. You told the truth!" (John 4:16-18).

The woman was stunned that Jesus knew her whole history and wondered if He could possibly be the Messiah. She called the man living with her and all the people in the village and the result of this was that they all believed in Jesus and acknowledged Him as Savior.

It's easy to keep your sins a secret from people. But with God it is impossible. He sees every one of your hidden sins and He doesn't tolerate any sin. "Nothing in all creation can hide from him. Everything is naked and exposed before His eyes," says the writer in Hebrews 4:13. Always remember that because God knows your sins, you are accountable to Him. Ask God to forgive you, and in future, live like He asks you to.

Heavenly Father, I realize that You know all about those things that I so painstakingly try to hide from others. Please forgive me! Amen.

God Sees through You

O LORD, You have examined my heart and know everything about me. You know when I sit down or stand up. You know my thoughts even when I'm far away. You know what I am going to say even before I say it, LORD. Ps. 139:1-2, 4

This psalm is a song of praise to the God who knows His children through and through, who knows everything about them, even their thoughts before they think them.

In verses 23 and 24, the psalmist expresses his approval that God knows him so personally and so intimately. He asks that God will test him to determine what he looks like inside, whether he is still on God's path. In verse 23 he prays, "Search me, O God, and know my heart; test me and know my anxious thoughts." And in *The Message*, the psalmist's request in verse 23 reads, "Investigate my life, O God, find out everything about me." In biblical times, the human heart was regarded as the center of human thinking.

God sees right through you; He knows you inside out. He knows what you think, even before you have formulated your thoughts. He knows about all the times you have disappointed Him, and yet He still loves you. You matter to Him. Even if people should reject you, He undertakes to protect you on all sides. How wonderful it is to belong to a God like ours!

Lord, You know me like the back of Your hand. You know everything about me and still You love me. It is my prayer that You will test me and see if I serve You in the right way. Amen.

Your Life Is an Open Book

The LORD sees clearly what a man does, examining every path he takes. An evil man is held captive by his own sins; they are ropes that catch and hold him. He will die for lack of self-control; he will be lost because of his great foolishness. Prov. 5:21-23

The writer of Proverbs cautions his readers to listen to their instructors, to stop doing wrong: they should stay away from immoral women and not cheat on their wives, but rejoice in them. Your life is exposed before the Lord. He knows your comings and goings and every step that you take, but a lack of self-control and your own foolishness can lead you down the wrong track.

Nobody knows what awaits us in the future, but God knows. He not only sees every step you take, but He also knows exactly what direction the path of your life will take. After all, your whole life lies before Him like an open book. For this reason, you ought to tread carefully on your path in life so that you don't end up on the wrong road in the process.

Make sure to stay on God's path and don't stray from it. The prophet Isaiah writes that if you stray from the right path, you will hear a voice behind you saying, "This is the way you should go" (Isa. 30:21). Listen very carefully for God's voice in your life and ask Him to keep you on the right track.

Father, my whole life lies open before You and You see every step I take. Keep me from wrongdoing so that I won't stray from Your path. Amen.

You Cannot Hide from God

"Am I a God who is only close at hand?" says the LORD. *"No,
I am far away at the same time. Can anyone hide from Me in
a secret place? Am I not everywhere in all the heavens and
earth?" says the* LORD. *Jer. 23:23-24*

God is near to His children and He promises never to
leave us: "The Lord your God will never leave you
nor forsake you" (Deut. 31:6). But because He is holy, He
is at the same time a God who is far away from sinners.
Nobody can hide from God in a secret place without
Him seeing them. He is present all over, everywhere, in
heaven and on earth.

The psalmist realized that he couldn't escape from
God. "I can never escape from Your spirit! I can never
get away from Your presence! If I go up to heaven, You
are there; if I go down to the grave, You are there. I could
ask the darkness to hide me and the light around me to
become night – but even in darkness I cannot hide from
You" (Ps. 139:7-8, 11-12, 16).

God is everywhere. He is always with you. Nothing
can ever take you away from Him. Even when you feel
as if God is far away, and darkness surrounds you, God
is with you and His hand will uphold you.

*Lord, I praise You for the promise that You are always with
me, that nothing can ever remove me from Your presence.
Amen.*

God sees Hagar

*Thereafter, Hagar used another name to refer to the L*ORD*, who had spoken to her. She said, "You are the God who sees me." She also said, "Have I truly seen the One who sees me?" So that well was named Beer-lahai-roi. Gen. 16:13-14*

When Sarai treated her servant badly, Hagar ran away. The angel of the Lord met her in the desert and asked her where she was from and where she was going. Hagar told him that her mistress had ill-treated her, but the angel replied that she should go back to her mistress and obey her. The angel also told her that she would have a son. She was to call him Ishmael (meaning "God hears"), because the Lord had heard her cry for help.

Then Hagar called on the name of the Lord, referring to Him as "the God who sees me." Although Hagar was a pagan woman, God noticed her and sent an angel to help her.

To this day, God sees every person who is in trouble. Even if you can't see God when you are going through a tough time, He can see you and you can rely on His help. In her difficult situation Hagar got to know the God of Abraham closely, and it very often happens like this in our case too. Only when there's no other way out, we see the God who sees us. The well where Hagar met the angel is called Beer-lahai-roi and this name means "well of the Living One who sees me."

Lord, thank You very much that You see me every time I am in a difficult situation, and that You reach out to me and help me, even when I don't deserve it at all. Amen.

Jesus and Nathanael

As they approached, Jesus said, "Now here is a genuine son of Israel – a man of complete integrity." "How do You know about me?" Nathanael asked. Jesus replied, "I could see you under the fig tree before Philip found you." John 1:47-48

When Philip told Nathanael that they had found the Messiah, Nathanael wanted to know whether anything good could come from Nazareth. Nazareth was a very small town and didn't have a very good reputation. Philip's response was, "Come and see for yourself" (v. 46).

When Jesus saw Nathanael approaching Him, He immediately knew who he was. And when Nathanael asked in astonishment where He knew him from, Jesus said, "I could see you under the fig tree before Philip found you."

This answer implies that Jesus must have had supernatural knowledge to form such an accurate opinion of Nathanael's character. Nathanael knew straight away that this was no ordinary man. Jesus had another special message for Nathanael: the people who follow Him would see heaven open up and angels descending on Him (see v. 51). With this He meant that God was revealed in Him.

Jesus also sees you; He knows your character and He knows who you are. If you want to get to know God better, you can meet Him in Jesus' life and behavior.

Lord Jesus, I want to confess like Nathanael that You are the Son of God, the King of Israel, and the King of my life. Thank You for always knowing where I am. Amen.

Jesus and Zacchaeus

So he ran ahead and climbed a sycamore-fig tree beside the road, for Jesus was going to pass that way. When Jesus came by, He looked up at Zacchaeus and called him by name. "Zacchaeus!" He said. "Quick, come down! I must be a guest in your home today." Luke 19:4-5

Zacchaeus was so short that he couldn't see Jesus through the crowds. He was, however, an important man – a chief tax collector. He wanted to meet Jesus so badly that he did something quite undignified – he climbed into a sycamore tree so that he could see Jesus.

The Jews didn't really mingle with the tax collectors, because they collected Roman taxes. Jesus, however, knew about the short tax collector and his fervent wish to see Him. Jesus stopped right under the tree Zacchaeus was sitting in. He not only saw Zacchaeus, He also knew his name. Zacchaeus couldn't believe his luck. This Jesus that he so very badly wanted to meet knew about him, knew his name and to top it all, invited Himself for a meal at Zacchaeus's house! Luke says that Zacchaeus received Jesus with great joy. Because Jesus noticed him, Zacchaeus undertook to give half of his possessions to the poor and if he had overcharged people on their taxes he would give them back four times as much.

When God takes notice of people He changes them. Are you willing to receive Jesus in your life with great joy and to let Him change you?

Lord Jesus, You take notice of me and know my name. I want to receive You into my life now with great joy. Amen.

To See God

"God blesses those whose hearts are pure, for they will see God." Matt. 5:8

"You're blessed when you get your inside world – your mind and heart – put right. Then you can see God in the outside world." Matt. 5:8 The Message

God blesses those whose hearts are pure, for they will see God," Jesus promises in His Sermon on the Mount. *Pure* means unblemished, faultless, blameless. And there is not one human being who measures up to this description. All of us are born sinful.

The severely tried Job yearned to see God in his life-time: "And after my body has decayed, yet in my body I will see God! I will see Him for myself. Yes, I will see Him with my own eyes. I am overwhelmed at the thought!" he says in Job 19:26-27. Only when Job recognized God for who He is, did God draw the curtain aside a little. Job confessed in Job 42:5, "I had only heard about You before, but now I have seen You with my own eyes."

If you would like to see God, if you want a pure heart, you will have to ask Jesus to wash your sins clean with His blood. You will also have to ask the Holy Spirit to make you aware of your sins. You must be prepared to confess those sins and give them up. Only then will this promise be addressed to you.

Lord, this is an awesome promise – that those whose hearts are pure will see You. Please give me a pure heart, so that I will see You face-to-face at Your second coming. Amen.

Whoever Sees Jesus, Sees God

Philip said, "Lord, show us the Father, and we will be satisfied." Jesus replied, "Have I been with you all this time, Philip, and yet you still don't know who I am? Anyone who has seen Me has seen the Father! So why are you asking Me to show Him to you?" John 14:8-9

I n Old Testament times no one could see God and live because of His holiness. Paul tried to explain this to Timothy: "He alone can never die, and He lives in light so brilliant that no human can approach Him. No human eye has ever seen Him, nor ever will. All honor and power to Him forever!" (1 Tim. 6:16).

When Jesus came to earth, He made His Father known, and ordinary humans could experience God in Him. Jesus was simultaneously God and man. John writes about Jesus in 1 John 1:1, "The One who existed from the beginning, whom we have heard and seen. We saw Him with our own eyes and touched Him with our own hands. He is the Word of life."

At His second coming every child of God will see Jesus. John writes, "Dear friends, we are already God's children, but He has not yet shown us what we will be like when Christ appears. But we do know that we will be like Him, for we will see Him as He really is" (1 John 3:2). Live in such a way that you will see Jesus with your own eyes one day!

Lord Jesus, I already yearn for Your second coming and look forward to it; the day that I will at last see You like You really are. Help me to live in such a way that it will be a reality for me. Amen.

Christmas Presents

They entered the house and saw the Child with His mother,
Mary, and they bowed down and worshiped Him. Then
they opened their treasure chests and gave Him gifts of gold,
frankincense, and myrrh. Matt. 2:11

Christmas is a time for giving presents – but instead of concentrating on buying other people extravagant, expensive presents, or looking forward to our own lavish gifts, we ought to focus on God's great gift to us – Jesus who came to set us free and to forgive our sins.

In our family we give very small Christmas presents so that the children don't get used to getting, and consequently expecting, expensive gifts. Make a point of giving fewer and smaller gifts this Christmas and rather tell your children that our real Gift at Christmas is Jesus.

Follow the wise men's example: kneel down before the Christ child and offer Him your praise and honor. I read somewhere that the wise men's gifts of gold, frankincense and myrrh are also symbolic: the frankincense of worship, the gold of your possessions and the myrrh of the hope that lives within you. Thus, this Christmas, offer Jesus your prayers and possessions, and fasten your hope on Him. Thank God for His Son – a gift too wonderful for words! (see 2 Cor. 9:15). Then you will have a very blessed Christmas this year.

Heavenly Father, this Christmas I want to praise You for
Your indescribable Gift: Your Son who came to the world to
die on a cross, so that I may have eternal life. Amen.

The Gifts that God Requires from Us

What can we bring to the LORD? What kind of offerings should we give Him? Should we bow before God with offerings of yearling calves? No, O people, the LORD has told you what is good, and this is what He requires of you: to do what is right, to love mercy, and to walk humbly with your God. Mic. 6:6, 8

Perhaps you wish that this Christmas you could offer God a tangible gift.

The prophet Micah considers what gifts he will take when he goes to kneel before God. First he tells us in Micah 6:7 what he thinks God does not want: He does not want offerings of rams or oil from us, neither does He want us to sacrifice our children like the heathens in Micah's time did.

Then Micah teaches us what type of gift is indeed worthy of God. God would like us to do what is right, to love mercy, and to live humbly before Him.

We can also give God tangible presents this year. In Matthew 25:40 Jesus says, "I tell you the truth, when you did it to one of the least of these My brothers and sisters, you were doing it to Me!" So find someone in need this Christmas and give that person gifts: food, clothes, provisions, your time and care. If we do that, we are in fact giving the gift to God.

Lord, help me to be just toward others, to show them love and mercy, to do what is right and to be considerate. Please show me who needs tangible gifts. Amen.

Jesus Reconciles People

Together as one body, Christ reconciled both groups to God by means of His death on the cross, and our hostility toward each other was put to death. Now all of us can come to the Father through the same Holy Spirit because of what Christ has done for us. Eph. 2:16, 18

With the advent of Jesus coming to earth, relationships were restored. The relationship between people and God, and also the relationship between man and man, was improved and people made peace with each other. Even Jews and Gentiles who lived in enmity with each other in Jesus' time were reconciled and joined together as one body by their shared faith in Him.

In particular, Christmas is the time when we build our own relationships: Families who don't see each other often get together to celebrate Christmas to commemorate the birth of Christ, who restores all relationships.

Don't you want to start today with your own reconciliation effort? It can start with a smile and a Christmas wish, or something more concrete like a food parcel or a contribution of money so that people who have less than you can celebrate Christmas. Why not look around you and decide how you will make a positive difference this Christmas?

Lord Jesus, You came to the world to bring about reconciliation. I want to make a positive effort towards this goal. Show me where to begin. Amen.

The Coming of the Light

The people who walk in darkness will see a great light. For those who live in a land of deep darkness, a light will shine. Isa. 9:2

Many years before Jesus' birth, Isaiah prophesied that someone would come who would destroy the darkness of sin on earth and bring light for God's children. With Jesus' birth this prophecy was fulfilled.

The Bible always describes light as positive; it is an indication of God's kingdom, while darkness is usually negative and refers to the kingdom of darkness. The message of Christmas is that God sent His Son to the world so that we need never again stumble along in darkness, but from that point on would have with us the living Light. Light is also synonymous with Christmas – Christmas lights glitter all over, in the streets, on Christmas trees and in store windows.

In Luke's version of the birth of Christ, the first sign of the angel was the radiance of God's glory surrounding the shepherds. Jesus testified that He is the Light of the world, but He also appoints us to be lights as well, lights that should shine in a dark world and that cannot be overcome by darkness.

Don't you want to do something positive about your calling to be a light? Let God's light shine from you and surround the people around you; testify about the Light so that you yourself can be a light for God.

Lord Jesus, thank You that You came to light up a dark world. Make me a light this Christmas, someone who will testify about You and radiate Your light. Amen.

Jesus, the Light-bearer

Because of God's tender mercy, the morning light from heaven is about to break upon us, to give light to those who sit in darkness and in the shadow of death, and to guide us to the path of peace. Luke. 1:78-79

Zechariah prophesied that the Child who was going to be born would be a Light-bearer. He would rise like the early morning sun and break on us from heaven to bring light to those who live in the dark and in the shadow of death. He would guide our footsteps on the path of peace.

At Jesus' birth the light indeed drove away the darkness of sin, because everyone who believes in Him receives forgiveness of sin and the promise of eternal life.

The world is experiencing a dark period at present. There is more bad news than good. Violence and crime are threatening to get out of hand and the economy is fragile. This Christmas we need Jesus, the Light-bearer, more than ever before. But because we believe in Him, we need not stay in the darkness.

Everything is not as negative as we see it at the moment. God's radiant future is waiting for every one of His children. Your troubles are eventually going to end in glory (see 2 Cor. 4:17).

Lord Jesus, thank You that everything is not the way I see it, that You still bring light in dark situations. You give me a bright future because I believe in You. Please bring me light this Christmas. Amen.

Life and Light

In the beginning the Word already existed. The Word was with God, and the Word was God. The Word gave life to everything that was created, and His life brought light to everyone. The light shines in the darkness, and the darkness can never extinguish it. John. 1:1, 4-5

T he only way that sinful humankind can live forever one day is through faith in Jesus, the Word that became flesh. Only in Him is life, the Life that is the light for the people. Jesus' light shines in the darkness, and can never be extinguished by the dark. His light is always stronger than the darkness of sin, and He makes eternal life possible for us.

"He has given us eternal life, and this life is in His Son. Whoever has the Son has life; whoever does not have God's Son does not have life" (1 John 5:11-12). It's as simple as that. Without faith in Jesus, eternal life is out of reach for you forever, but faith in Him brings you life and light.

It is God's will that you would let your light shine for Him this Christmas. Underline Isaiah 60:1-2 in your Bible: "Arise, shine (your name), for your light has come, and the glory of the LORD rises upon you. See, darkness covers the earth ... but the LORD rises upon you." This Christmas, live in God's light and pass it on to everyone you come into contact with.

Lord Jesus, in You are light and life. Please make it possible for me this Christmas to live in Your light and to pass it on to others. Amen.

Immanuel, God Is with Us

"Look! The virgin will conceive a child! She will give birth to a Son, and they will call Him Immanuel, which means 'God is with us.'" Matt. 1:23

I n Isaiah 7:14, God promised His people that their Messiah would one day be born to a virgin, "The Lord Himself will give you the sign. Look! The virgin will conceive a child! She will give birth to a Son and will call him Immanuel (which means 'God is with us')."

With Jesus' birth, Isaiah's prophecy was fulfilled. The young Mary became pregnant by the power of God that conceived the life in her, and the Child that was born is indeed Immanuel, God with us.

Jesus came to show us what God looks like; He displays the qualities of His Father. By His death on the cross He made it possible for us to be God's children. He paid the full ransom for the sins of each of us on the cross, so that God can now forgive those sins.

He was raised from the dead to ensure that His children would not have to endure eternal death, but so that we would also one day rise in a new life. Even after His ascension He is still with us through His Holy Spirit. He lives in us, teaches and leads us daily, and even prays for us. Thus you can rest assured that He will always be with you.

Lord Jesus, thank You for the assurance that I never have to get by without You and that You will be with me up until the day that You come again to fetch me. Amen.

God Can Be Vulnerable

We live under constant danger of death because we serve Jesus, so that the life of Jesus will be evident in our dying bodies. 2 Cor. 4:11

Jesus was prepared to become human for us. This is why we celebrate Christmas. While He was on earth, He shared the same experiences we do. At times He was sad and upset, vulnerable and tired. At His birth, Jesus was as helpless as a newborn Baby. G. K. Chesterton writes, "The hands that made the sun and the stars were too small to reach the big heads of the cattle. In the manger God experienced what it is like to be helpless like a baby." At the end of His life, Jesus was again helpless. This time He was nailed to a cross. And He did this to demonstrate God's love for us.

Nothing on earth can separate us from God's love that is in Jesus. We also suffer here on earth, but to a much lesser degree than Jesus. We share in His suffering and death in our own bodies, yet the power of His resurrection flows through our lives.

Decide this Christmas to live in such a way that you make Jesus' life visible through your conduct.

Lord Jesus, I praise You that You came to show me how great God's love is for me. During this Christmastime I want to live for You so that others will see You through my conduct. Amen.

One Last Chance

"Finally, the owner sent his son, thinking, 'Surely they will respect my son.' So they grabbed him, dragged him out of the vineyard, and murdered him." Matt. 21:37, 39

I n this parable Jesus tells the story of a landowner who leased his vineyard to tenant farmers. When he sent servants to them to collect his share of the crop, the farmers killed these servants. At last, the landowner sent his son to the tenants, because he thought they would not harm him. But the farmers murdered him too.

This parable explains in detail how people receive God's message. In the olden days He spoke through His prophets, but now He speaks through His Son. In the Old Testament dispensation, the people didn't want to listen to the prophets. Some of them were killed because the people didn't want to hear God's message. But God loves us too much to give up on His salvation plan – He sent His Son to the world, so that everyone who believes in Him would not perish, but receive eternal life. And what was the reaction of the people who Jesus was prepared to die for? They refused to listen to His message, and crucified Him.

Every Christmas you get another chance to listen to God's Son, to believe in Him and make Him the Lord of your life. This Christmas you owe God an answer. Have you made His Son part of your life yet?

Lord Jesus, forgive me that I sometimes listen so unenthusiastically to the message You came to deliver. This Christmas I want to reaffirm my faith in You. Amen.

Goodness, Peace and Joy

The Kingdom of God is not a matter of what we eat or drink, but of living a life of goodness and peace and joy in the Holy Spirit. So then, let us aim for harmony in the church and try to build each other up. Rom. 14:17, 19

The kingdom of God is where God's sovereignty is acknowledged. Every one of God's children is a citizen of that kingdom. God's kingdom implies three things, Paul writes to the church in Rome: goodness, peace and joy.

These qualities are synonymous with Christmas. When the "good news that will bring great joy" (Luke 2:10) is announced by the angel, the angel chorus sings of peace on earth for all people who please God. We proclaim this message of joy every Christmas: the birth of the Messiah! God's kingdom has come close.

Jesus still makes peace possible for us – peace with God and peace with each other. We may be, no we *must* be, glad about this. In Jesus, God comes close to us. Make it your aim this Christmas to obey God and to spread His goodness, peace and joy among all the people you come across.

This Christmas I would like to wish you Paul's prayer to the church in Colosse: "Let the peace that comes from Christ rule in your hearts. For as members of one body you are called to live in peace. And always be thankful" (Col. 3:15).

Lord Jesus, Your birth makes peace and joy possible for humankind. Help me this Christmas to radiate Your goodness, to be joyful and to live in peace with others. Amen.

The Savior Is Born

Suddenly, an angel of the Lord appeared among them, and the radiance of the Lord's glory surrounded them. They were terrified, but the angel reassured them. "Don't be afraid!" he said. "I bring you good news that will bring great joy to all people. The Savior – yes, the Messiah, the Lord – has been born today in Bethlehem, the city of David!" Luke 2:9-11

At Jesus' birth, the angel who brings the news of great joy to the shepherds uses three names for the Child that has been born: Savior, Christ and Lord. These three names emphasize the importance of the Child. This Child was the long-awaited Savior who would save His people from their sins.

He is also Christ, the Messiah. This title is from the Old Testament where it was used for the one who was anointed by God. The third name, *Lord*, indicates that Jesus is King, Ruler over everything and everybody.

The angels' song that follows the angel's announcement sings of two things: Glory to God and peace on earth. We are inclined to focus only on the peace because we have become so tired of the current unrest and conflict. However, before God can give us peace, we must first bring Him the glory that is due to Him.

Make a point this Christmas of glorifying God as your Savior, your Messiah and your King. Put His glory first, then He will guarantee you His peace.

Lord Jesus, I want to glorify You as my Savior, my Messiah and my King. Please grant me Your peace this Christmas season. Amen.

The Revelation of God's Love

God is love. God showed how much He loved us by sending
His one and only Son into the world so that we might have
eternal life through Him. 1 John 4:8-9

The fact that Jesus came into the world and died on the cross is the most significant revelation of God's love for humankind. John puts it in a nutshell in the most well-known verse in the Bible, "For God so loved the world that He gave His one and only Son, that whoever believes in Him shall not perish but have eternal life" (John 3:16).

God proves His love for you in Jesus. God is the Source of all love and He makes Himself visible in the fact that believers love one another.

Jesus came to the world to demonstrate God's love to you. He is God's greatest act of love to people. Because He died in your place, you may now live forever if you believe in Him. You ought to let that love spill over onto all other people. God sacrificed His Son so that you may receive the gift of eternal life.

You will most probably give many presents to people today and also receive quite a few – but remember that God's Son is the greatest of all Christmas gifts. This is the main reason why we give each other Christmas presents today – to show our gratitude for God's gift through which He revealed His love for us.

Lord Jesus, I praise You that You came to make God's love
clear to me. Make it possible for me to love like You do, and to
pass Your message of love on to other people. Amen.

Your Love Must Overflow

I pray that your love will overflow more and more, and that you will keep on growing in knowledge and understanding. For I want you to understand what really matters, so that you may live pure and blameless lives until the day of Christ's return. Phil. 1:9-10

Of all the months of the year, December can be singled out as the genuine month of love. All the preparations for Christmas call for loads of love – especially from the women of the house! We show our family our love and caring through delicious meals and carefully chosen gifts. This is the time that family members renew the bond of love when they visit together, chat and catch up on everything.

It is my hope that Paul's prayer for the church in Philippi will be true for you this Christmas. May your love may grow in understanding and depth of insight, so that you would recognize the things that are of value.

But may it not end here. You should do your best to work on your love for your family, your friends, for people you don't know and especially for God, so that it will grow every day. As your love grows in understanding and as you become attuned to the feelings and thoughts of others, you will understand the needs of people better and be able to respond to them. This Christmas, share God's love with the people around you.

Lord Jesus, I pray that my love will overflow more and more, that I will keep on growing in Your love and understanding and depth of insight for the needs of others, and that I may discern which things are truly important. Amen.

Love that Is Prepared to Give

If we love our Christian brothers and sisters, it proves that we have passed from death to life. But a person who has no love is still dead. Anyone who hates another brother or sister is really a murderer at heart. And you know that murderers don't have eternal life within them. 1 John 3:14-15

True love is love that is prepared to give without holding back. God gave His Son on that first Christmas and about thirty years later Jesus gave His life so that you and I could be God's children. For this reason God expects us to be prepared to give also, because we love. We may no longer just say we love each other; we must show it by our actions (see 1 John 3:18).

The month of Christmas is also especially a month of giving. We give each other presents and we are more attuned to one another's needs. If this is not the case, something is very wrong somewhere. If you have earthly possessions and you are able to help others and yet have no feeling for the needy, the love of God cannot be in you.

It is because God loves the world that He was prepared to give His Son to die on a cross, and it is precisely because Jesus loves you so much that He was prepared to give His life. Show your love for others this Christmas by giving: giving to those who can give you nothing in return; giving to those who deserve your love the least.

Lord Jesus, You were prepared to give Your life so that I could live forever. Make me willing to give so that other people will see Your love in me. Amen.

Love that Keeps on Growing

May the Lord make your love for one another and for all people grow and overflow, just as our love for you overflows. May He, as a result, make your hearts strong, blameless, and holy as you stand before God our Father when our Lord Jesus comes again with all His holy people. 1 Thess. 3:12-13

T oday's Scripture reading is in fact a testimonial that Timothy wrote for the church of Thessalonica about their love and faith. It is Paul's prayer that their love for one another will overflow, that their love and faith will grow more and more, and that God will give them inner strength so that they will be strong, blameless and holy when Jesus comes again.

When you have Jesus' love in your heart and life, and that love grows every day, you will also grow in the process of sanctification. You will become more and more like Jesus. And this process of being made holy is not something that happens in an instant; it is a lifelong process. Your love may not stagnate either. It is God's wish that your love for Him and for others will keep on growing, so that it will eventually overflow.

Practice loving; live in such a way that other people will see by the things you do and the things you say that you love God and other people sincerely. Then God will give you inner strength, so that you will be holy and blameless at Jesus' second coming.

Lord, I want my love for You and other people to grow. I want to become more and more like You, so that one day when You come to fetch me, I will be blameless and holy before You. Amen.

An Honorable and Pleasing Life

We ask God to give you complete knowledge of His will and
to give you spiritual wisdom and understanding. Then the
way you live will always honor and please the Lord.
Col. 1:9-10

Here Paul gives a stirring description of what a Christian's life should look like from day to day. By means of the wisdom and insight we get only from the Holy Spirit, we must try to know God's will so that in future we will live to God's glory by doing only the things that please Him.

Karen Watson, a young American missionary, wrote the following letter to her church minister; it was read at her funeral after she was murdered in Iraq: "Care more than some think is wise. Risk more than some think is safe. Dream more than some think is practical. Expect more than some think is possible."

How about it? Are you prepared to live up to Karen's credo in the year ahead? If so, pray that God will give you His knowledge, wisdom and insight so that you can honor Him with your life. In so doing you will be able to do what He expects of you, and in this way make headway on the path of sanctification.

God undertakes to make His power available to you so that you will have all the patience and endurance you need in all circumstances (see Col. 1:11).

Father, I pray that You make Your will known to me through
the wisdom and insight that Your Spirit gives me so that in
the year that lies ahead I shall live to honor You and obey
Your will. Amen.

The Whole Year Through

It is a land the Lord your God cares for; the eyes of the Lord your God are continually on it from the beginning of the year to its end. Deut. 11:12

I n Deuteronomy 11, Moses told the people how God looked after them in the past, and also predicted that He would do so in the future as well. God freed them from slavery in Egypt, took care of them in the desert and saved them from the enemy. If they obeyed God, He would let them live long in the land that He would give them. God would take care of the land; He would watch over it throughout the year.

God is still the same God who provides for His children and holds their future in His hands. The promise in our Scripture reading today is a beautiful, reassuring promise. We often worry about what will happen to our country, but it is unnecessary. God promises to look after His children from New Year's Day right through to New Year's Eve.

Tomorrow is New Year's Eve and then follows New Year's Day, the right time to make this promise your own. Live confidently and believe that God will meet your needs today, but also in the future that lies ahead of you. Thank the Lord that He has taken care of you day and night over the past year, and pray for His blessing on the new year that is just around the corner.

Heavenly Father, thank You for looking after me this year from New Year's Day right up to New Year's Eve. Please bless me in this year that lies ahead. Amen.

A Commission for the New Year

Now the LORD speaks – the One … who commissioned me to bring Israel back to Him. My God has given me strength. He says, "I will make you a light to the Gentiles, and you will bring My salvation to the ends of the earth." Isa. 49:5-6

The prophet Isaiah was given an important commission: God made him a light for the nations, so that His message of salvation would reach the ends of the earth. He also undertook to give Isaiah strength so that he would be able to carry out this important mission in God's power.

In Matthew 28:19-20, Jesus gives His handful of disciples a seemingly impossible task: "Therefore, go and make disciples of all the nations, baptizing them in the name of the Father and the Son and the Holy Spirit. Teach these new disciples all the commands I have given you."

We sometimes feel at the end of a year that we didn't really do anything worthwhile. If you rely on God's power in your life, this will never be true of you. The Lord will never give you a command and not provide you with the power you need to obey it. If you stay close to Him, any task or challenge that awaits you in the new year, any disaster that might strike you, any problem that you may encounter, will be possible for you to handle. If you tackle it in His power, you will always be more than a winner.

Lord Jesus, thank You that I will be able to successfully carry out any task that You give me. Please be with me in the year ahead. Amen.

Reading List

1. Brazelton, K. 2005. *Pathway to Purpose for Women.* Cape Town: Struik Christian Media.
2. Cowman, LB. 1997. *Streams in the Desert.* Grand Rapids: Michigan.
3. Keating, K. 1989. *The Little Book of Hugs.* Australia: Harper Collins.
4. Lucado, Max. 2001. *Six Hours One Friday.* Cape Town: Struik Christian Media.
5. MacArthur, J. 2002. *The Keys to Spiritual Growth.* Vereeniging: Christian Art Publishers.
6. Mandela, N. 1995. *Long Walk to Freedom.* London: Little, Brown and Company.
7. Nouwen, Henry. 1996. *Bread for the Journey.* London: Darton, Longman and Todd Ltd.
8. Nouwen, Henry. 2000. *Reaching Out.* Wellington: Lux Verbi BM.
9. Ortberg, J. 2003. *Everybody's Normal Till You Get to Know Them.* Grand Rapids, MI: Zondervan.
10. Yancey, Philip. 2003. *Reaching for the Invisible God.* Jeppestown: Jonathan Ball.